2nd Conference of the Asia-Pacific Chapter of the Association for Computational Linguistics and the 12th International Joint Conference on Natural Language Processing (AACL-IJCNLP 2022)

Student Research Workshop

Online
20 November 2022

ISBN: 978-1-7138-6312-0

Printed from e-media with permission by:

Curran Associates, Inc.
57 Morehouse Lane
Red Hook, NY 12571

Some format issues inherent in the e-media version may also appear in this print version.

Printed with permission by Curran Associates, Inc. (2023)

Association for Computational Linguistics
209 N. Eighth Street
Stroudsburg, Pennsylvania 18360

Phone: 1-570-476-8006
Fax: 1-570-476-0860

acl@aclweb.org

Additional copies of this publication are available from:

Curran Associates, Inc.
57 Morehouse Lane
Red Hook, NY 12571 USA
Phone: 845-758-0400
Fax: 845-758-2633
Email: curran@proceedings.com
Web: www.proceedings.com

AACL-IJCNLP 2022

The 2nd Conference of the Asia-Pacific Chapter of the Association for Computational Linguistics and the 12th International Joint Conference on Natural Language Processing

Proceedings of the Student Research Workshop

November 20, 2022
Online

Message from the General Chairs

Welcome to the AACL-IJCNLP 2022 Student Research Workshop (SRW)!

The AACL-IJCNLP 2022 SRW is held in conjunction with the 2nd Conference of the Asia-Pacific Chapter of the Association for Computational Linguistics (AACL) and the 12th International Joint Conference on Natural Language Processing conference (IJCNLP).

The AACL-IJCNLP 2022 SRW provides a forum for student researchers who are investigating various areas related to Computational Linguistics and Natural Language Processing. The workshop provides an excellent opportunity for student participants to present their work and receive valuable feedback from the international research community as well as from selected panelists - experienced researchers, specifically assigned according to the topic of their work, who will prepare in-depth comments and questions in advance of the presentation. The workshop's goal is to aid students at multiple stages of their education: including undergraduate, master's, junior, and senior PhD students.

This year's submissions were organized into three different categories. Two of the three categories are general research papers and thesis proposals, following the tradition established by the previous SRWs:

- General research papers: Papers in this category can describe completed work, or work in progress with preliminary results. For these papers, the first author must be a current graduate or undergraduate student.

- Thesis proposals: This category is appropriate for advanced students who have decided on a thesis topic and wish to get feedback on their proposal and broader ideas for their continuing work.

In this year's workshop, we also introduced a special theme category, **Human-Centered NLP**:

- The rising prevalence of living along with artificial intelligence has brought lots of benefits to people's daily life. However, it also poses a challenge of building reliable, explainable, and empathic tools to provide better service, from essential natural language applications (e.g., machine translation, and text classification) to mental support. Especially during the current pandemic, people are more likely to feel alone and rely upon technology. This, together with the advances in the field of Natural Language Processing, has motivated the exploration of human-centered technology. In this special theme, we invite submissions that address diverse human-centered questions, particularly encouraging bringing together perspectives and methods from NLP and affective computing to improve individuals' lives physically and mentally. Topics of interest include (but are not limited to): (1) affective systems to understand human emotion and respond to their emotional feedback; (2) sentiment analysis in social media, e-commerce data, etc.; (3) human factors in the NLP evaluation system; (4) reliable and explainable NLP models; (5) ethics in NLP, including debiasing, detoxification, etc.

We received a total of 40 submissions: 38 general research papers, 1 thesis proposal, and 1 human-centered NLP paper. We accepted 14 general research papers, one thesis proposal, and one human-centered NLP paper, resulting in an overall acceptance rate of 40%. The decision-making process was competitive, but we were delighted that all accepted submissions have great creativity and make contributions to their fields. The accepted submissions are diverse not only in topics but also in terms of student demographics. In addition to the accepted ones, we wish each author of every submission the best of luck in their future endeavors.

Following previous SRWs, we also provided the pre-submission mentoring program for participants. The mentoring program offers students the opportunity to get feedback by a mentor prior to submitting their work for review. 12 papers participated in the pre-submission mentoring program. We would like to thank the 12 pre-submission mentors that spend their time and effort to help improve the work of the student authors. We would also like to thank all members of the program committee for their in-depth, detailed review and constructive suggestions for each submission. We are especially grateful to all the emergency reviewers who provide timely support and submit their high-quality feedback. Carrying on the practice of the AACL-IJCNLP 2020 SRW, we also include an SRW Keynote and an SRW Best Paper Award in this workshop.

Preparing a workshop is never an easy business. Many thanks to our faculty advisors, Sebastian Ruder and Xiaojun Wan, who provided enormous help and inspiring suggestions through the preparation of this workshop. Special thanks to Boaz Shmueli and Yin Jou Huang, the co-chairs of the AACL-IJCNLP 2020 SRW, who shared their invaluable experience in preparing the workshop. We are also grateful to Yulan He for her constant and timely support. A huge shout out to Yanran Li, who agreed to give the SRW keynote. We sincerely appreciate all of the organizers of the AACL-IJCNLP conference for their effort. And of course, we would like to thank all the student authors and participants who submitted their work to the workshop. This workshop cannot be successful without any of them.

We hope you enjoy the AACL-IJCNLP 2022 SRW!

Organizing Committee

Student Research Workshop Co-Chairs

- Hanqi Yan, University of Warwick, UK
- Zonghan Yang, Tisnghua University, China

Faculty Advisors

- Sebastian Ruder
- Xiaojun Wan

Pre-submission Mentors

- François Charton
- Sedigheh Eslami
- Mor Geva
- Jian Guan
- Itika Gupta
- Yanran Li
- Bin Liang
- Yusheng Su
- Zhixing Tan
- Huiyuan Yang
- Xiaoqing Zheng

Program Committee

- Piush Aggarwal
- Evelin Amorim
- Ali Araabi
- Ehsaneddin Asgari
- Valerio Basile
- Anjali Bhavan

- Ronald Cardenas
- Jonathan P. Chang
- Xinchi Chen
- Sijie Cheng
- Qinyuan Cheng
- David Chiang
- Ganqu Cui
- Xiang Dai
- Min-Yuh Day
- Alok Debnath
- Louise Deléger
- Qingxiu Dong
- John Dougrez-Lewis
- Heba Elfardy
- Micha Elsner
- Matthew Engelhard
- Zheng Fang
- Qiaozi Gao
- Tirthankar Ghosal
- Udo Hahn
- Hardy Hardy
- Christopher Homan
- Dirk Hovy
- Shengding Hu
- Hen-Hsen Huang
- Kaiyu Huang
- Jeff Jacobs
- Masoud Jalili Sabet
- Ganesh Jawahar
- Zara Kancheva
- Philipp Koehn
- Varun Kumar

- Artuur Leeuwenberg
- Lei Li
- Jasy Suet Yan Liew
- Xiaokai Liu
- Xuebo Liu
- Valentin Malykh
- Xiaoyue Mi
- Tsvetomila Mihaylova
- Gosse Minnema
- Pavankumar Reddy Muddireddy
- Kenton Murray
- Masaaki Nagata
- Mitra Pabitra
- Endang Pamungkas
- Lucy Park
- Mah Parsa
- Ivaylo Radev
- Sree Harsha Ramesh
- Vikas Raunak
- Arijit Sehanobish
- Sunayana Sitaram
- Kevin Small
- Richard Sproat
- Yusheng Su
- Zhaoyue Sun
- Shabnam Tafreshi
- Liling Tan
- Keegan Te Taka
- Laure Thompson
- Yan Wang
- Xinyu Wang
- Yuzhong Wang

- Jun Wang
- Jiashuo Wang
- Shuo Wang
- Xing Wang
- Bonnie Webber
- Jheng-Long Wu
- Zhenglu Yang
- Zeyuan Yang
- Michael Yoder
- Yao Zhang
- Xinran Zhang
- Byoung-Tak Zhang
- Xikun Zhang
- Wenjia Zhang
- Linhai Zhang
- Ce Zheng
- Zhong Zhou
- Qinhong Zhou
- Pierre Zweigenbaum

Table of Contents

Conference Program

Sunday, November 20, 2022

14:00–15:00 ***Keynotes***

15:00–16:20 **Oral Session I**

15:00–15:20 *Emotional Intensity Estimation based on Writer's Personality*
Haruya Suzuki, Sora Tarumoto, Tomoyuki Kajiwara, Takashi Ninomiya, Yuta Nakashima and Hajime Nagahara

15:20–15:40 *Bipartite-play Dialogue Collection for Practical Automatic Evaluation of Dialogue Systems*
Shiki Sato, Yosuke Kishinami, Hiroaki Sugiyama, Reina Akama, Ryoko Tokuhisa and Jun Suzuki

15:40–16:00 *Toward Building a Language Model for Understanding Temporal Commonsense*
Mayuko Kimura, Lis Kanashiro Pereira and Ichiro Kobayashi

16:40–18:40 **Oral Session II**

17:00–17:20 *Optimal Summaries for Enabling a Smooth Handover in Chat-Oriented Dialogue*
Sanae Yamashita and Ryuichiro Higashinaka

17:20–17:40 *MUTE: A Multimodal Dataset for Detecting Hateful Memes*
Eftekhar Hossain, Omar Sharif and Mohammed Moshiul Hoque

18:00–18:20 *A Simple and Fast Strategy for Handling Rare Words in Neural Machine Translation*
Nguyen-Hoang Minh-Cong, Vinh Thi Ngo and Van Vinh Nguyen

18:20–18:40 *C3PO: A Lightweight Copying Mechanism for Translating Pseudocode to Code*
Vishruth Veerendranath, Vibha Masti, Prajwal Anagani and Mamatha HR

Sunday, November 20, 2022 (continued)

19:40–21:40 Oral Session III

19:40–20:00 *Outlier-Aware Training for Improving Group Accuracy Disparities*
Li-Kuang Chen, Canasai Kruengkrai and Junichi Yamagishi

20:00–20:20 *An Empirical Study on Topic Preservation in Multi-Document Summarization*
Mong Yuan Sim, Wei Emma Zhang and Congbo Ma

20:20–20:40 *Detecting Urgency in Multilingual Medical SMS in Kenya*
Narshion Ngao, Zeyu Wang, Lawrence Nderu, Tobias Mwalili, Tal August and Keshet Ronen

20:40–21:00 *Language over Labels: Contrastive Language Supervision Exceeds Purely Label-Supervised Classification Performance on Chest X-Rays*
Anton Wiehe, Florian Schneider, Sebastian Blank, Xintong Wang, Hans-Peter Zorn and Christian Biemann

21:00–21:20 *Dynamic Topic Modeling by Clustering Embeddings from Pretrained Language Models: A Research Proposal*
Anton Eklund, Mona Forsman and Frank Drewes

21:20–21:40 *Concreteness vs. Abstractness: A Selectional Preference Perspective*
Tarun Tater, Diego Frassinelli and Sabine Schulte im Walde

21:40–22:20 Poster Session

22:20–22:30 ***Best Paper Award and Closing Remarks***

Emotional Intensity Estimation based on Writer's Personality

Haruya Suzuki[†] **Sora Tarumoto**[†] **Tomoyuki Kajiwara**[†]
Takashi Ninomiya[†] **Yuta Nakashima**[‡] **Hajime Nagahara**[‡]
[†]Ehime University [‡]Osaka University
{suzuki@ai.,tarumoto@ai.,kajiwara@,ninomiya@}cs.ehime-u.ac.jp
{n-yuta,nagahara}@ids.osaka-u.ac.jp

Abstract

We propose a method for personalized emotional intensity estimation based on a writer's personality test for Japanese text. Existing emotion analysis models are difficult to accurately estimate the writer's subjective emotions behind the text. We personalize the emotion analysis using not only the text but also the writer's personality information. Experimental results show that personality information improves the performance of emotional intensity estimation. Furthermore, a hybrid model combining the existing personalized method with ours achieved state-of-the-art performance.

1 Introduction

Emotional intensity estimation (Strapparava and Mihalcea, 2007; Bostan et al., 2020; Kajiwara et al., 2021) is one of the major challenges in the natural language processing community with many applications in dialogue systems (Tokuhisa et al., 2008) and social media mining (Stieglitz and Dang-Xuan, 2013). Emotional intensity estimation predicts the (often discretized) intensities of finer-grained emotions, such as Ekman's basic emotions, i.e., *joy*, *sadness*, *surprise*, *anger*, *fear*, and *disgust* (Ekman, 1992) and Plutchik's basic emotions, i.e., *joy*, *sadness*, *expectation*, *surprise*, *anger*, *fear*, *disgust*, and *trust* (Plutchik, 1980).

WRIME[1] (Kajiwara et al., 2021; Suzuki et al., 2022) is a corpus from Social Networking Service (SNS) text in Japanese for emotional intensity estimation. As exemplified in Table 1, the corpus adopts Plutchik's basic emotions from *both* the writers' (*subjective*) and the readers' (*objective*) points of view. Their experimental results showed that estimating subjective emotion is more difficult than objective emotion. This fact renders an additional challenge to subjective emotional intensity estimation. That is, there can be a latent factor that modulates the superficial emotion perceived from the text *per se*.

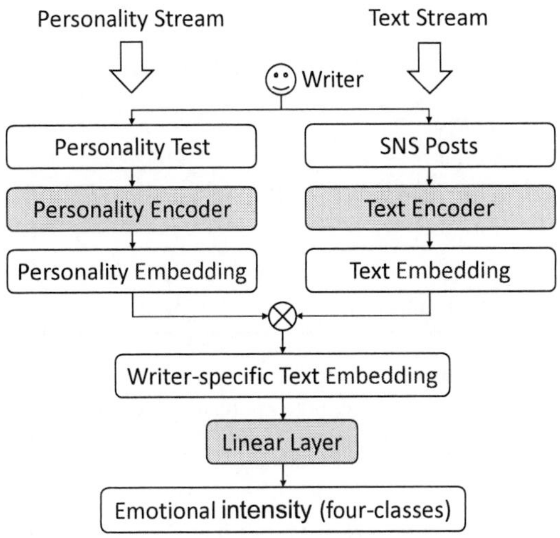

Figure 1: An overview of the proposed method.

A straightforward hypothesis to explain the difference is that *the writer's personality affects their writing*. This hypothesis seems plausible as the same text can have different meanings depending on who wrote it, the contexts such as the writer's preceding SNS text and the circumstance the writer is in, etc; the writer's personality can influence all these aspects and can alter how they author text.

This hypothesis inspires us to design a model specialized for subjective emotion. The model uses the personality test result of each writer, which is fortunately included in the corpus. Specifically, given the personality test result, which is answers to 60 questions (Saito et al., 2001) based on the Big Five personality five-factor model (Goldberg, 1992), we embed 60 answers into a high-dimensional feature vector. Our model, shown in Figure 1 combines feature vectors from the SNS text and the personality to improve the estimation performance.

[1]https://github.com/ids-cv/wrime

Proceedings of the AACL-IJCNLP 2022 Student Research Workshop, pages 1–7
November 20, 2022.

I often have expectations for people I meet in real life, not on the web, and am a little disappointed due to overly high expectations. What should I do?								
	Joy	Sadness	Anticipation	Surprise	Anger	Fear	Disgust	Trust
Subjective	0	3	0	0	0	0	0	0
Objective A	0	1	0	0	0	0	1	0
Objective B	0	1	2	0	0	0	0	0
Objective C	0	2	0	0	0	0	0	0
BERT	0	1	1	0	0	0	3	0
+ Personality	0	3	0	0	0	0	0	0

Why can't people who work hard be rewarded for their efforts? It's so frustrating.								
	Joy	Sadness	Anticipation	Surprise	Anger	Fear	Disgust	Trust
Subjective	0	3	0	0	2	0	1	0
Objective A	0	2	0	0	0	2	2	0
Objective B	0	2	0	0	0	0	3	0
Objective C	0	3	0	0	0	0	0	0
BERT	0	3	0	0	0	0	0	0
+ Personality	0	3	0	0	2	0	3	0

Table 1: The upper rows of each table show examples of emotional intensity labels, consisting of subjective and objective ones, where three annotators (A–C) were invited for this sample (0: none, 1: weak, 2: medium, 3: strong). The lower part of each table shows the prediction results of the baseline model and our method.

Experimental results on the WRIME corpus show that our model performs better than both Bag-of-Words (BoW) and BERT (Devlin et al., 2019) baselines without personality information, which suggests the advantage of using writers' personality information for subjective emotional intensity estimation. Furthermore, a hybrid model combining the existing personalized method (Milkowski et al., 2021) with ours achieved state-of-the-art performance in emotional intensity estimation. The performance is on par with the performance of our human annotators.

2 Related Work

Human emotions are subjective and have personal biases depending on many factors such as the first language, age, education (Wich et al., 2020; Al Kuwatly et al., 2020), gender (Bolukbasi et al., 2016; Tatman, 2017), race (Sap et al., 2019; Davidson et al., 2019), and personality (Kajiwara et al., 2021). Due to the nature of such personal biases, writers may express different emotions even if they wrote the same text (Milkowski et al., 2021; Ngo et al., 2022). Taking into account the emotional differences between writers is important for a high-quality emotional analysis.

Personalized emotion analysis has been studied in recent years. Milkowski et al. (2021) personalized the emotion analysis by focusing on the labeling variation among annotators. They proposed Personal Emotional Bias (PEB) as a measure of labeling variation and showed that such user-specific information contributes to emotional intensity estimation. Kajiwara et al. (2021) personalized the emotion analysis by focusing on the personality of the text writer. They considered personality information based on the Big Five personality five-factor model (Goldberg, 1992) in a simple way (concatenation or attention) and showed that such user-specific information contributes to emotional intensity estimation. This study advances the latter approach and proposes a more effective method to model personality information for this task.

3 Methods

As argued in Section 1, we hypothesize that the writer's personality influences how they express themselves. We thus propose to leverage the personality of the writer as auxiliary information, especially for subjective emotional intensity estimation.

Figure 1 shows the overall structure of our model, which consists of the *text stream* and *personality stream*, fused together for estimating personality-aware emotional intensities. The text stream is the feature extractor of a basic emotional intensity estimation model, and the personality stream can also be seen as the feature extractor of regression model, trained to predict individual personality traits of the Big Five taxonomy (Goldberg, 1992).

3.1 Text Stream

Our text stream is a part of simple BERT pre-trained model (Devlin et al., 2019)-based emotional intensity classifiers. The 768-dimensional feature vector $\boldsymbol{h}_\text{t}$ corresponding to `[CLS]` token is fed into a linear classifier for each emotion to predict one of the four-level intensities of the emotion (as in Table 1). We use $\boldsymbol{h}_t$ as text features.

3.2 Personality Stream

The WRIME (Kajiwara et al., 2021; Suzuki et al., 2022) corpus provides a personality assessment result for each writer during the curation process. This personality assessment is based on the Big Five model (Goldberg, 1992), and our writers were asked to answer 60 questions related to talkativeness, anxiousness, etc. (Saito et al., 2001) over a seven-point scale. The answers are collectively mapped into continuous likeliness values (Big Five Scales) of the writer having the five personality traits (i.e. *extraversion*, *neuroticism*, *openness*, *conscientiousness*, and *agreeableness*).

For embedding a writer's personality in a feature vector, we mimic the process of computing the likeliness values from the 60 answers using a 3-layer multilayer perceptron with a 60-dimensional input layer and a 5-dimensional output layer, as shown in Figure 2. The middle layer's dimensionality is 768, which is the same as the output of BERT. We use the middle layer as personality feature $\boldsymbol{h}_p$.

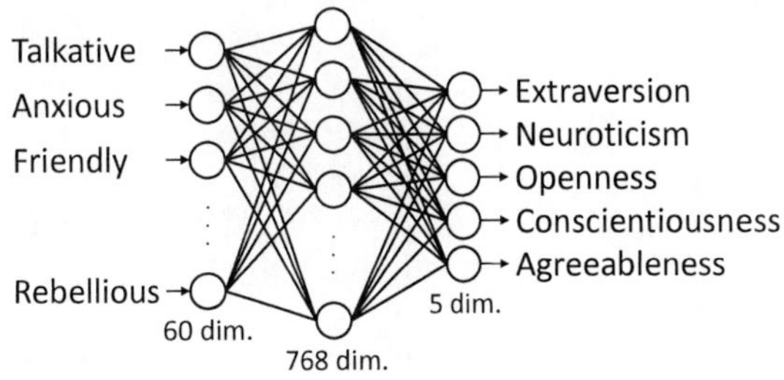

Figure 2: Mapping from 60 answers to Big Five personality traits.

3.3 Fusion of Text and Personality Streams

The feature vectors $\boldsymbol{h}_t$ and $\boldsymbol{h}_p$ are fused for personality-aware emotional intensity estimation, where the dimensionalities of the feature vectors are both $d = 768$. We exploratively evaluate the following four approaches for fusion.

1. **Difference** uses $\boldsymbol{h}_\text{diff} = |\boldsymbol{h}_t - \boldsymbol{h}_p|$ as a fused vector. This approach retains the dimensionality of the fused vector $\boldsymbol{h}$.
2. **Product** applies the element-wise multiplication $\boldsymbol{h}_\text{prod} = \boldsymbol{h}_t \odot \boldsymbol{h}_p$. This approach retains the dimensionality of the fused vector $\boldsymbol{h}$.
3. **Concatenation** is given by $\boldsymbol{h}_\text{conc} = [\boldsymbol{h}_t, \boldsymbol{h}_p]$, where $[\cdot, \cdot]$ is the operator for concatenation. This approach doubles the fused vector's dimensionality.
4. **All** concatenate all these fused vectors, i.e., $\boldsymbol{h}_\text{all} = [\boldsymbol{h}_\text{diff}, \boldsymbol{h}_\text{prod}, \boldsymbol{h}_\text{conc}]$. This approach results in a $4d$-dimensional fused vector.

For fusion approach $f \in \{\text{diff}, \text{prod}, \text{conc}, \text{all}\}$, emotional intensity is estimated by

$$\boldsymbol{y}_e = \text{softmax}(\boldsymbol{W}_e \boldsymbol{h}_f + \boldsymbol{b}_e), \qquad (1)$$

where $\boldsymbol{y}_e \in [0, 1]^4$ is the confidences of four intensity levels for emotion e in Plutchik's basic emotions (Plutchik, 1980), and $\boldsymbol{W}_e \in \mathbb{R}^{4 \times D_f}$ and $\boldsymbol{b}_e \in \mathbb{R}^4$ are parameters of the classifier for emotion e (D_f is size of fused vector for approach f).

4 Experiments

Using WRIME (Kajiwara et al., 2021; Suzuki et al., 2022), a corpus for estimating the emotion analysis in Japanese, we conduct an experiment to evaluate a four-class (i.e. none, weak, medium, and strong) classification of writers' emotional intensity.

4.1 Setting

4.1.1 Dataset

For a fair comparison with the previous work (Milkowski et al., 2021), we first split 35,000 SNS posts by 60 writers into two parts: One is for training/evaluating the models, while the other is for computing the user representation in PEB. Following Milkowski et al. (2021), the latter part thus contains past 15% of SNS posts authored by each writer. The former is further split into training, validation, and evaluation sets. The training, validation, and evaluation sets respectively contain 25,500 posts from 40 writers, 2,125 posts from 10 writers, and 2,125

	Joy	Sadness	Anticipation	Surprise	Anger	Fear	Disgust	Trust	Overall
BoW	0.307	0.181	0.151	0.132	0.165	0.145	0.178	0.080	0.227
+ Difference	0.313	0.206	0.164	0.144	0.151	0.117	0.168	0.108	0.229
+ Product	0.293	0.233	0.139	0.145	0.164	0.154	0.200	0.037	0.231
+ Concat	0.294	0.217	0.148	0.120	0.144	0.145	0.188	0.101	0.236
+ All	0.300	0.231	0.169	0.111	**0.167**	0.108	0.178	0.097	0.230
+ Pc	0.293	0.193	0.153	0.121	0.135	0.153	0.151	0.066	0.219
+ Pa	0.310	0.192	0.130	0.121	0.138	0.093	0.180	0.067	0.213
+ PEB	0.329	0.292	**0.207**	0.198	0.147	0.174	0.181	**0.142**	0.260
+ Personality (All)	**0.336**	**0.312**	0.199	**0.200**	0.147	**0.185**	**0.249**	0.115	**0.281**
BERT	0.551	0.419	0.352	0.341	0.375	0.302	0.431	0.206	0.437
+ Difference	0.559	0.444	0.368	0.336	0.381	0.313	0.410	0.225	0.440
+ Product	0.573	0.468	0.363	**0.351**	0.384	0.311	**0.439**	0.240	0.459
+ Concat	0.558	0.453	0.332	0.331	0.359	0.303	0.433	0.222	0.444
+ All	0.573	**0.476**	0.373	0.345	0.404	**0.328**	0.425	0.153	0.454
+ Pc	0.564	0.443	0.377	0.310	0.358	0.290	0.403	**0.243**	0.438
+ Pa	0.560	0.430	0.359	0.322	0.392	0.284	0.413	0.206	0.429
+ PEB	0.576	0.455	0.377	0.336	**0.421**	0.327	0.429	0.198	0.451
+ Personality (All)	**0.588**	0.469	**0.389**	0.343	0.394	0.311	0.451	0.214	**0.462**
Annotator 1	0.622	0.461	0.423	0.348	0.363	0.333	0.394	0.089	0.439
Annotator 2	0.633	0.526	0.432	0.339	0.386	0.361	0.442	0.153	0.465
Annotator 3	0.624	0.450	0.459	0.396	0.374	0.380	0.467	0.134	0.463

Table 2: Quadratic weighted kappa of the writer's subjective emotional intensity estimation.

posts from 10 writers. We employ quadratic weighted kappa[2] (Cohen, 1968) as our evaluation metric, which assesses the agreement between the estimated and correct labels, considering the ordinal nature of our labels.

4.1.2 Implementation Details

For the text steam, we evaluated the two models.

- **BoW** extracts bag-of-words from a post and estimates emotional intensity by linear regression model. MeCab (IPADIC-2.7.0)[3] (Kudo et al., 2004) is used for word segmentation.
- **BERT** is a Japanese BERT[4] (Devlin et al., 2019) with a structure of 12 layers, 12 attention heads, and 768 dimensions, pre-trained with mask language modeling objectives on 86 million Japanese Twitter posts.

The BoW model is implemented using scikit-learn[5] (Pedregosa et al., 2011). The HuggingFace Transformers (Wolf et al., 2020) is used to implement the BERT model. BERT is fine-tuned using the cross entropy loss with the batch size of 32 posts and the dropout rate of 0.1. The learning rate is set to 2e-5 with the Adam optimizer (Kingma and Ba, 2015). Early stopping is used for training and training stops when the metric (quadratic weighted kappa) of the validation set does not improve for 3 epochs. For linear regressor of the BoW model is trained with the learning rate of 0.01.

Both BoW and BERT models are coupled with writers' personality features in Section 3.2 by the four fusion approaches. For this personality embedding, the multilayer perceptron shown in Figure 2 with sigmoid activation is trained for 1,000 epochs with the SGD optimizer and the mean squared error loss.

4.1.3 Comparative Methods

We compare the following three existing methods with the proposed method.

- **Pc (Kajiwara et al., 2021)** uses $h_c = W_c[\boldsymbol{u}, \boldsymbol{v}]$ as a feature vector, where $\boldsymbol{v}$ is a 768-dimensional textual representation corresponding to the `[CLS]` token of BERT and $\boldsymbol{u}$ is a 786-dimensional personality representation computed by a linear mapping from the

[2] https://scikit-learn.org/stable/modules/generated/sklearn.metrics.cohen_kappa_score.html

[3] https://taku910.github.io/mecab/

[4] https://github.com/hottolink/hottoSNS-bert

[5] https://scikit-learn.org/

5-dimensional Big Five personality traits. We use Equation (1) as classifier with replacing $\boldsymbol{h}_f$ with $\boldsymbol{h}_c$.

- **Pa (Kajiwara et al., 2021)** employs the scaled dot-product attention (Vaswani et al., 2017) as $\boldsymbol{h}_a = \text{attention}(\boldsymbol{W}^Q\boldsymbol{u}, \boldsymbol{W}^K\boldsymbol{v}, \boldsymbol{W}^V\boldsymbol{v})$ for feature extraction, so that textual representation corresponding to the `[CLS]` token of BERT can be weighted based on the writer's personality. Emotional intensity estimation is done in the same way as Pc but with $\boldsymbol{h}_a$.

- **PEB (Milkowski et al., 2021)** extracts features by $\boldsymbol{h}_{\text{PEB}} = \boldsymbol{W}_{\text{PEB}}[\boldsymbol{z}, \boldsymbol{v}']$, where $\boldsymbol{v}'$ is a textual representation given by linearly transforming $\boldsymbol{v}$ into a 50-dimensional vector and $\boldsymbol{z}$ is a user representation given by linear transformation of a 8-dimensional vector representing annotation bias for each emotion into a 50-dimensional vector. Again, Equation (1) is used with $\boldsymbol{h}_{\text{PEB}}$ for emotional estimation.

4.2 Results

Table 2 shows the experimental results. The scores are the average of quadratic weighted kappa values over three training runs, where we trained the models five times with different parameter initialization and excluded the maximum and minimum kappa values. The table is divided into three blocks: The top two are for the emotional intensity estimation models, while the bottom block shows the human performance of three annotators in the WRIME corpus (Kajiwara et al., 2021; Suzuki et al., 2022). Note that these annotators do not know the writer's personality or past posts.

Compared to the BoW model, the BERT model consistently achieves higher performance. This is a reasonable result for two reasons: feature extraction with BoW cannot take context into account, and BoW does not have the benefit of a large-scale corpus such as the one used for pre-training BERT.

The proposed methods showed improvement in many emotions compared to the baseline model, which does not take the writer's personality into account. Our Difference method improved performance on five out of eight emotions for BoW and on six emotions for BERT. Our Product method improved performance on half of the eight emotions for BoW and consistently improved performance on all emotions for BERT. While our Concat method only improved performance on three out of eight emotions for BoW, it improved on five emotions for BERT. Our All method improved performance on half of the eight emotions for BoW and on six emotions for BERT. Furthermore, the proposed methods consistently improved performance in the overall evaluation. These experimental results confirm the effectiveness of the proposed methods for estimating subjective emotional intensity with the writer's personality information.

Next, we discuss the results of a comparison of the proposed and existing methods. The existing methods for Pc and Pa (Kajiwara et al., 2021) did not show significant improvement from each baseline model in the overall evaluation in this experimental setting. Although these existing methods utilize the writer's personality similar to our method, they differ in the method for feature extraction from the personality information. In contrast, our methods consistently improved performance in the overall evaluation.

Another existing method, PEB (Milkowski et al., 2021), achieves higher performance than our methods for BoW and comparable performance to our methods for BERT in the overall evaluation. Because our method, which takes into account the personality of the writer, and PEB, which takes into account labeling variations, take different approaches to personalize emotional intensity estimation, we can expect synergies from their combination. The bottom methods in Table 2, using $\boldsymbol{h}_{\text{hybrid}} = [\boldsymbol{h}_{\text{diff}}, \boldsymbol{h}_{\text{prod}}, \boldsymbol{h}_{\text{conc}}, \boldsymbol{h}_{\text{PEB}}]$ instead of $\boldsymbol{h}_f$, achieved the best performance for both BoW and BERT models in the overall evaluation. Furthermore, BERT with both writer's personality and PEB achieved performance comparable to the human annotators in the overall evaluation. These experimental results demonstrate the usefulness of personality information in emotional intensity estimation and the effectiveness of our feature extraction method from the personality test.

The bottom row of each table in Table 1 shows examples of output from our model. By taking into account the personality of the writer, we succeeded in emphasizing the emotional intensity of *sadness* in the upper example and *anger* in the lower example, respectively. In the personality test, these writers answered strongly to the questions "pessimistic" and "irascible," respectively.

5 Conclusions

To improve the performance of estimating subjective emotional intensity by writers, we propose an emotional intensity estimation model that takes into account the writer's personality information. In the proposed method, we first extracted feature representations from the results of a personality test based on the Big Five personality five-factor model. Then, we fused that personality features with textual features from BoW or BERT to personalize the emotional intensity estimation. Experimental results on subjective emotional intensity estimation in Japanese SNS text reveal the effectiveness of the proposed methods in taking into account the personality of the writer.

Currently, our method requires writers to answer a 60-item personality test. Therefore, our future work includes studying methods for estimating the writer's personality from their past posts, and how to combine them with the present method.

Acknowledgements

This work was supported by Innovation Platform for Society 5.0 from Japan Ministry of Education, Culture, Sports, Science and Technology (JPMXP0518071489).

References

Hala Al Kuwatly, Maximilian Wich, and Georg Groh. 2020. Identifying and Measuring Annotator Bias Based on Annotators' Demographic Characteristics. In *Proceedings of the Fourth Workshop on Online Abuse and Harms*, pages 184–190.

Tolga Bolukbasi, Kai-Wei Chang, James Zou, Venkatesh Saligrama, and Adam Kalai. 2016. Man is to Computer Programmer as Woman is to Homemaker? Debiasing Word Embeddings. In *Proceedings of the 30th Conference on Neural Information Processing Systems*, pages 4356–4364.

Laura Ana Maria Bostan, Evgeny Kim, and Roman Klinger. 2020. GoodNewsEveryone: A Corpus of News Headlines Annotated with Emotions, Semantic Roles, and Reader Perception. In *In Proceedings of the 12th Language Resources and Evaluation Conference*, pages 1554–1566.

Jacob Cohen. 1968. Weighted Kappa: Nominal Scale Agreement Provision for Scaled Disagreement or Partial Credit. *Psychological Bulletin*, 70(4):213–220.

Thomas Davidson, Debasmita Bhattacharya, and Ingmar Weber. 2019. Racial Bias in Hate Speech and Abusive Language Detection Datasets. In *Proceedings of the Third Workshop on Abusive Language Online*, pages 25–35.

Jacob Devlin, Ming-Wei Chang, Kenon Lee, and Kristina Toutanova. 2019. BERT: Pre-training of Deep Bidirectional Transformers for Language Understanding. In *Proceedings of the 2019 Conference of the North American Chapter of the Association for Computational Linguistics: Human Language Technologies*, pages 4171–4186.

Paul Ekman. 1992. A General Psychoevolutionary Theory of Emotion. *Cognition and Emotion*, 6(3–4):169–200.

Lewis R Goldberg. 1992. The Development of Markers for the Big-Five Factor Structure. *Psychological Assessment*, 4(1):26–42.

Tomoyuki Kajiwara, Chenhui Chu, Noriko Takemura, Yuta Nakashima, and Hajime Nagahara. 2021. WRIME: A New Dataset for Emotional Intensity Estimation with Subjective and Objective Annotations. In *Proceedings of the 2021 Conference of the North American Chapter of the Association for Computational Linguistics: Human Language Technologies*, pages 2095–2104.

Diederik P. Kingma and Jimmy Lei Ba. 2015. Adam: A Method for Stochastic Optimization. In *Proceedings of the 3rd International Conference on Learning Representations*.

Taku Kudo, Kaoru Yamamoto, and Yuji Matsumoto. 2004. Applying Conditional Random Fields to Japanese Morphological Analysis. In *Proceedings of the 2004 Conference on Empirical Methods in Natural Language Processing*, pages 230–237.

Piotr Milkowski, Marcin Gruza, Kamil Kanclerz, Przemyslaw Kazienko, Damian Grimling, and Jan Kocon. 2021. Personal Bias in Prediction of Emotions Elicited by Textual Opinions. In *Proceedings of the 59th Annual Meeting of the Association for Computational Linguistics and the 11th International Joint Conference on Natural Language Processing: Student Research Workshop*, pages 248–259.

Anh Ngo, Agri Candri, Teddy Ferdinan, Jan Kocon, and Wojciech Korczynski. 2022. StudEmo: A Non-aggregated Review Dataset for Personalized Emotion Recognition. In *Proceedings of the 1st Workshop on Perspectivist Approaches to NLP*, pages 46–55.

Fabian Pedregosa, Gaël Varoquaux, Alexandre Gramfort, Vincent Michel, Bertrand Thirion, Olivier Grisel, Mathieu Blondel, Peter Prettenhofer, Ron Weiss, Vincent Dubourg, Jake Vanderplas, Alexandre Passos, David Cournapeau, Matthieu Brucher, Matthieu Perrot, and Édouard Duchesnay. 2011. Scikit-learn: Machine Learning in Python. *Journal of Machine Learning Research*, 12(85):2825–2830.

Robert Plutchik. 1980. A General Psychoevolutionary Theory of Emotion. *Theories of Emotion*, 1:3–31.

Takako Saito, Tomoyasu Nakamura, Toshihiko Endo, and Madoka Yokoyama. 2001. Standardization of Big Five Scales Using the Adjective Check List. *Kyushu University Psychological Research*, 2:135–144.

Maarten Sap, Dallas Card, Saadia Gabriel, Yejin Choi, and Noah A. Smith. 2019. The Risk of Racial Bias in Hate Speech Detection. In *Proceedings of the 57th Annual Meeting of the Association for Computational Linguistics*, pages 1668–1678.

Stefan Stieglitz and Linh Dang-Xuan. 2013. Emotions and Information Diffusion in Social Media — Sentiment of Microblogs and Sharing Behavior. *Journal of Management Information Systems*, 29(4):217–248.

Carlo Strapparava and Rada Mihalcea. 2007. SemEval-2007 Task 14: Affective Text. In *Proceedings of the Fourth International Workshop on Semantic Evaluations*, pages 70–74.

Haruya Suzuki, Yuto Miyauchi, Kazuki Akiyama, Tomoyuki Kajiwara, Takashi Ninomiya, Noriko Takemura, Yuta Nakashima, and Hajime Nagahara. 2022. A Japanese Dataset for Subjective and Objective Sentiment Polarity Classification in Micro Blog Domain. In *Proceedings of the 13th International Conference on Language Resources and Evaluation*, pages 7022–7028.

Rachael Tatman. 2017. Gender and Dialect Bias in YouTube's Automatic Captions. In *Proceedings of the First ACL Workshop on Ethics in Natural Language Processing*, pages 53–59.

Ryoko Tokuhisa, Kentaro Inui, and Yuji Matsumoto. 2008. Emotion Classification Using Massive Examples Extracted from the Web. In *Proceedings of the 22nd International Conference on Computational Linguistics*, pages 881–888.

Ashish Vaswani, Noam Shazeer, Niki Parmar, Jakob Uszkoreit, Llion Jones, Aidan N Gomez, Łukasz Kaiser, and Illia Polosukhin. 2017. Attention is All you Need. In *Advances in Neural Information Processing Systems*, pages 5998–6008.

Maximilian Wich, Hala Al Kuwatly, and Georg Groh. 2020. Investigating Annotator Bias with a Graph-Based Approach. In *Proceedings of the Fourth Workshop on Online Abuse and Harms*, pages 191–199.

Thomas Wolf, Lysandre Debut, Victor Sanh, Julien Chaumond, Clement Delangue, Anthony Moi, Pierric Cistac, Tim Rault, Remi Louf, Morgan Funtowicz, Joe Davison, Sam Shleifer, Patrick von Platen, Clara Ma, Yacine Jernite, Julien Plu, Canwen Xu, Teven Le Scao, Sylvain Gugger, Mariama Drame, Quentin Lhoest, and Alexander Rush. 2020. Transformers: State-of-the-Art Natural Language Processing. In *Proceedings of the 2020 Conference on Empirical Methods in Natural Language Processing: System Demonstrations*, pages 38–45.

Bipartite-play Dialogue Collection for Practical Automatic Evaluation of Dialogue Systems

Shiki Sato[1,*] Yosuke Kishinami[1,*] Hiroaki Sugiyama[2] Reina Akama[1,3]
Ryoko Tokuhisa[1] Jun Suzuki[1,3]
[1]Tohoku University [2]NTT Communication Science Laboratories [3]RIKEN
{shiki.sato.d1,akama,tokuhisa,jun.suzuki}@tohoku.ac.jp
yosuke.kishinami.q8@dc.tohoku.ac.jp, h.sugi@ieee.org

Abstract

Automation of dialogue system evaluation is a driving force for the efficient development of dialogue systems. This paper introduces the *bipartite-play* method, a dialogue collection method for automating dialogue system evaluation. It addresses the limitations of existing dialogue collection methods: (i) inability to compare with systems that are not publicly available, and (ii) vulnerability to cheating by intentionally selecting systems to be compared. Experimental results show that the automatic evaluation using the bipartite-play method mitigates these two drawbacks and correlates as strongly with human subjectivity as existing methods.

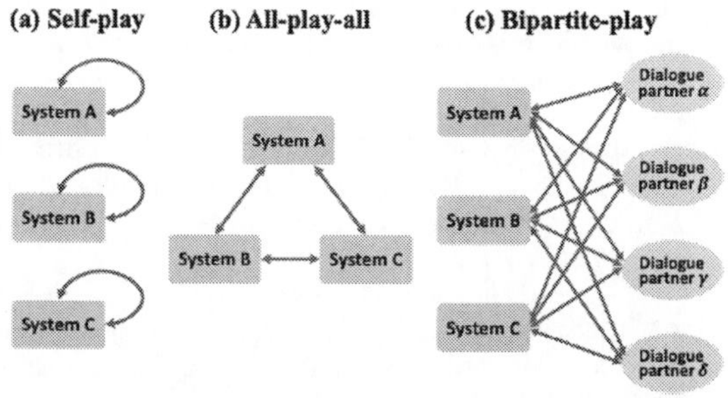

Figure 1: Dialogue collection methods. Here, the evaluation targets are System A, B, and C. (a) Self-play collects dialogues by talking to themselves (e.g., A-A and B-B). (b) All-play-all collects dialogues with other evaluation targets (e.g., A-B and A-C). (c) Our bipartite-play collects dialogues with fixed dialogue partners separated from the evaluation targets (e.g., A-α and A-β).

1 Introduction

The performance evaluation of dialogue systems is a crucial and challenging research topic for the dialogue research community. The community recommends human evaluation as the primary evaluation method, which is the gold standard but is time-consuming and costly. Moreover, reproducing the evaluation results is mostly impractical due to the unavailability of maintaining identical evaluators or identical evaluation conditions. Human evaluation is therefore unsuitable for evaluating daily updates of developing dialogue systems or comparing systems with non-public ones. Thus, constructing a better automatic evaluation method, which is both highly reproducible and low cost, is desirable. In particular, automating interactive evaluation, not static evaluation such as BLEU (Papineni et al., 2002), is attracting an increasing interest as static evaluation cannot capture diverse aspects of dialogue systems (Ghandeharioun et al., 2019).

An interactive evaluation framework consists of two phases: first, *collecting* the dialogues in which the systems to be evaluated (hereinafter called evaluation targets) talk to others (hereinafter called dialogue partners), then *rating* evaluation targets based on the quality of their utterances in the collected dialogues. Regarding the collecting (i.e., automating dialogue partners), **self-play** and **all-play-all** (Figure 1 (a) and (b)) are the current promising methods; All-play-all collects dialogues among multiple evaluation targets, while self-play collects dialogues with itself. Recently, Yang et al. (2022) have reported that all-play-all correlates with human evaluation strongly. However, all-play-all is not perfect and has at least two potential drawbacks: (i) the difficulty of comparison with publicly inaccessible systems and (ii) the vulnerability to cheating by choice of evaluation targets, i.e., with whom the evaluation target will talk (Section 3).

This paper addresses the above two drawbacks of the all-play-all method while maintaining the all-play-all method's high correlation with human rating. Specifically, we propose the **bipartite-play** method, i.e., fixing and sharing a set of dialogue partners across studies as shown in Figure 1 (c) instead of assigning other evaluation targets as partners as shown in Figure 1 (b) (Section 4). The bipartite-play method offers (i) a fair comparison

*Both authors contributed equally to this paper.

Proceedings of the AACL-IJCNLP 2022 Student Research Workshop, pages 8–16
November 20, 2022.

with publicly inaccessible systems as long as its developers use our method and (ii) prevention of cheating by an intentional choice of evaluation targets. Our experiments show that the bipartite-play method strongly correlates with humans as the all-play-all method while preventing the potential drawbacks in the all-play-all method.

2 Related Work

2.1 Automatic dialogue collection

Self-play. The self-play method collects dialogues where evaluation targets talk to themselves, i.e., $i \times 1 \times j$ dialogues in which collecting j dialogues for each of i evaluation targets. This method is cost-effective for interactive dialogue system evaluation since it does not require human interactions (Ghandeharioun et al., 2019; Deriu and Cieliebak, 2019). However, since there are few dialogue partners, it does not fully expose the characteristics of evaluation targets (Yang et al., 2022).

All-play-all. The all-play-all method collects dialogues between multiple evaluation targets, i.e., $i \times (i-1) \times j$ dialogues when collecting j dialogues for each of i evaluation targets (considering speaker order). This method also requires no human interactions. Compared to the self-play method, the all-play-all method's dialogue partners are more diverse since it collects dialogues with other evaluation targets that result in various dialogues (Deriu et al., 2020; Yang et al., 2022). Additionally, direct interactions with evaluation targets make them easy to compare. Yang et al. (2022) experimentally showed that the evaluation using the all-play-all method correlates with human evaluation stronger than the self-play method.

2.2 Automatic dialogue rating

Compared with methods relying on reference responses (e.g., BLEU (Papineni et al., 2002), ROUGE (Lin, 2004), METEOR (Lavie and Agarwal, 2007), Greedy Matching (Rus and Lintean, 2012), Vector Extrema (Forgues et al., 2014), and ADEM (Lowe et al., 2017)), reference-free methods, such as USR (Mehri and Eskenazi, 2020b), GPT-2 based evaluation (Pang et al., 2020), FED (Mehri and Eskenazi, 2020a), and DynaEval (Zhang et al., 2021), have attracted greater interest from the research community. For example, FED allows fine-grained practical evaluation of the system utterances without high-cost preparation, such as training an evaluation model; it assesses system utterances for given dimensions, such as Fluency and Specificity, by guessing whether positive or negative responses are valid to the system utterance in terms of language model score (see Section 5.1). We also focus on reference-free evaluation, especially the FED metric, to automate the rating part of the interactive evaluation, as preparing references for automatically collected dialogues is impractical.

3 Limitations of All-play-all Method

The all-play-all method enables effective dialogue collection for system comparison, as described in Section 2. However, we point out that the current all-play-all method cannot handle the following two cases: First, when the group of evaluation targets includes unavailable systems. Since all-play-all requires the collection of dialogues with all evaluation targets, it is impossible to compare systems that are not released or that cannot be run by many researchers due to such computational resources. Second, when one attempts to boost their system's performance by deploying an unfair evaluation setting. Our experiments (Section 6) reveal that one can intentionally improve the automatic evaluation results of desired systems by choosing evaluation targets to be compared when using the all-play-all method. If these potential drawbacks can be overcome, existing automated evaluation methods could be enhanced to be more versatile and practical.

4 Proposed Method: Bipartite-play

We introduce a new automatic dialogue collection method, called bipartite-play method, which updates the two aforementioned limitations.

Evaluation targets vs fixed dialogue partners. Considering the two drawbacks of the all-play-all method (Section 3), we propose fixing and sharing a set of publicly accessible systems as dialogue partners rather than assigning other evaluation targets as partners. Our idea is that even if evaluation targets do not talk to each other directly, dialogues in which evaluation targets talk to the same (shared) partners should be effective for system comparison. In this setting, the diversity of dialogue partners can be maintained by ensuring the diversity of predetermined dialogue partners set. Sharing a set of dialogue partners allows a fair comparison with publicly inaccessible systems as long as its developers use our method. Furthermore, predetermining a set of dialogue partners prevents cheating by an intentional choice of evaluation targets.

Bipartite-play dialogue collection. Given i evaluation targets, the bipartite-play method collects $i \times k \times j$ dialogues by having evaluation targets interact j times with each of the k various dialogue partners predetermined for evaluation.

5 Bipartite-play based Evaluation Framework

Subsequently, we introduce bipartite-play to the interactive dialogue evaluation framework. We combine the dialogue collection based on the bipartite-play method with FED (Mehri and Eskenazi, 2020a), which is one of the modern and effective dialogue rating methods.

5.1 System evaluation procedure

Based on the m collected dialogues by the bipartite-play method, We assess an evaluation target for a dimension v. Specifically, we first evaluate the performance for v in a dialogue using the average score of the system's utterances. We then determine the system's whole performance for v using the average score of m dialogues. We compute the system utterances score using FED. This rating method evaluates the system's utterances for v by guessing whether positive or negative responses for v are valid in terms of the language model as a response to the system's utterance. The validity of each positive and negative response is automatically evaluated using a large-scale dialogue system. The evaluation value of v of the evaluation target's utterance r for a context c is calculated as follows:

$$\sum_{p \in \mathcal{P}_v} D(c+r, p; \theta) - \sum_{n \in \mathcal{N}_v} D(c+r, n; \theta), \quad (1)$$

where $\mathcal{P}_v$ and $\mathcal{N}_v$ are the set of positive and negative responses for v, respectively. $D(c, \cdot; \theta)$ is a function that calculates the probability of generating a response to c using a large-scale dialogue system with parameters θ.

5.2 Preliminary experiment

We assess evaluation targets based on dimensions frequently deployed in recent research (Deriu et al., 2020; Adiwardana et al., 2020): Fluency, Specificity, and Sensibleness, additionally Overall. The applicability of FED to these dimensions is unclear as Mehri and Eskenazi (2020a) cover only some of these dimensions. Therefore, as a preliminary experiment, we determine whether the FED evaluation for these dimensions correlates with humans.

Dimension	FED	w/o neg	w/o pos
Fluency	0.121	−0.145	0.171
Specificity	−0.022	−0.364	0.340
Sensibleness	0.370	-	0.370
Overall	0.329	−0.367	0.386

Table 1: Spearman's rank correlation coefficients of the FED with human evaluation. "w/o pos" and "w/o neg" are the FED evaluations calculated without positive and negative responses respectively. "w/o neg" for Sensibleness is a missing value.

Dataset. We created the dataset by collecting dialogues between the dialogue system and humans, then annotating the collected dialogues with a human evaluation score. Crowdsourcing[1] was employed in two processes. First, we collected dialogues between the 11 systems deployed as evaluation targets for the experiments in Section 6 and humans. We obtained 50 dialogues for each system, for 550 dialogues in total.[2] We then asked five workers to evaluate each collected dialogue with a five-point Likert scale for the question about each of the four dimensions.[3]

FED evaluation settings. We used the positive and negative responses manually created by Mehri and Eskenazi (2020a), and our additional responses for the FED evaluation. Also, we used Blender 9B from ParlAI (Miller et al., 2017) as a large-scale dialogue system to calculate FED scores. We used the four dimensions for which human evaluation scores were annotated in the constructed dataset.

Results of FED evaluation. Table 1 shows Spearman's rank correlation coefficients between the FED and human evaluation results. We found that the FED evaluation using only the negative response correlates to some extent with human evaluation. Although Mehri and Eskenazi (2020a) proposed a method using positive and negative responses, we use only negative responses in subsequent experiments based on these results. Also, we

[1] `https://www.mturk.com/`

[2] Starts with the human's *Hi!* and continues for six turns.

[3] We asked workers *Are Bot's responses fluent and grammatically correct?* (Fluency), *Are Bot's responses specific and explicit in the given context?* (Specificity), *Are Bot's responses sensible?* (Sensibleness), and *Is the overall impression of the chatbot good?* (Overall), and they answered from *Strongly disagree* (score 1) to *Strongly agree* (score 5).

Evaluation targets:	Tfm-3B-Rdt-Bsm, Tfm-3B-Rdt-Msc, Tfm-3B-R2c-Bsm, Tfm-3B-Rdt-Lgu, GPT-345M-Wtx-Rdt, Tfm-89M-Ddc-Nft, Tfm-89M-Ddc-Crm, Tfm-89M-Ddc-Ddg, Tfm-89M-Ddc-Rdt, Tfm-89M-Ddc-Twt, PEn-256M-Rdt-Bst
Partner systems:	Tfm-3B-Rdt-Slf, Tfm-3B-Rdt-Lgt, Tfm-3B-Rdt-Img, Tfm-3B-Rdt-Sfr, Tfm-1B-Rdt-Bsm, GPT-117M-Wtx-Rdt, GPT-762M-Wtx-Rdt, Tfm-406M-Rdt-Bsm, Tfm-406M-R2c-Bsm, Brt-406M-Rbt-Woi, Trm-89M-Ddc-Wow, Trm-89M-Ddc-Lgt, Trm-89M-Ddc-Emp, Trm-89M-Ddc-Cv2, Trm-89M-Rdt-Wow, Trm-89M-Rdt-Cv2, Trm-88M-Rdt-Bst, Trm-88M-Rdt-Cv2, PEn-256M-Rdt-Cv2, PEn-256M-Rdt-Emp, PEn-256M-Rdt-Wow, PEn-256M-Rdt-All, PEn-256M-Rdt-Bsm, B+F-256M-Rbt-Wow

∗Tfm: Transformer (Vaswani et al., 2017). GPT: DialoGPT (Zhang et al., 2020). PEn: PolyEncoder (Humeau et al., 2020). Brt: Bart (Lewis et al., 2020). B+F: FiD (Izacard and Grave, 2021) with Brt. Rdt: Pushshift Reddit Dataset (Baumgartner et al., 2020). R2c: R2C2 dataset (Shuster et al., 2022). Wtx: WebText dataset (Radford et al., 2019). Ddc: DodecaDialogue dataset (Shuster et al., 2020b). Rbt: Training dataset of RoBERTa (Liu et al., 2019). Bsm: Smith et al. (2020)'s multi-task dataset. Msc: Multi-Session Chat dataset (Xu et al., 2022). Lgu: LIGHT dataset (Urbanek et al., 2019) for unlikelihood training. Nft: No finetune. Crm: Cornell Movie-Dialogs Corpus (Danescu-Niculescu-Mizil and Lee, 2011). Ddg: DailyDialog dataset (Li et al., 2017). Twt: Tweets collected by Shuster et al. (2020b). Bst: BlendedSkillTalk dataset (Smith et al., 2020). Slf: Dialogues collected using the self-play method by Smith and Williams (2021). Lgt: LIGHT dataset. Img: Image-Chat dataset (Shuster et al., 2020a). Sfr: SaFeRDialogues dataset (Ung et al., 2022). Woi: Wizard of the Internet dataset (Komeili et al., 2022). Wow: Wizard of Wikipedia dataset (Dinan et al., 2019b). Emp: EmpatheticDialogues. All: Cv2+Emp+Wow. Cv2: ConvAI2 dataset (Dinan et al., 2019a).

Table 2: Dialogue systems for our experiments: 11 evaluation targets and 24 partner systems. Each system name represents [architecture]-[number of model parameters]-[pretrain data]-[finetune data].

found that the FED evaluation of Fluency correlates poorly with human evaluation, while the other dimensions correlate relatively well with human evaluation. However, the agreement rate for human evaluation is extremely low, and we consider Fluency evaluation with consistent results difficult even for humans.[4] One possible reason is that all systems have a high Fluency in neural response generation, so the difference in the Fluency of dialogues for each sample is small. Therefore, in the evaluation experiment of Section 6, we do not evaluate the Fluency dimension.

6 Experiments: System Evaluation

We show that the interactive automatic evaluation using the bipartite-play method correlates with humans as strongly as the all-play-all method, which has been reported to be an effective dialogue collection method but requires access to all evaluation targets. We first rank prepared evaluation targets by interactive human evaluation and then measure the correlation with the rankings by interactive automatic evaluations in the three dialogue collection methods: self-play, all-play-all, and bipartite-play.

6.1 Experimental settings

Dialogue systems. Table 2 shows the set of 11 evaluation targets and the set of 24 partner systems for the bipartite-play method with diverse architectures and training data from ParlAI.

Dialogue collection settings. For each of the three dialogue collection methods, We set the target-partner pairs for the self-play method, the all-play-all method, and the bipartite-play method. The resulting pairs are $11 \times 1 = 11$, $11 \times (11-1) = 110$, and $11 \times 24 = 264$, respectively. A pair's systems exchange utterances five times to form one dialogue following two given initial utterances, which we extracted from the initial parts of dialogues in the test set of the EmpatheticDialogues dataset (Rashkin et al., 2019). The evaluation target of each pair talks first. We found that ranking the 11 systems with the self-play method required 1,000 dialogues of each pair to converge in our settings, while the all-play-all method and the bipartite-play method required each pair's 600 dialogues; we used these numbers of dialogues for the experiments.

Interactive human evaluation. We compute each evaluation target's score for each of the three dimensions (i.e., Specificity, Sensibleness, and Overall) by averaging the manually annotated scores of 50 dialogues in Section 5.2. We then rank evaluation targets based on their averaged scores.

6.2 System evaluation results

Table 3 shows Spearman's rank correlation coefficients of the automatic evaluations with the human evaluation. First, the automatic evaluation using the all-play-all method had a stronger correlation with humans than the self-play method; this is consistent with Yang et al. (2022)'s results. Second, the automatic evaluation with the bipartite-play method achieved the exact high correlation as the all-play-all method. This shows that the bipartite-play method enables reliable interactive automatic evaluation without direct interaction between evaluation targets.

Not requiring direct interaction makes system comparison across studies much easier. For in-

[4]To compute inter-annotator agreement, we randomly divided the five annotators into two groups and calculated Spearman's rank correlation coefficients between those groups. The results were 0.603 (Fluency), 0.835 (Specificity), 0.857 (Sensibleness), and 0.831 (Overall).

Method	Specificity	Sensibleness	Overall
Self-play	0.83	0.70	0.77
All-play-all	**0.90**	**0.75**	**0.85**
Bipartite-play	**0.90**	**0.75**	**0.85**

Table 3: Spearman's rank correlation coefficients of the automatic evaluations using the three dialogue collection method with the human evaluation.

stance, with the same settings as our experiment, one can indirectly compare their systems with our evaluation targets by comparing systems' FED scores. As one of the reference values, we present the FED scores of Tfm-3B-Rdt-Bsm, referred to as Blender 3B (Roller et al., 2021): 11.99 (Specificity), 14.48 (Sensibleness), and 3.99 (Overall).

6.3 Qualitative analysis of bipartite-play

Tables 4 and 5 show dialogue examples of Tfm-89M-Ddc-Ddg (an evaluation target) collected using the bipartite-play method. Tfm-89M-Ddc-Ddg talked with Tfm-1B-Rdt-Bsm, a high-performance system (Table 4), and GPT-117M-Wtx-Rdt, which is guessed to have relatively low performance in the set of dialogue partners (Table 5).

Collecting dialogues. Tfm-89M-Ddc-Ddg returned valid responses to high-quality utterances of Tfm-1B-Rdt-Bsm (Table 4). However, Tfm-89M-Ddc-Ddg generated semantically inappropriate responses (bolded parts) to low-quality utterances of GPT-117M-Wtx-Rdt (Table 5). These examples suggest that Tfm-89M-Ddc-Ddg can handle high-quality inputs but may be vulnerable to low-quality ones. Therefore, the bipartite-play method can reveal the diverse features of evaluation targets.

Rating dialogues. Regarding Tfm-89M-Ddc-Ddg, the scores of the dialogues in Tables 4 and 5 for the Overall dimension were 4.00 and 3.81, respectively; FED assigned higher scores to better dialogues than to mediocre ones. In these examples, FED succeeded in assigning appropriate ratings.

7 Discussion

The interactive automatic evaluation using the bipartite-play method correlates with humans as strongly as the all-play-all method, as described in Section 6, without direct interaction with evaluation targets. Additionally, we present another reason to use the bipartite-play method: one can sometimes cheat by choice of evaluation targets when using the all-play-all method.

A:	I love being in the "flow" – whether it's in speaking to a group of people or working to help facilitate meetings.
B:	What kind of work do you do?
A:	i'm a sales manager at a trading company.
B:	That sounds like a lot of fun. I bet you meet lots of interesting people. Do you like it?
A:	i love it. i get to meet new people all the time.
B:	That's great! I'm glad you enjoy it. It sounds like you have a great job.
A:	thanks. i've got a lot to learn.
B:	It's always good to learn new things. What else do you like to do in your spare time?
A:	i like to play chess. how about you?
B:	I love chess as well. My favorite game to play is checkers. Have you ever played that?
A:	no, i haven't . but i'd like to try.
B:	It's a great game. You should give it a try. If you like chess, you'll love it.

Table 4: Example of dialogue between an evaluation target (A; Tfm-89M-Ddc-Ddg) and one of the dialogue partners (B; Tfm-1B-Rdt-Bsm).

A:	I love being in the "flow" – whether it's in speaking to a group of people or working to help facilitate meetings.
B:	What kind of work do you do?
A:	i'm a sales manager at a trading company.
B:	What type of job do you have? I'm looking to get a job as a software engineer in the next year or two.
A:	i work in **the marketing department**. we've been in business for a long time.
B:	Where do you work? I'd love to be a part of the marketing team for a company like that. I'd be happy to work with you.
A:	i work at a small company in the midwest.
B:	Where are you guys located? I'm in the Midwest and would love to work for a small business like that. Thanks!
A:	we're in **los angeles**. we have a lot of offices here.
B:	Are you located in the US? If so, where are you located? If not, what state are you in? Thanks!
A:	yes, we are in the u.s. and we are located in california.
B:	Are you in the U.S.? If so, what state do you live in? Thanks for your help!!

Table 5: Example of dialogue between an evaluation target (A; Tfm-89M-Ddc-Ddg) and one of the dialogue partners (B; GPT-117M-Wtx-Rdt). The evaluation target generated semantically inappropriate responses (bolded parts) to low-quality utterances of the partner.

7.1 How can we cheat on all-play-all?

We found that dialogues where systems frequently speak about the same things tend to receive low ratings from the FED evaluation described in Section 5.2. This can be a desirable evaluation property since human evaluation is known to have the same tendency (Li et al., 2020). Therefore, we hypothesize that one could worsen a particular system's ranking by forming an unfair set of evaluation targets where the system is likely to talk about repeated things.

7.2 Cheating examples

We show cheating using the all-play-all method following the above hypothesis. Specifically, based on Yang et al. (2022)'s observation that systems tend to speak repeated things in self-play (i.e., when talking with extremely similar systems), we attempt to worsen the ranking of a particular system by having the system talk with different but similar systems.

Settings. We form an unfair set of evaluation targets by collecting four systems, i.e., one whose rank we attempt to improve (favored system), another whose rank we attempt to worsen (unfavored system), and two systems similar to the unfavored system. We then check whether the ranking relationship between favored and unfavored ones changes from that of the original all-play-all evaluation (fair evaluation) in Section 6. In this unfair evaluation, unfavored systems have to construct dialogues with similar systems three out of four times, where repeated utterances are likely to occur as in self-play. We prepared two combinations of the unfavored system and its similar system: a series of DialoGPT (GPT-345M-Wtx-Rdt is the unfavored system, whose similar systems are GPT-124M-Wtx-Rdt and GPT-774M-Wtx-Rdt) and a series of Blender (Tfm-3B-Rdt-Bsm is the unfavored system, whose similar systems are Tfm-406M-Rdt-Bsm and Tfm-1B-Rdt-Bsm). We assigned each of all ten evaluation targets for the experiments in Section 6 except the unfavored one (GPT-345M-Wtx-Rdt or Tfm-3B-Rdt-Bsm) as a favored system. We focused on evaluation for Specificity, where the self-play property especially affects the results of automatic evaluation using the self-play method.

Results. Table 6 shows the change in the ranking relationship between favored and unfavored systems. The results show that we succeeded in intentionally improving the favored systems' ranking in some cases. In this way, when using the all-play-all method, one can improve the automatic evaluation results of their systems by choice of evaluation targets. The bipartite-play method, fixing and sharing a set of diverse partner systems, is one of the practical methods to prevent this cheating.

Fair \ Unfair	Favored wins	Favored loses
Favored wins	6	**0**
Favored loses	**2**	2

(a) Evaluation of 10 systems with DialoGPT series.

Fair \ Unfair	Favored wins	Favored loses
Favored wins	1	**0**
Favored loses	**2**	7

(b) Evaluation of 10 systems with Blender series.

Table 6: Changes in the ranking relationship between favored versus unfavored systems by deploying unfair evaluation target sets instead of the original fair set. "Favored wins" means that a favored system was rated higher than the unfavored system. In both situations with the two unfair sets, the ranking was overturned in favor of the two favored systems out of ten.

8 Conclusion

In this paper, we proposed the bipartite-play method as a dialogue collection method. The bipartite-play method can address the impossibility of comparison with publicly inaccessible systems and the vulnerability to cheating by intentional choice evaluation targets to improve the all-play-all method. For the proposed method, no dialogue with evaluation targets is required, thereby facilitating system comparison across studies and possibly enabling comparison with inaccessible systems. Our experiments showed that, compared with the evaluation using the all-play-all method, the automatic evaluation using the bipartite-play method correlates just as strongly with humans.

Although we formed a set of the bipartite-play method's partner systems for the experiments considering its diversity of architectures and training data, it may still have some vulnerabilities. In future work, we will explore the property of the bot-bot dialogue further and refine the set of partner systems for the bipartite-play method.

Acknowledgements

This work was mainly done under the NTT-Tohoku University collaborative research agreement. This work was also partly supported by JSPS KAKENHI Grant Numbers JP19H05693, JP21J22383, and JP22K17943 (training large-scale dialogue models, English proofreading, and registration fees).

References

Daniel Adiwardana, Minh-Thang Luong, David R. So, Jamie Hall, Noah Fiedel, Romal Thoppilan, Zi Yang, Apoorv Kulshreshtha, Gaurav Nemade, Yifeng Lu, and Quoc V. Le. 2020. Towards a Human-like Open-Domain Chatbot. In *aiXiv preprint arXiv:2001.09977*.

Jason Baumgartner, Savvas Zannettou, Brian Keegan, Megan Squire, Jeremy Blackburn, and Pushshift Io. 2020. The Pushshift Reddit Dataset. In *Proceedings of the International AAAI Conference on Web and Social Media (ICWSM2020)*, volume 14, pages 830–839.

Cristian Danescu-Niculescu-Mizil and Lillian Lee. 2011. Chameleons in Imagined Conversations: A New Approach to Understanding Coordination of Linguistic Style in Dialogs. In *Proceedings of the 2nd Workshop on Cognitive Modeling and Computational Linguistics (CMCL2011)*, pages 76–87.

Jan Deriu and Mark Cieliebak. 2019. Towards a Metric for Automated Conversational Dialogue System Evaluation and Improvement. In *Proceedings of the 12th International Conference on Natural Language Generation (INLG)*, pages 432–437.

Jan Deriu, Don Tuggener, Pius von Däniken, Jon Ander Campos, Alvaro Rodrigo, Thiziri Belkacem, Aitor Soroa, Eneko Agirre, and Mark Cieliebak. 2020. Spot The Bot: A Robust and Efficient Framework for the Evaluation of Conversational Dialogue Systems. In *Proceedings of the 2020 Conference on Empirical Methods in Natural Language Processing (EMNLP)*, pages 3971–3984.

Emily Dinan, Varvara Logacheva, Valentin Malykh, Alexander Miller, Kurt Shuster, Jack Urbanek, Douwe Kiela, Arthur Szlam, Iulian Serban, Ryan Lowe, Shrimai Prabhumoye, Alan W. Black, Alexander Rudnicky, Jason Williams, Joelle Pineau, Mikhail Burtsev, and Jason Weston. 2019a. The Second Conversational Intelligence Challenge (ConvAI2). In *aiXiv preprint arXiv:1902.00098*.

Emily Dinan, Stephen Roller, Kurt Shuster, Angela Fan, Michael Auli, and Jason Weston. 2019b. Wizard of Wikipedia: Knowledge-Powered Conversational agents. In *Proceedings of the 7th International Conference on Learning Representations (ICLR2019)*, pages 1–16.

Gabriel Forgues, Joelle Pineau, Jean-Marie Larchevêque, and Réal Tremblay. 2014. Bootstrapping dialog systems with word embeddings. In *Nips modern machine learning and natural language processing workshop*.

Asma Ghandeharioun, Judy Hanwen Shen, Natasha Jaques, Craig Ferguson, Noah Jones, Agata Lapedriza, and Rosalind Picard. 2019. Approximating Interactive Human Evaluation with Self-Play for Open-Domain Dialog Systems. In *Proceedings of the 2019 Conference on Neural Information Processing Systems (NeurIPS)*.

Samuel Humeau, Kurt Shuster, Marie-Anne Lachaux, and Jason Weston. 2020. Poly-encoders: Architectures and Pre-training Strategies for Fast and Accurate Multi-sentence Scoring.

Gautier Izacard and Edouard Grave. 2021. Leveraging Passage Retrieval with Generative Models for Open Domain Question Answering. In *Proceedings of the 16th Conference of the European Chapter of the Association for Computational Linguistics (EACL): Main Volume*, pages 874–880.

Mojtaba Komeili, Kurt Shuster, and Jason Weston. 2022. Internet-Augmented Dialogue Generation. In *Proceedings of the 60th Annual Meeting of the Association for Computational Linguistics (ACL2022)*, volume 1, pages 8460–8478.

Alon Lavie and Abhaya Agarwal. 2007. METEOR: An Automatic Metric for MT Evaluation with High Levels of Correlation with Human Judgments. In *Proceedings of the Second Workshop on Statistical Machine Translation*, pages 228–231.

Mike Lewis, Yinhan Liu, Naman Goyal, Marjan Ghazvininejad, Abdelrahman Mohamed, Omer Levy, Ves Stoyanov, Luke Zettlemoyer, and Facebook Ai. 2020. BART: Denoising Sequence-to-Sequence Pre-training for Natural Language Generation, Translation, and Comprehension. In *Proceedings of the 58th Annual Meeting of the Association for Computational Linguistics (ACL2020)*, pages 7871–7880.

Margaret Li, Stephen Roller, Ilia Kulikov, Sean Welleck, Y-Lan Boureau, Kyunghyun Cho, and Jason Weston. 2020. Don' t Say That! Making Inconsistent Dialogue Unlikely with Unlikelihood Training. In *Proceedings of the 58th Annual Meeting of the Association for Computational Linguistics (ACL2020)*, pages 4715–4728.

Yanran Li, Hui Su, Xiaoyu Shen, Wenjie Li, Ziqiang Cao, Shuzi Niu, and Hong Kong. 2017. DailyDialog: A Manually Labelled Multi-turn Dialogue Dataset. In *Proceedings of the Eighth International Joint Conference on Natural Language Processing (IJCNLP2017)*, pages 986–995.

Chin-Yew Lin. 2004. ROUGE: A Package for Automatic Evaluation of Summaries. In *Text Summarization Branches Out*, pages 74–81, Barcelona, Spain. Association for Computational Linguistics.

Yinhan Liu, Myle Ott, Naman Goyal, Jingfei Du, Mandar Joshi, Danqi Chen, Omer Levy, Mike Lewis, Luke Zettlemoyer, Veselin Stoyanov, and Paul G Allen. 2019. RoBERTa: A Robustly Optimized BERT Pretraining Approach. In *aiXiv preprint arXiv:1907.11692*.

Ryan Lowe, Michael Noseworthy, Iulian Vlad Serban, Nicolas Angelard-Gontier, Yoshua Bengio, and Joelle Pineau. 2017. Towards an Automatic Turing Test:

Learning to Evaluate Dialogue Responses. In *Proceedings of the 55th Annual Meeting of the Association for Computational Linguistics (Volume 1: Long Papers)*, pages 1116–1126.

Shikib Mehri and Maxine Eskenazi. 2020a. Unsupervised Evaluation of Interactive Dialog with DialoGPT. In *Proceedings of the 21th Annual Meeting of the Special Interest Group on Discourse and Dialogue (SIGDIAL)*, pages 225–235.

Shikib Mehri and Maxine Eskenazi. 2020b. USR: An Unsupervised and Reference Free Evaluation Metric for Dialog Generation. In *Proceedings of the 58th Annual Meeting of the Association for Computational Linguistics*, pages 681–707.

Alexander H. Miller, Will Feng, Adam Fisch, Jiasen Lu, Dhruv Batra, Antoine Bordes, Devi Parikh, and Jason Weston. 2017. ParlAI: A Dialog Research Software Platform. In *Proceedings of the 2017 Conference on Empirical Methods in Natural Language Processing (EMNLP): System Demonstrations*, pages 79–84.

Bo Pang, Erik Nijkamp, Wenjuan Han, Linqi Zhou, Yixian Liu, and Kewei Tu. 2020. Towards Holistic and Automatic Evaluation of Open-Domain Dialogue Generation. In *Proceedings of the 58th Annual Meeting of the Association for Computational Linguistics*, pages 3619–3629.

Kishore Papineni, Salim Roukos, Todd Ward, and Wei-Jing Zhu. 2002. BLEU: a method for automatic evaluation of machine translation. In *Proceedings of the 40th Annual Meeting of the Association for Computational Linguistics (ACL2002)*, pages 311–318, Morristown, NJ, USA. Association for Computational Linguistics.

Alec Radford, Jeff Wu, Rewon Child, David Luan, Dario Amodei, and Ilya Sutskever. 2019. Language Models are Unsupervised Multitask Learners. *OpenAI Blog*.

Hannah Rashkin, Eric Michael Smith, Margaret Li, and Y. Lan Boureau. 2019. Towards Empathetic Open-domain Conversation Models: A New Benchmark and Dataset. In *Proceedings of 57th Annual Meeting of the Association for Computational Linguistics, Proceedings of the Conference (ACL2019)*, pages 5370–5381.

Stephen Roller, Emily Dinan, Naman Goyal, Da Ju, Mary Williamson, Yinhan Liu, Jing Xu, Myle Ott, Kurt Shuster, Eric M. Smith, Y. Lan Boureau, and Jason Weston. 2021. Recipes for Building an Open-Domain Chatbot. In *Proceedings of the 16th Conference of the European Chapter of the Association for Computational Linguistics (EACL)*, pages 300–325.

Vasile Rus and Mihai Lintean. 2012. A Comparison of Greedy and Optimal Assessment of Natural Language Student Input Using Word-to-Word Similarity Metrics. In *Proceedings of the Seventh Workshop on Building Educational Applications Using NLP*, pages 157–162, Montréal, Canada. Association for Computational Linguistics.

Kurt Shuster, Samuel Humeau, Antoine Bordes, and Jason Weston. 2020a. Image-Chat: Engaging Grounded Conversations. In *Proceedings of the 58th Annual Meeting of the Association for Computational Linguistics (ACL2020)*, pages 2414–2429.

Kurt Shuster, Da Ju, Stephen Roller, Emily Dinan, Y-Lan Boureau, and Jason Weston. 2020b. The Dialogue Dodecathlon: Open-Domain Knowledge and Image Grounded Conversational Agents. In *Proceedings of the 58th Annual Meeting of the Association for Computational Linguistics (ACL2020)*, pages 2453–2470.

Kurt Shuster, Mojtaba Komeili, Leonard Adolphs, Eth Zürich, Stephen Roller, Arthur Szlam, and Jason Weston. 2022. Language Models that Seek for Knowledge: Modular Search & Generation for Dialogue and Prompt Completion. In *aiXiv preprint arXiv: 2203.13224 (2022)*.

Eric Michael Smith and Adina Williams. 2021. Hi, my name is Martha: Using names to measure and mitigate bias in generative dialogue models. In *aiXiv preprint arXiv:2109.03300 (2021)*.

Eric Michael Smith, Mary Williamson, Kurt Shuster, Jason Weston, and Y-Lan Boureau. 2020. Can You Put it All Together: Evaluating Conversational Agents' Ability to Blend Skills. In *Proceedings of the 58th Annual Meeting of the Association for Computational Linguistics (ACL2020)*, pages 2021–2030.

Megan Ung, Jing Xu, and Y-Lan Boureau. 2022. SaFeRDialogues: Taking Feedback Gracefully after Conversational Safety Failures. In *Proceedings of the 60th Annual Meeting of the Association for Computational Linguistics (ACL2022)*, volume 1, pages 6462–6481.

Jack Urbanek, Angela Fan, Siddharth Karamcheti, Saachi Jain, Samuel Humeau, Emily Dinan, Tim Rocktäschel, Douwe Kiela, Arthur Szlam, and Jason Weston. 2019. Learning to Speak and Act in a Fantasy Text Adventure Game. In *Proceedings of the 2019 Conference on Empirical Methods in Natural Language Processing and the 9th International Joint Conference on Natural Language Processing (EMNLP-IJCNLP)*, pages 673–683.

Ashish Vaswani, Noam Shazeer, Niki Parmar, Jakob Uszkoreit, Llion Jones, Aidan N. Gomez, Łukasz Kaiser, and Illia Polosukhin. 2017. Attention is All you Need. In *Advances in Neural Information Processing Systems 30 (NIPS2017)*, pages 5998–6008.

Jing Xu, Arthur Szlam, and Jason Weston. 2022. Beyond Goldfish Memory: Long-Term Open-Domain Conversation. In *Proceedings of the 60th Annual Meeting of the Association for Computational Linguistics (ACL2022)*, volume 1, pages 5180–5197.

Ruolan Yang, Zitong Li, Haifeng Tang, and Kenny Q Zhu. 2022. ChatMatch: Evaluating Chatbots by Autonomous Chat Tournaments. In *Proceedings of the 60th Annual Meeting of the Association for Computational Linguistics (ACL2022)*, volume 1, pages 7579–7590.

Chen Zhang, Yiming Chen, Luis Fernando D'Haro, Yan Zhang, Thomas Friedrichs, Grandee Lee, and Haizhou Li. 2021. DynaEval: Unifying Turn and Dialogue Level Evaluation. In *Proceedings of the 59th Annual Meeting of the Association for Computational Linguistics and the 11th International Joint Conference on Natural Language Processing (Volume 1: Long Papers)*, pages 5676–5689.

Yizhe Zhang, Siqi Sun, Michel Galley, Yen-Chun Chen, Chris Brockett, Xiang Gao, Jianfeng Gao, Jingjing Liu, and William B. Dolan. 2020. DIALOGPT : Large-Scale Generative Pre-training for Conversational Response Generation. In *Proceedings of the 58th Annual Meeting of the Association for Computational Linguistics (ACL): System Demonstrations*, pages 270–278.

Toward Building a Language Model for Understanding Temporal Commonsense

Mayuko Kimura[1] **Lis Kanashiro Pereira**[2] **Ichiro Kobayashi**[3]
Ochanomizu University, Japan
[1,3]{g1720512,koba}@is.ocha.ac.jp
[2]kanashiro.pereira@ocha.ac.jp

Abstract

The ability to capture temporal commonsense relationships for time-related events expressed in text is a very important task in natural language understanding. However, pre-trained language models such as BERT, which have recently achieved great success in a wide range of natural language processing tasks, are still considered to have poor performance in temporal reasoning. In this paper, we focus on the development of language models for temporal commonsense inference over several pre-trained language models. Our model relies on multi-step fine-tuning using multiple corpora and masked language modeling to predict masked temporal indicators that are crucial for temporal commonsense reasoning. We also experimented with multi-task learning and build a language model that can improve performance on multiple time-related tasks. In our experiments, multi-step fine-tuning using the general commonsense knowledge task as an auxiliary task produced the best results. We obtained a significant improvement in accuracy over standard fine-tuning in the temporal commonsense inference task and on other time-related tasks.

1 Introduction

Commonsense reasoning is crucial for natural language processing (NLP). Commonsense is the basic level of practical knowledge that is commonly shared among most people[1]. A specific type of commonsense is temporal commonsense. Temporal commonsense refers to the common knowledge about various temporal aspects of events, such as duration, frequency, and temporal order.

Capturing temporal commonsense relations for time-related events expressed in sentences is a very important task in natural language understanding. However, pre-trained language models such as BERT (Devlin et al., 2019), which have recently achieved significant results in a wide range of NLP tasks, are still said to perform poorly in temporal reasoning (Ribeiro et al., 2020). For example, given two events, "going on a vacation" and "going for a walk," most humans know that "vacation is longer and occurs less frequently than walks," or that "going on a walk is more frequent than going on a vacation. However, it is difficult for computers to make inferences based on such commonsense knowledge.

In this paper, we focus on the development of a language model for understanding temporal commonsense. In a prior study (Kimura et al., 2021), BERT was used, and in this study, we also use RoBERTa (Liu et al., 2019b) and ALBERT (Lan et al., 2019), which are improved models of BERT. We use them for multi-step fine-tuning using multiple corpora and continual pre-training by performing the masked language modeling (MLM) task (Devlin et al., 2019) on the target dataset. MLM task is a fill-in-the-blank task that has been employed as a pre-training task for various language models.

For multi-step fine-tuning, we thought an additional stage of fine-tuning on an intermediate related supervised task might help improve performance because temporal datasets usually have only a small amount of training data available. For continual pre-training on the target dataset, we aimed to resolve the domain mismatch between the pre-trained models and the target task, and make the model better weight temporal indicators and event triggers for our downstream tasks. In addition, we apply multi-task learning to further improve our model's generalization performance.

Our contributions are summarized as follows:

- We propose a language model for understanding temporal commonsense that effectively leverages continual pre-training, multi-step fine-tuning, and multi-task learning.
- We conducted multi-step fine-tuning and continual pre-training by performing the MLM

[1]https://csrr-workshop.github.io/

Proceedings of the AACL-IJCNLP 2022 Student Research Workshop, pages 17–24
November 20, 2022.

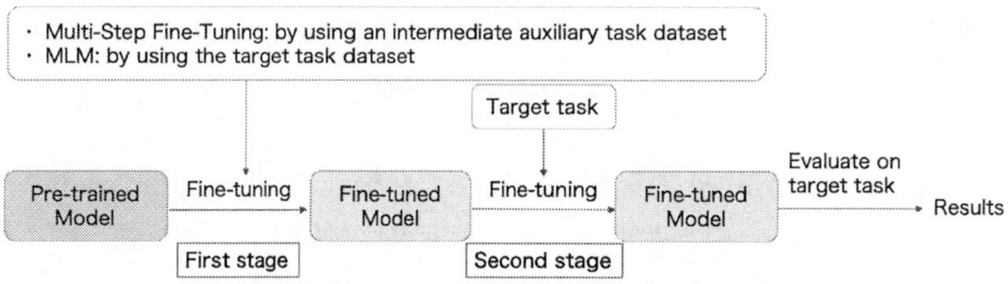

Figure 1: Overview of the multi-step fine-tuning and continual pre-training methods.

task on the target dataset on three pre-trained language models (BERT, RoBERTa, and ALBERT).

- We achieved the best performance with multi-step fine-tuning using the general commonsense knowledge task as auxiliary task on ALBERT.
- Although we focus on temporal commonsense reasoning, we also examined and confirmed the effectiveness of our multi-task learning model on several other temporal-related tasks.

2 Related Work

Although research on temporal inference has been conducted for a long time, in recent years, many studies have been proposed on temporal expression extraction (Lee et al., 2014; Vashishtha et al., 2019), temporal relation extraction (Ning et al., 2017, 2018b), and the construction of timelines (Leeuwenberg and Moens, 2018). As for temporal commonsense, there are studies focusing on the duration of events (Vempala et al., 2018; Vashishtha et al., 2019), the temporal order of events (Ning et al., 2018a), and so forth. Zhou et al. (2020) proposed methods for constructing language models that produce representations of events for relevant tasks such as duration comparison, parent-child relations, event coreference and temporal question-answering tasks.

In particular, some recent works have focused on the construction of challenging benchmarks for temporal commonsense inference. The Story Cloze Test (Mostafazadeh et al., 2016) dataset focuses on the typical temporal and causal relationships between events. TORQUE (Ning et al., 2020) is a machine reading comprehension dataset that focuses on the temporal ordering of events. MC-TACO (Zhou et al., 2019) is a challenging multiple choice temporal commonsense reasoning task that focuses on temporal properties such as duration and ordering of events. TIMEDIAL (Qin et al., 2021) is a dataset consisting of dialogues containing temporal information and is a complex temporal commonsense inference task using multi-turn dialogues.

In addition, pre-trained language models such as BERT have succeeded on broad-coverage probing benchmarks. However, in the case of domain mismatch between the pre-trained model and the target task, these models may still suffer catastrophic accuracy degradation.

In this study, we focus on temporal commonsense reasoning and attempt to improve the performance of the pre-trained language model for understanding temporal commonsense. Our model effectively leverages continual pre-training, multi-step fine-tuning, and multi-task learning. It substantially outperforms the standard fine-tuning approach.

3 Temporal Commonsense Reasoning Task: MC-TACO

MC-TACO is a dataset that entirely focuses on a specific reasoning capability: temporal commonsense. MC-TACO considers five temporal properties: (1) duration (how long an event takes), (2) temporal ordering (typical order of events), (3) typical time (when an event occurs), (4) frequency (how often an event occurs), and (5) stationarity (whether a state is maintained for a very long time or indefinitely). It contains 13k tuples, each consisting of a sentence, a question, and a candidate answer, that should be judged as plausible or not. The sentences are taken from different sources such as news, Wikipedia and textbooks. An example from this dataset is below. The correct answers are in **bold**.

Paragraph: He layed down on the chair and pawed at her as she ran in a circle under it.
Question: How long did he paw at her?
a) **2 minutes** b) 2 days
c) 90 minutes e) **7 seconds**
Reasoning Type: Duration

We mainly use the MC-TACO dataset for evaluating the performance of our model. In the later sections, we also show evaluation on additional temporal-related tasks.

4 Methods

We focus on exploring different training techniques, i.e., multi-step fine-tuning, continual pre-training, and multi-task learning, for building our language model for understanding temporal commonsense. Each technique is detailed below.

4.1 Multi-Step Fine-Tuning

Multi-step fine-tuning (4.1) aims to supplement the language model pre-training with an intermediate fine-tuning stage on supervised tasks that are related to the target dataset. It has been shown to improve model robustness and performance, especially for data-constrained scenarios (Phang et al., 2018; Camburu et al., 2019). We first fine-tune models on carefully selected auxiliary tasks and datasets. This model's parameters are further refined by fine-tuning on the MC-TACO dataset.

4.2 Continual pre-training on the target dataset

As mentioned in Section 2, performing continual pre-training using the target dataset can be useful to adapt the pre-trained model to the target task. Based on this, we have applied the MLM task (Devlin et al., 2019) using MC-TACO on pre-trained language models before performing standard fine-tuning. The MLM task, which is used in the pre-training of language models, is performed by randomly replacing a subset of tokens by a special token (e.g., [MASK]), and asks the model to predict them.

An overview of the multi-step fine-tuning and continual pre-training methods is shown in Figure 1.

4.3 Multi-Task Learning

Multi-task learning (MTL) aims to improve the generalization performance of the model by learning multiple related tasks simultaneously. It has become increasingly popular in NLP because it can improve the performance of related tasks by exploiting their commonalities and differences (Zhang et al., 2022). In this study, we use MT-DNN (Liu et al., 2019a) to perform MTL and evaluate the model's performance on multiple time-related tasks. MT-DNN is a multi-task learning framework that can incorporate models such as BERT and RoBERTa as the shared text encoding layers (shared across all tasks), while the top layers are task-specific. We used the pre-trained BERT, RoBERTa, and ALBERT models to initialize its shared layers and refined them via MTL on multiple time-related tasks.

	BERT (large)	RoBERTa (large)	ALBERT (xxlarge)
Parameters	334M	355M	235M
Layers	24	24	12
Hidden	1024	1024	4096
Embedding	1024	1024	128
Pre-training data size	16GB	160GB	16GB

Table 1: Summary of each pre-trained language model used in our experiments.

5 Experiments

5.1 Text Encoders

In our previous study (Kimura et al., 2021), we used BERT-base as the text encoder. In this study, we explore the use of BERT-large, RoBERTa-large and ALBERT-xxlarge models. RoBERTa is an improved version of BERT, and has succeeded in significantly improving on BERT's accuracy by adjusting the hyperparameters, changing the pre-training method, and increasing the amount of data for training, while keeping BERT's mechanism intact. ALBERT is also an improved model of BERT, and is a lightweight, high-performance language model that has surpassed the accuracy of BERT by changing the type of pre-training task and how to handle parameters. The summary of each pre-trained language model is shown in Table 1. In pre-training, BERT and ALBERT use the English Wikipedia and BookCorpus, and RoBERTa uses CC-News, OpenWebText and Stories datasets in addition to them (Liu et al., 2019b).

5.2 Datasets

We use MC-TACO as the main training and evaluation dataset. In addition, we use the TimeML, CosmosQA, and SWAG datasets as auxiliary datasets in the multi-step fine-tuning setting. A summary of each dataset is provided below and in Table 2.

TimeML (Pan et al., 2006): This dataset is specifically about duration of an event in a span of text. The task is to decide whether a given event has a duration longer or shorter than a day. An example from this dataset showing a sentence with an event (in bold) that has a duration shorter than a day is below:

	train	val	test	huggingface model implementation	MT-DNN implementation
MC-TACO	-	3,783	9,442	*ForSequenceClassification	Pairwise Text Classification
TimeML	1,248	-	1,003	*ForSequenceClassification	Pairwise Text Classification
MATRES	12,716	-	838	*ForSequenceClassification	Single-Sentence Classification
CosmosQA	25,588	3,000	7,000	*ForMultipleChoice	Relevance Ranking
SWAG	73,546	20,006	20,005	*ForMultipleChoice	Relevance Ranking

Table 2: Summary of the datasets and their model implementations used in our experiments. We use huggingface for the multi-step fine-tuning and continual pre-training experiments, and MT-DNN for the multi-task learning experiments. The * symbol in the huggingface model implementation column stands for Bert, Roberta or Albert, depending on the text encoder we use. When using MT-DNN, we use the Single-Sentence Classification, Pairwise Text Classification, or Relevance Ranking implementations.

In Singapore, stocks **hit** a five year low.

CosmosQA (Huang et al., 2019): We propose to enrich the temporal commonsense reasoning task training by leveraging data from the general commonsense knowledge task. Since the commonsense reasoning task commonly also involves reasoning about temporal events, e.g., what event(s) might happen before or after the current event, we hypothesize that temporal reasoning might benefit from it. CosmosQA is a general commonsense knowledge task. This task focuses on reading between the lines of a story where the causes and effects of events are not explicitly mentioned and is a four-choice multiple-choice question. An example from the CosmosQA dataset is below. The correct answer is in **bold**.

> *Paragraph*: Did some errands today. My prime objectives were to get textbooks, find computer lab, find career services, get some groceries, turn in payment plan application, and find out when KEES money kicks in. I think it acts as a refund at the end of the semester at Murray, but I would be quite happy if it would work now.
> *Question*: What happens after I get the refund?
> *Option 1*: **I can pay my bills.**
> *Option 2*: I can relax.
> *Option 3*: I can sleep.
> *Option 4*: None of the above choices.

SWAG (Zellers et al., 2018): SWAG is also a general commonsense knowledge task. The task is to choose the correct ending among four options that leverages commonsense knowledge. An example from this dataset is below. The correct answer is in **bold**.

> *Question*: On stage, a woman takes a seat at the piano. She
> *Option 1*: sits on a bench as her sister plays with the doll.
> *Option 2*: smiles with someone as the music plays.
> *Option 3*: is in the crowd, watching the dancers.
> *Option 4*: **nervously sets her fingers on the keys.**

	max seq_len	train batch_size	num train_epoch	learning rate
BERT				
standard fine-tuning	128	16	5	1e-5
TimeML	128	16	4	2e-5
CosmosQA	256	32	1	2e-5
SWAG	256	32	2	2e-5
MLM	128	32	3	3e-5
RoBERTa				
standard fine-tuning	128	16	20	1e-5
TimeML	128	16	6	2e-5
CosmosQA	512	16	1	1e-5
SWAG	256	32	2	1e-5
MLM	128	8	3	5e-5
ALBERT				
standard fine-tuning	128	16	6	1e-5
TimeML	128	16	6	2e-5
CosmosQA	256	16	2	1e-5
SWAG	256	16	1	1e-5
MLM	128	8	3	5e-5

Table 3: Hyperparameter settings.

5.3 Implementation Details

The hyperparameter settings used in our experiments are shown in Table 3. For each dataset, we select the best parameters based on validation experiments. The parameters for MLM using the target dataset are based on the values originally used in the pre-training of the language model.

The bert-large-uncased, roberta-large and albert-xxlarge-v2 models were used, and the Exact Match (EM) and F1 scores were employed as the evaluation metrics. The EM is the probability of correctly labeling all answers to each question, and the F1-

fine-tuned on	EM [%]	F1 [%]
BERT		
standard fine-tuning	42.6 (42.9)	70.9 (71.0)
TimeML→MC-TACO	44.8 (43.7)	72.8 (70.8)
CosmosQA→MC-TACO	**46.3** (43.6)	73.4 (70.7)
SWAG→MC-TACO	46.2 **(44.7)**	**73.6 (72.6)**
RoBERTa		
standard fine-tuning	53.8 (54.4)	75.3 **(77.6)**
TimeML→MC-TACO	51.3 (51.1)	75.7 (76.1)
CosmosQA→MC-TACO	**55.6 (55.2)**	**78.1** (77.3)
SWAG→MC-TACO	53.1 (53.9)	76.1 (77.3)
ALBERT		
standard fine-tuning	55.0 (54.6)	77.1 (77.9)
TimeML→MC-TACO	51.8 (51.3)	77.9 (75.5)
CosmosQA→MC-TACO	**59.5 (58.9)**	**80.3 (78.7)**
SWAG→MC-TACO	52.8 (51.3)	77.3 (74.6)

Table 4: Test results on multi-step fine-tuning. The 5-fold cross-validation results using the validation dataset are shown in parenthesis ().

	EM [%]	F1 [%]
BERT		
standard fine-tuning	42.6 (42.9)	70.9 (71.0)
MLM (MC-TACO)	45.2 (45.0)	72.5 (71.9)
RoBERTa		
standard fine-tuning	53.8 (54.4)	75.3 (77.6)
MLM (MC-TACO)	51.2 (54.4)	76.2 (77.5)
ALBERT		
standard fine-tuning	55.0 (54.6)	77.1 (77.9)
MLM (MC-TACO)	**59.2 (58.3)**	**79.9 (78.2)**

Table 5: Test results on MLM with target dataset. The 5-fold cross-validation results using the validation dataset are shown in parenthesis ().

score measures the average overlap between one's predictions and the ground truth (Zhou et al., 2020).

The model implementations we used in our experiments are speficied in Table 2. We use huggingface for the multi-step fine-tuning and continual pre-training experiments, and MT-DNN for the multi-task learning experiments.

5.4 Results

Multi-Step Fine-Tuning

The results of the multi-step fine-tuning experiments are shown in Table 4. The results show that changing the language model from BERT to RoBERTa and ALBERT improves accuracy. Overall, the best results were obtained when we used ALBERT.

Continual pre-training on the target dataset

Table 5 shows the results when we perform MLM on the target dataset. The results show that the accuracy also improved by changing the model used from BERT to RoBERTa and ALBERT. The best results were also obtained when ALBERT was used (with an EM score of 59.2% and an F1-score of 79.9% on the test set).

Multi-Task Learning

We used MC-TACO, TimeML, CosmosQA, and MATRES (Ning et al., 2018c) as auxiliary training data and evaluated on the time-related datasets (MC-TACO, TimeML, and MATRES). MATRES is a time-related task that focuses on the ordering of events in a sentence and events annotated with a temporal relation (BEFORE, AFTER, EQUAL, VAGUE). An example of a sentence from this dataset with two events (in bold) that hold the BEFORE relation is below:

> At one point , when it **(e1:became)** clear controllers could not contact the plane, someone **(e2:said)** a prayer.

We performed MTL using ALBERT, which obtained the best results in our previous experiments, shown in Table 4 and Table 5. These results are shown in Table 6. While there was an improvement in accuracy with MTL on MATRES, there were differences on MC-TACO depending on the auxiliary dataset used for training, and no improvement on TimeML.

5.5 Discussion

The experimental results show that changing the text encoder used from BERT to RoBERTa and ALBERT improves the accuracy of both multi-step fine-tuning using an auxiliary dataset (Table 4, with an EM score on the test set increasing from 46.3% to 55.6% and 59.5%, respectively) and of continual pre-training on the target dataset (Table 5, with an EM score on the test set increasing from 45.2% to 51.2% to 59.2%, respectively). These results indicate a significant improvement over the BERT baseline. This is a natural result considering that RoBERTa and ALBERT are improved models of BERT and have better performance than BERT on benchmarks such as GLUE.

RoBERTa is an improved model of BERT, with about 10 times the data size used for pre-training. We think that pre-training on a large amount of data improves performance in solving tasks that require commonsense.

The best results were obtained when ALBERT was used (with an EM score on the test set of 59.5%, in Table 4, and an EM score on the test set of 59.2%, in Table 5). The reason for this might also be the difference in its pre-training method. ALBERT's pre-training method employs Sentence Order Prediction (SOP) in addition to MLM. SOP is a binary classification task that determines whether two text segments are in the correct order, and focuses on

Train dataset \ Evalation dataset	MC-TACO EM [%]	MC-TACO F1 [%]	TimeML acc [%]	MATRES acc [%]
MC-TACO	57.6	80.6	-	-
MC-TACO, TimeML	**58.1**	79.7	81.0	-
MC-TACO, MATRES	57.3	80.1	-	**75.4**
MC-TACO, CosmosQA	**59.2**	80.4	-	-
MC-TACO, TimeML, MATRES	56.3	78.8	79.2	**76.3**
MC-TACO, TimeML, CosmosQA	53.0	76.5	79.9	-
MC-TACO, MATRES, CosmosQA	53.6	78.6	-	**76.8**
MC-TACO, TimeML, MATRES, CosmosQA	53.4	78.2	77.7	**76.8**
TimeML	-	-	81.1	-
TimeML, MATRES	-	-	79.4	**77.2**
TimeML, CosmosQA	-	-	80.4	-
TimeML, MATRES, CosmosQA	-	-	78.8	**76.2**
MATRES	-	-	-	74.6
MATRES, CosmosQA	-	-	-	**74.7**

Table 6: Test results on MTL using MT-DNN. Single-task learning results using MT-DNN are in blue, and those exceeding the accuracy of single-task learning are in **bold**.

modeling inter-sentence coherence. We hypothesize that this pre-training task enables the model to acquire additional temporal knowledge needed to solve the MC-TACO task.

Focusing on the results of multi-step fine-tuning using RoBERTa (Table 4), we can see that the proposed method improves the standard fine-tuning accuracy in many cases (with an EM score on the test set increasing from 53.8% to 55.6%, and a F1-score on the test set increasing from 75.3% to 75.7%, 78.1%, and 76.1%), but the increase in accuracy is smaller than that of BERT and ALBERT. The reason is that RoBERTa uses a much larger number of data for pre-training than BERT or ALBERT, and a large corpus is learned at the time of pre-training, thus multi-step fine-tuning may not be effective.

Note here that EM measures how many questions a system is able to correctly label all candidate answers (Zhou et al., 2019). EM is a stricter metric and we consistently obtain lower EM scores than F1 scores in our experiments.

The results of the MTL experiments (Table 6) were somewhat unstable, with the accuracy improving in some cases (e.g., an EM score on the test set of 59.2% with the model that trains with MC-TACO and CosmosQA and evaluates on MC-TACO) and worsening in others (e.g., an EM score on the test set of 53.0% with the model that trains with MC-TACO and TimeML and CosmosQA and evaluates on MC-TACO), depending on the dataset used. Task affinity is important for MTL, and performance may deteriorate if unrelated tasks are learned at the same time. In addition, we found it surprising that all multi-task settings lead to improved accuracy on MATRES. MATRES is a task that treats verbs in sentences as events and predicts their order. However, there are many temporal expressions other than verbs in natural language sentences (e.g., *before*, *after*, *when*, *first*, etc.), and in order to predict the order of events, not only verbs but also various parts of speech and other factors such as duration might be effective. We hypothesize this is why MTL improves the accuracy on MATRES. We think it is necessary to further analyze why these results are obtained in cases where accuracy improves and in cases where it does not.

6 Conclusion

In this paper, we focused on the development of a language model for temporal commonsense reasoning, and tried to develop a language model for understanding temporal commonsense. We conducted multi-step fine-tuning, continual pre-training, and multi-task learning on BERT, RoBERTa, and ALBERT, using several datasets. We confirmed that the multi-step fine-tuning model that uses the general commonsense knowledge task as an auxiliary task was often better than that obtained by ordinary fine-tuning and we were able to construct a language model that understands temporal commonsense. Comparing BERT, RoBERTa, and ALBERT, ALBERT produced the best results overall.

For future work, we plan to further investigate multi-task learning. In multi-task learning, we would like to visualize attention scores, for example, and pursue what setting can improve generalization performance. Also, we plan to construct a new general-purpose language model that performs well in a variety of time-related tasks.

References

Oana-Maria Camburu, Vid Kocijan, Thomas Lukasiewicz, and Yordan Yordanov. 2019. A surprisingly robust trick for the winograd schema challenge.

Jacob Devlin, Ming-Wei Chang, Kenton Lee, and Kristina Toutanova. 2019. BERT: Pre-training of deep bidirectional transformers for language understanding. In *Proceedings of the 2019 Conference of the North American Chapter of the Association for Computational Linguistics: Human Language Technologies, Volume 1 (Long and Short Papers)*, pages 4171–4186, Minneapolis, Minnesota. Association for Computational Linguistics.

Lifu Huang, Ronan Le Bras, Chandra Bhagavatula, and Yejin Choi. 2019. Cosmos QA: Machine reading comprehension with contextual commonsense reasoning. In *Proceedings of the 2019 Conference on Empirical Methods in Natural Language Processing and the 9th International Joint Conference on Natural Language Processing (EMNLP-IJCNLP)*, pages 2391–2401, Hong Kong, China. Association for Computational Linguistics.

Mayuko Kimura, Lis Kanashiro Pereira, and Ichiro Kobayashi. 2021. Towards a language model for temporal commonsense reasoning. In *Proceedings of the Student Research Workshop Associated with RANLP 2021*, pages 78–84, Online. INCOMA Ltd.

Zhenzhong Lan, Mingda Chen, Sebastian Goodman, Kevin Gimpel, Piyush Sharma, and Radu Soricut. 2019. Albert: A lite bert for self-supervised learning of language representations. *arXiv preprint arXiv:1909.11942*.

Kenton Lee, Yoav Artzi, Jesse Dodge, and Luke Zettlemoyer. 2014. Context-dependent semantic parsing for time expressions. In *Proceedings of the 52nd Annual Meeting of the Association for Computational Linguistics (Volume 1: Long Papers)*, pages 1437–1447, Baltimore, Maryland. Association for Computational Linguistics.

Artuur Leeuwenberg and Marie-Francine Moens. 2018. Temporal information extraction by predicting relative time-lines. In *Proceedings of the 2018 Conference on Empirical Methods in Natural Language Processing*, pages 1237–1246, Brussels, Belgium. Association for Computational Linguistics.

Xiaodong Liu, Pengcheng He, Weizhu Chen, and Jianfeng Gao. 2019a. Multi-task deep neural networks for natural language understanding. In *Proceedings of the 57th Annual Meeting of the Association for Computational Linguistics*, pages 4487–4496, Florence, Italy. Association for Computational Linguistics.

Yinhan Liu, Myle Ott, Naman Goyal, Jingfei Du, Mandar Joshi, Danqi Chen, Omer Levy, Mike Lewis, Luke Zettlemoyer, and Veselin Stoyanov. 2019b. Roberta: A robustly optimized bert pretraining approach. *arXiv preprint arXiv:1907.11692*.

Nasrin Mostafazadeh, Nathanael Chambers, Xiaodong He, Devi Parikh, Dhruv Batra, Lucy Vanderwende, Pushmeet Kohli, and James Allen. 2016. A corpus and cloze evaluation for deeper understanding of commonsense stories. In *Proceedings of the 2016 Conference of the North American Chapter of the Association for Computational Linguistics: Human Language Technologies*, pages 839–849, San Diego, California. Association for Computational Linguistics.

Qiang Ning, Zhili Feng, and Dan Roth. 2017. A structured learning approach to temporal relation extraction. In *Proceedings of the 2017 Conference on Empirical Methods in Natural Language Processing*, pages 1027–1037, Copenhagen, Denmark. Association for Computational Linguistics.

Qiang Ning, Zhili Feng, Hao Wu, and Dan Roth. 2018a. Joint reasoning for temporal and causal relations. In *Proceedings of the 56th Annual Meeting of the Association for Computational Linguistics (Volume 1: Long Papers)*, pages 2278–2288, Melbourne, Australia. Association for Computational Linguistics.

Qiang Ning, Hao Wu, Rujun Han, Nanyun Peng, Matt Gardner, and Dan Roth. 2020. TORQUE: A reading comprehension dataset of temporal ordering questions. In *Proceedings of the 2020 Conference on Empirical Methods in Natural Language Processing (EMNLP)*, pages 1158–1172, Online. Association for Computational Linguistics.

Qiang Ning, Hao Wu, Haoruo Peng, and Dan Roth. 2018b. Improving temporal relation extraction with a globally acquired statistical resource. In *Proceedings of the 2018 Conference of the North American Chapter of the Association for Computational Linguistics: Human Language Technologies, Volume 1 (Long Papers)*, pages 841–851, New Orleans, Louisiana. Association for Computational Linguistics.

Qiang Ning, Hao Wu, and Dan Roth. 2018c. A multi-axis annotation scheme for event temporal relations. In *Proceedings of the 56th Annual Meeting of the Association for Computational Linguistics (Volume 1: Long Papers)*, pages 1318–1328, Melbourne, Australia. Association for Computational Linguistics.

Feng Pan, Rutu Mulkar-Mehta, and Jerry R Hobbs. 2006. Extending timeml with typical durations of events. In *Proceedings of the Workshop on Annotating and Reasoning about Time and Events*, pages 38–45.

Jason Phang, Thibault Févry, and Samuel R Bowman. 2018. Sentence encoders on stilts: Supplementary training on intermediate labeled-data tasks. *arXiv preprint arXiv:1811.01088*.

Lianhui Qin, Aditya Gupta, Shyam Upadhyay, Luheng He, Yejin Choi, and Manaal Faruqui. 2021. TIMEDIAL: Temporal commonsense reasoning in dialog.

In *Proceedings of the 59th Annual Meeting of the Association for Computational Linguistics and the 11th International Joint Conference on Natural Language Processing (Volume 1: Long Papers)*, pages 7066–7076, Online. Association for Computational Linguistics.

Marco Tulio Ribeiro, Tongshuang Wu, Carlos Guestrin, and Sameer Singh. 2020. Beyond accuracy: Behavioral testing of nlp models with checklist. *arXiv preprint arXiv:2005.04118*.

Siddharth Vashishtha, Benjamin Van Durme, and Aaron Steven White. 2019. Fine-grained temporal relation extraction. In *Proceedings of the 57th Annual Meeting of the Association for Computational Linguistics*, pages 2906–2919, Florence, Italy. Association for Computational Linguistics.

Alakananda Vempala, Eduardo Blanco, and Alexis Palmer. 2018. Determining event durations: Models and error analysis. In *Proceedings of the 2018 Conference of the North American Chapter of the Association for Computational Linguistics: Human Language Technologies, Volume 2 (Short Papers)*, pages 164–168, New Orleans, Louisiana. Association for Computational Linguistics.

Rowan Zellers, Yonatan Bisk, Roy Schwartz, and Yejin Choi. 2018. SWAG: A large-scale adversarial dataset for grounded commonsense inference. In *Proceedings of the 2018 Conference on Empirical Methods in Natural Language Processing*, pages 93–104, Brussels, Belgium. Association for Computational Linguistics.

Zhihan Zhang, Wenhao Yu, Mengxia Yu, Zhichun Guo, and Meng Jiang. 2022. A survey of multi-task learning in natural language processing: Regarding task relatedness and training methods.

Ben Zhou, Daniel Khashabi, Qiang Ning, and Dan Roth. 2019. "going on a vacation" takes longer than "going for a walk": A study of temporal commonsense understanding. In *Proceedings of the 2019 Conference on Empirical Methods in Natural Language Processing and the 9th International Joint Conference on Natural Language Processing (EMNLP-IJCNLP)*, pages 3363–3369, Hong Kong, China. Association for Computational Linguistics.

Ben Zhou, Qiang Ning, Daniel Khashabi, and Dan Roth. 2020. Temporal common sense acquisition with minimal supervision. In *Proceedings of the 58th Annual Meeting of the Association for Computational Linguistics*, pages 7579–7589, Online. Association for Computational Linguistics.

Optimal Summaries for Enabling a Smooth Handover in Chat-Oriented Dialogue

Sanae Yamashita　　**Ryuichiro Higashinaka**
Graduate School of Informatics, Nagoya University
yamashita.sanae.w7@s.mail.nagoya-u.ac.jp
higashinaka@i.nagoya-u.ac.jp

Abstract

In dialogue systems, one option for creating a better dialogue experience for the user is to have a human operator take over the dialogue when the system runs into trouble communicating with the user. In this type of handover situation (we call it intervention), it is useful for the operator to have access to the dialogue summary. However, it is not clear exactly what type of summary would be the most useful for a smooth handover. In this study, we investigated the optimal type of summary through experiments in which interlocutors were presented with various summary types during interventions in order to examine their effects. Our findings showed that the best summaries were an abstractive summary plus one utterance immediately before the handover and an extractive summary consisting of five utterances immediately before the handover. From the viewpoint of computational cost, we recommend that extractive summaries consisting of the last five utterances be used.

1 Introduction

Dialogue systems are widely utilized in chatbots and call centers to respond automatically to users (Pappas et al., 2015; Sheehan et al., 2020). However, it is often difficult for such systems to deliver fully autonomous dialogue. To ensure a good dialogue experience, human operators sometimes need to intervene in a dialogue if communication difficulties arise. We call this process handover or intervention and define it as joining a dialogue in the middle to achieve the original objective of the dialogue.

In this study, we investigate which type of summary should be presented to the human operator in an intervention for a smooth handover. Specifically, we conducted a large-scale experiment focused on chat dialogues to investigate the most useful summary for handover among seven types of dialogue summaries consisting of abstractive, extractive, and keyword summaries. Our findings showed that the best summaries were an abstractive summary plus one utterance immediately before the handover and an extractive summary consisting of five utterances immediately before the handover. From the viewpoint of computational cost, we recommend that extractive summaries consisting of the last five utterances be used.

2 Related Work

The handover in dialogues from systems to human operators has been researched extensively in the context of call routing. In call routing, the dialogue is transferred to an appropriate operator and the system hands over the dialogue (Gorin et al., 1997; Walker et al., 2000). However, there has been little research on the actual type of information to be shown to an operator during call routing.

Various frameworks have been proposed in which a semi-autonomous dialogue system performs most of the dialogue and hands over to a human operator when necessary (Glas et al., 2012; Kawahara et al., 2021; Kawasaki and Ogawa, 2021; Kawai et al., 2022). However, it is not clear exactly what type of information or summary would be the most useful for a smooth handover.

Automatic summarization has long been studied (Mani, 2001; Rennard et al., 2022), and various datasets have been released (Carletta et al., 2006; Janin et al., 2003; Zhong et al., 2021b) and are currently in use (Goo and Chen, 2018; Zhong et al., 2021a). Recently, large-scale pre-trained language models have been utilized to generate abstractive summaries (Chen and Yang, 2020; Liu et al., 2021) using a large corpus of summaries (Gliwa et al., 2019; Chen et al., 2021; Liu and Chen, 2021). In this study, we examine what kind of summary is useful for a specific situation: handover.

Proceedings of the AACL-IJCNLP 2022 Student Research Workshop, pages 25–31
November 20, 2022. ©2022 Association for Computational Linguistics

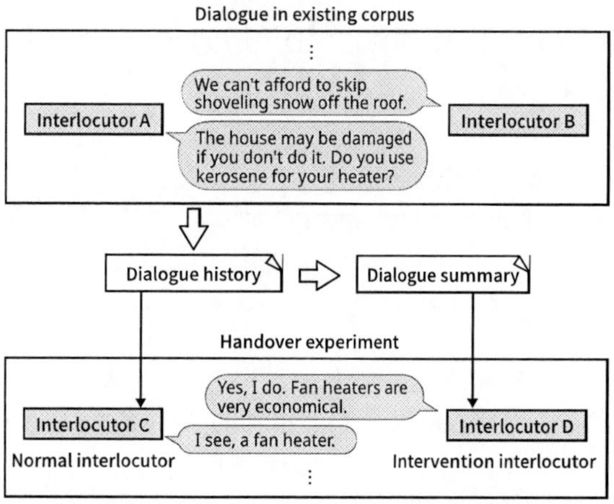

Figure 1: Overview of handover experiment.

3 Approach

To determine the type of summaries needed for a smooth handover in dialogue, our approach is to present a variety of summaries to the operator during the intervention process, examine the smoothness of the dialogue after the intervention, and quantify the effects of each summary type.

To this end, it would be best to collect dialogues in a situation where one interlocutor changes to another in the middle of the dialogue. However, such experimentation would be extremely costly. Therefore, in this paper, we simulate the dialogue handover. Specifically, instead of performing the handover in real-time, we present the dialogue history of an existing dialogue to one of the interlocutors and a summary of that dialogue to the other interlocutor and have them continue the dialogue. We call this experiment a handover experiment.

Figure 1 shows an overview of the handover experiment. As a dialogue history, we prepared a chat dialogue between two interlocutors, A and B, from an existing corpus. The participants in the handover experiment are interlocutors C and D. Interlocutor C is given the dialogue history and interlocutor D is given the dialogue summary created from the dialogue history, and they continue the dialogue on the basis of the information given to each. In this paper, we refer to interlocutor C as the "normal" interlocutor and interlocutor D as the "intervention" interlocutor.

We investigated the usefulness of a summary by utilizing various summary types and analyzing their effects. The questionnaire responses of interlocutors and the number of dialogue breakdowns (Higashinaka et al., 2016) (a state in which dialogue cannot be continued smoothly) after the handover were used for the quantification of the effects. To cover typical summaries, we focused on the following summary types.

- **Abstractive summary**
  An abstractive summary is created by reconstructing important information from a document (Zhong et al., 2021a; Liu and Chen, 2021).

- **Extractive summary**
  An extractive summary is created by extracting important sentences from a document (Nallapati et al., 2016; See et al., 2017).

- **Keyword summary**
  A keyword summary is created by extracting important keywords from a document (Kawahara et al., 2021; Kawasaki and Ogawa, 2021).

4 Handover Experiment

4.1 Existing Corpus

We randomly selected 20 dialogues from an existing chat corpus[1] (Higashinaka et al., 2020). These dialogues are text chats between two people for a total of at least 20 utterances, each of which is about 50 characters in length. In the dialogues, the interlocutors chat freely on any topic of their choice. The dialogues are in Japanese.

4.2 Preparing Dialogue History

We define dialogue history as the past utterance logs from the beginning of the dialogue to a certain point in time. To ensure variations in the progress of the dialogue, we prepared short dialogue histories (from the beginning to the 9th or 11th utterance) and long dialogue histories (from the beginning to the 15th or 17th utterance). For each of the 20 extracted dialogues, we prepared dialogue histories of two different lengths, for a total of 40 dialogue histories.

4.3 Preparing Dialogue Summary

As detailed below, we prepared two types of abstractive summary, three types of extractive summary, and one type of keyword summary. Also, as a control condition, the entire dialogue history was used as one type of summary.

[1] https://github.com/dsbook/dsbook/blob/master/dialogue_data.zip

(i) Abstractive summary (Abs) Abstractive summary manually created from the whole dialogue history. We manually prepared the summaries because we are interested in how the types of summaries affect the handover; if we use automatically generated summaries, we thought that the noise might make it difficult to evaluate the exact effect of this summary type. We recruited 30 workers through crowdsourcing[2] and had them create 40 summaries corresponding to the 40 dialogue histories. The quality of these summaries was verified by a separate crowd sourcing experiment in which we confirmed that the quality was adequate (average rating: 4.4 on a 5-point Likert scale).

(ii) Abstractive summary + last utterance (AbsLast1)
Abstractive summary manually created from the dialogue history except for the last utterance plus the last utterance; the last utterance was included to facilitate the handover. Abstractive summaries were created manually in the same way as Abs.

(iii) Keyword + last utterance (KeyLast1)
A list of keywords (proper nouns) in the dialogue history plus the last utterance. To extract proper nouns, we used MeCab[3] (version 0.996) with the NEologd dictionary[4] (Release 20200827-01), which covers an extensive amount of proper nouns extracted from the Internet. The last utterance was included to facilitate the handover.

(iv)–(vi) Extractive summary consisting of last few utterances (ExtLast1, ExtLast3, ExtLast5)
Extractive summary created by extracting the last one, three, or five utterances immediately before the handover. We utilized a LEAD-like method (Wasson, 1998; Grenander et al., 2019) focusing on the last utterances of the dialogue history, which should contain important information for a handover.

(vii) Dialogue history (control condition)
Entire dialogue history as a summary.

Table 1 lists the average number of characters in each dialogue summary. Note that they are in varying lengths; we did not control the lengths of the summary deliberately because we wanted to first verify the types of summary for optimal handover in dialogue.

	No. of characters in summary
(i) Abs	46.8
(ii) AbsLast1	88.9
(iii) KeyLast1	76.4
(iv) ExtLast1	44.7
(v) ExtLast3	130.5
(vi) ExtLast5	209.5
(vii) Dialogue history	485.9

Table 1: Average number of characters in a dialogue summary.

Questionnaire item
Contextual appropriateness
Inconsistency (normal interlocutor only)
Speech style (normal interlocutor only)
Confidence (intervention interlocutor only)
Informativeness
Motivation to utter
Semantic comprehension
Naturalness
Continuity

Table 2: Questionnaire items used in this study.

4.4 Questionnaire

A questionnaire (Table 2) was administered to both the normal and intervention interlocutors to evaluate whether the handover dialogue was a success. The normal interlocutors evaluated the utterance quality of the intervention interlocutors, while the intervention interlocutors evaluated their own utterances, as we were interested in the intervention interlocutors' utterances to better understand the process and difficulty of intervention. We referenced the work of Finch and Choi (2020) here. Specifically, we utilized the questionnaire items focusing on coherence (inconsistency, speech style, contextual appropriateness, and semantic comprehension) and informativeness from their work and added items on the motivation to utter and the confidence of the utterance of the intervention interlocutor. To determine overall dialogue satisfaction, we also added an item for naturalness, which is commonly used in dialogue system evaluations (Hung et al., 2009). We also added an item for continuity, since it is important that an intervention interlocutor be able to continue a dialogue adequately in the handover experiment.

[2] https://crowdworks.jp
[3] https://taku910.github.io/mecab
[4] https://github.com/neologd/mecab-ipadic-neologd

Item	Abs	AbsLast1	KeyLast1	ExtLast1	ExtLast3	ExtLast5	Dialogue history
Contextual appropriateness	4.19	*4.54*	4.29	4.34	*4.54*	**4.66***	4.66
Consistency	4.24	*4.40*	4.16	4.34	4.41	**4.64***	4.38
Speech style	*4.62*	*4.62*	4.59	**4.69**	4.58	4.60	4.62
Informativeness	4.28	4.31	4.28	*4.39*	4.30	**4.47**	4.35
Motivation to utter	4.39	*4.44*	4.39	4.41	**4.46**	4.39	4.40
Semantic comprehension	4.75	*4.81*	4.78	4.74	4.68	**4.89**	4.81
Naturalness	4.51	*4.64*	4.59	4.50	4.61	**4.72**	4.62
Continuity	4.29	*4.51*	4.39	4.47	4.42	**4.60**	4.41

Table 3: Questionnaire results for normal interlocutors. The highest score for each item is shown in bold and the second highest in italics with an underline except for dialogue history. Consistency scores are calculated by 6 – inconsistency score. * denotes a significant difference at the 5% level over Abs or KeyLast1.

Item	Abs	AbsLast1	KeyLast1	ExtLast1	ExtLast3	ExtLast5	Dialogue history
Contextual appropriateness	4.39	4.41	*4.45*	4.18	**4.46**	4.44	4.45
Confidence	*4.25*	4.19	4.15	4.05	**4.30**	4.21	4.32
Informativeness	*3.89*	3.85	3.86	3.65	**3.94**	**3.94**	3.99
Motivation to utter	4.08	3.89	*4.09*	3.98	3.95	**4.15**	4.08
Semantic comprehension	4.72	4.64	4.66	4.69	*4.74*	**4.76**	4.72
Naturalness	**4.59**	4.40	4.42	4.38	4.53	*4.58*	4.47
Continuity	**4.39**	4.29	4.34	4.25	**4.39**	*4.35*	4.41

Table 4: Questionnaire results for intervention interlocutors. The highest score for each item is shown in bold and the second highest in italics with an underline except for dialogue history.

4.5 Conducting Handover Experiment

We combined the seven types of summary and 40 dialogue histories to create a total of 280 dialogue-summary patterns. To cover them, we recruited 280 pairs of interlocutors (560 interlocutors in total) through crowdsourcing and collected a total of 560 dialogues by having each pair conduct a dialogue twice. Eighty dialogues were collected per summary type.

In each pair of participants, one was randomly assigned as a normal interlocutor and the other as an intervention interlocutor. First, participants had sufficient time (three minutes) to read the dialogue history or summary presented on the screen. Each pair then conducted a text chat based on the information presented. The utterances were alternated between the intervention interlocutor and the normal interlocutor, in that order. As we wanted the intervention interlocutors to keep the conversation going for some time, each pair performed a total of 20 utterances after the intervention point. Each pair conducted two dialogues within one hour. After each dialogue, participants indicated their degree of agreement with the questionnaire items (Table 2) on a 5-point Likert scale.

4.6 Questionnaire Results

Table 3 shows the questionnaire results for the normal interlocutors. Overall, AbsLast1 and ExtLast5 had higher scores for all items. The scores for Abs and KeyLast1 tended to be low. We conducted Wilcoxon rank sum tests (with Bonferroni correction) between these two and ExtLast5, which had the highest score, and found a significant difference at the 5% level between ExtLast5 and Abs in terms of contextual appropriateness and between ExtLast5 and KeyLast1 in terms of consistency. These findings indicate that ExtLast5 is the most useful for handover in terms of contextual appropriateness and consistency. No significant differences were found between the other questionnaire items.

Table 4 shows the questionnaire results for the intervention interlocutors. No significant differences were found in any of the questionnaire items. Throughout, the scores for KeyLast1 and ExtLast1 were low. It seems that uttering based on keywords was difficult because it was unclear how the keywords were used in the dialogue history, making it difficult to continue the dialogue. Note that, although dialogue history should show the highest score with no information lost, it was not the case; this was probably because of the high cognitive load needed to comprehend the whole dialogue, although we thought we provided the interlocutors with ample time to read through the materials.

To summarize: the questionnaire results indicate that AbsLast1 and ExtLast5 are useful for handover, while Abs, KeyLast1, and ExtLast1 are unsuitable.

Error type	Abs	AbsLast1	KeyLast1	ExtLast1	ExtLast3	ExtLast5	Dialogue history
Context (102)							
Unclear intention	**7**	0	**7**	0	2	1	0
Topic transition error	**8**	0	2	0	6	0	3
Lack of information	1	0	**3**	0	0	0	0
Self-contradiction	2	3	**6**	0	1	1	0
Contradiction	5	0	5	3	3	2	**6**
Repetition	**16**	0	1	3	3	2	0
Response (49)							
Ignore question	**4**	1	3	0	1	0	1
Ignore expectation	**16**	3	12	0	4	2	2
Utterance (4)							
Grammatical error	0	0	0	0	**2**	0	0
Wrong information	0	0	0	0	**1**	**1**	0
Total	59	7	39	6	23	9	12

Table 5: Annotated error types causing dialogue breakdown. The number in parentheses represents the total number for that error scope. The largest number for each error type is shown in bold.

5 Analysis

In this section, we investigate why AbsLast1 and ExtLast5 received the highest scores in the questionnaire. Specifically, we first identified utterances in which dialogue breakdown occurred and classified them according to an existing taxonomy of errors in chat-oriented dialogue systems (Higashinaka et al., 2021), and then clarified the types of errors most common for each summary type. The specific procedures are described below.

5.1 Identification of Failure Utterances

First, for analysis, we took ten dialogue samples of the handover dialogue for each type of dialogue summary, resulting in 70 dialogue samples.

To identify which utterances were causing dialogue breakdowns, we annotated utterances of intervention interlocutors (700 utterances in all) as to whether they presented any discomfort. The annotators were provided with the dialogue history, the dialogue during the intervention, and each sampled utterance and then asked to specify whether they felt uncomfortable with the sampled utterances on a 4-point scale (1: not uncomfortable, 2: slightly uncomfortable, 3: uncomfortable, 4: clearly uncomfortable). Thirty annotators were recruited through crowdsourcing and utterances for which at least half of them (15 or more) responded that they felt at least a little uncomfortable (2 or more on the 4-point scale) were considered problematic. These utterances were determined as the cause of dialogue breakdown.

5.2 Annotation of Error Types

As the taxonomy of errors, we used the taxonomy consisting of 17 error types for chat-oriented dialogue proposed by Higashinaka et al. (2021).

5.3 Analysis of Dialogue Breakdowns

A total of 35 utterances were determined to be dialogue-breakdown-causing. Since dialogue breakdowns are unlikely to occur in human-human dialogue, failure utterances are rare and worthy of analysis. Five annotators were recruited through crowdsourcing and asked to label the error types for these utterances in a multi-labeling manner. The total number of error types annotated for the utterances by the five annotators was 155.

Table 5 lists the number of error types for each dialogue summary type. In terms of the total number of error types, AbsLast1, ExtLast1, and ExtLast5 had the fewest (7, 6, and 9, respectively), indicating that they were non-problematic for the handover. In contrast, there were many errors when Abs, KeyLast1, and ExtLast3 were presented (59, 39, and 23, respectively), indicating that they were unsuitable.

When Abs was presented, there were eight topic transition errors and 16 repetitions. Dialogue summaries other than Abs contained one utterance immediately before the handover, and when those dialogue summaries were presented, there were fewer topic transition errors and repetitions, confirming that presenting the last utterance was helpful.

When KeyLast1 was presented, there were three instances of lack of information and six of self-contradiction. These errors occurred more than twice as often as when the other kinds of summaries were presented. We presume that many of these dialogue breakdowns occurred because the meaning of the keywords was not clear. This suggests the importance of surrounding context (not only a keyword) for sufficiently understanding the content of dialogue for smooth handover.

6 Conclusion

In this study, we conducted a large-scale experiment to determine which summaries are the most useful for handing over a chat dialogue from seven types of dialogue summary consisting of abstractive, extractive, and keyword summaries. Our findings showed that the best summaries were an abstractive summary plus one utterance immediately before the handover and an extractive summary consisting of five utterances immediately before the handover. From the viewpoint of computational cost, summaries that do not require learning, such as keyword summary and extractive summary, are useful. Considering the results of the questionnaire and the analysis of dialogue breakdowns, we conclude that presenting the extractive summary consisting of the last five utterances is currently the most useful.

As future work, it will be necessary to perform experiments to verify the effects of summary lengths. We also want to perform similar experiments with automatically generated summaries so that we can grasp the utility of abstractive summaries in actual handover situations. In addition, we would like to verify the actual usefulness of the summaries by conducting real-time handover experiments. Although we targeted chat dialogues in this study, useful summaries for dialogues other than chat, such as task-oriented dialogue, should also be investigated.

References

Jean Carletta, Simone Ashby, Sebastien Bourban, Mike Flynn, Mael Guillemot, Thomas Hain, Jaroslav Kadlec, Vasilis Karaiskos, Wessel Kraaij, Melissa Kronenthal, Guillaume Lathoud, Mike Lincoln, Agnes Lisowska, Iain McCowan, Wilfried Post, Dennis Reidsma, and Pierre Wellner. 2006. The AMI meeting corpus: A pre-announcement. In *Proceedings of the Second International workshop on Machine Learning for Multimodal Interaction*, pages 28–39.

Jiaao Chen and Diyi Yang. 2020. Multi-view sequence-to-sequence models with conversational structure for abstractive dialogue summarization. In *Proceedings of the 2020 Conference on Empirical Methods in Natural Language Processing*, pages 4106–4118.

Yulong Chen, Yang Liu, Liang Chen, and Yue Zhang. 2021. DialogSum: A real-life scenario dialogue summarization dataset. In *Findings of the Association for Computational Linguistics: ACL-IJCNLP 2021*, pages 5062–5074.

Sarah E. Finch and Jinho D. Choi. 2020. Towards unified dialogue system evaluation: A comprehensive analysis of current evaluation protocols. In *Proceedings of the 21th Annual Meeting of the Special Interest Group on Discourse and Dialogue*, pages 236–245.

Dylan F Glas, Takayuki Kanda, Hiroshi Ishiguro, and Norihiro Hagita. 2012. Teleoperation of multiple social robots. *IEEE Transactions on Systems, Man, and Cybernetics-Part A: Systems and Humans*, 42(3):530–544.

Bogdan Gliwa, Iwona Mochol, Maciej Biesek, and Aleksander Wawer. 2019. SAMSum corpus: A human-annotated dialogue dataset for abstractive summarization. In *Proceedings of the 2nd Workshop on New Frontiers in Summarization*, pages 70–79.

Chih-Wen Goo and Yun-Nung Chen. 2018. Abstractive dialogue summarization with sentence-gated modeling optimized by dialogue acts. In *Proceedings of 2018 IEEE Spoken Language Technology Workshop*, pages 735–742.

Allen L Gorin, Giuseppe Riccardi, and Jeremy H Wright. 1997. How may I help you? *Speech communication*, 23(1):113–127.

Matt Grenander, Yue Dong, Jackie Chi Kit Cheung, and Annie Louis. 2019. Countering the effects of lead bias in news summarization via multi-stage training and auxiliary losses. In *Proceedings of the 2019 Conference on Empirical Methods in Natural Language Processing and the 9th International Joint Conference on Natural Language Processing*, pages 6019–6024.

Ryuichiro Higashinaka, Masahiro Araki, Hiroshi Tsukahara, and Masahiro Mizukami. 2021. Integrated taxonomy of errors in chat-oriented dialogue systems. In *Proceedings of the 22nd Annual Meeting of the Special Interest Group on Discourse and Dialogue*, pages 89–98.

Ryuichiro Higashinaka, Kotaro Funakoshi, Yuka Kobayashi, and Michimasa Inaba. 2016. The dialogue breakdown detection challenge: Task description, datasets, and evaluation metrics. In *Proceedings of the Tenth International Conference on Language Resources and Evaluation*, pages 3146–3150.

Ryuichiro Higashinaka, Michimasa Inaba, and Masahiro Mizukami. 2020. *Creating a Dialogue System with Python*. Ohmsha. (In Japanese).

Victor Hung, Miguel Elvir, Avelino Gonzalez, and Ronald DeMara. 2009. Towards a method for evaluating naturalness in conversational dialog systems. In *Proceedings of 2009 IEEE International Conference on Systems, Man and Cybernetics*, pages 1236–1241.

Adam Janin, Don Baron, Jane Edwards, Dan Ellis, David Gelbart, Nelson Morgan, Barbara Peskin, Thilo Pfau, Elizabeth Shriberg, Andreas Stolcke, et al. 2003. The ICSI meeting corpus. In *Proceedings of 2003 IEEE International Conference on Acoustics, Speech, and Signal Processing*, volume 1, pages I–I.

Tatsuya Kawahara, Naoyuki Muramatsu, Kenta Yamamoto, Divesh Lala, and Koji Inoue. 2021. Semi-autonomous avatar enabling unconstrained parallel conversations—seamless hybrid of woz and autonomous dialogue systems—. *Advanced Robotics*, 35(11):657–663.

Haruki Kawai, Yusuke Muraki, Kenta Yamamoto, Divesh Lala, Koji Inoue, and Tatsuya Kawahara. 2022. Simultaneous job interview system using multiple semi-autonomous agents. In *Proceedings of the SIGdial 2022 Conference*, pages 107–110.

Kazuyoshi Kawasaki and Kohei Ogawa. 2021. Development of simultaneous summarizing technology of multiple sites context for multiple agent teleoperation system. In *Proceedings of the 36th Annual Conference of the Japanese Society for Artificial Intelligence*, pages 2F1–GS–9–04. (In Japanese).

Zhengyuan Liu and Nancy Chen. 2021. Controllable neural dialogue summarization with personal named entity planning. In *Proceedings of the 2021 Conference on Empirical Methods in Natural Language Processing*, pages 92–106.

Zhengyuan Liu, Ke Shi, and Nancy Chen. 2021. Coreference-aware dialogue summarization. In *Proceedings of the 22nd Annual Meeting of the Special Interest Group on Discourse and Dialogue*, pages 509–519.

Inderjeet Mani. 2001. *Automatic summarization*, volume 3. John Benjamins Publishing.

Ramesh Nallapati, Bowen Zhou, Cicero dos Santos, Caglar Gulcehre, and Bing Xiang. 2016. Abstractive text summarization using sequence-to-sequence RNNs and beyond. In *Proceedings of The 20th SIGNLL Conference on Computational Natural Language Learning*, pages 280–290.

Dimitris Pappas, Ion Androutsopoulos, and Haris Papageorgiou. 2015. Anger detection in call center dialogues. In *Proceedings of 2015 6th IEEE International Conference on Cognitive Infocommunications*, pages 139–144.

Virgile Rennard, Guokan Shang, Julie Hunter, and Michalis Vazirgiannis. 2022. Abstractive meeting summarization: A survey. *Computing Research Repository*, arXiv:2208.04163.

Abigail See, Peter J. Liu, and Christopher D. Manning. 2017. Get to the point: Summarization with pointer-generator networks. In *Proceedings of the 55th Annual Meeting of the Association for Computational Linguistics (Volume 1: Long Papers)*, pages 1073–1083.

Ben Sheehan, Hyun Seung Jin, and Udo Gottlieb. 2020. Customer service chatbots: Anthropomorphism and adoption. *Journal of Business Research*, 115:14–24.

Marilyn Walker, Irene Langkilde, Jerry Wright, Allen Gorin, and Diane Litman. 2000. Learning to predict problematic situations in a spoken dialogue system: Experiments with How May I Help You? In *Proceedings of the 1st Meeting of the North American Chapter of the Association for Computational Linguistics*, pages 210–217.

Mark Wasson. 1998. Using leading text for news summaries: Evaluation results and implications for commercial summarization applications. In *Proceedings of the 17th International Conference on Computational Linguistics*, volume 2, pages 1364–1368.

Ming Zhong, Yang Liu, Yichong Xu, Chenguang Zhu, and Michael Zeng. 2021a. Dialoglm: Pre-trained model for long dialogue understanding and summarization. *Computing Research Repository*, arXiv:2109.02492.

Ming Zhong, Da Yin, Tao Yu, Ahmad Zaidi, Mutethia Mutuma, Rahul Jha, Ahmed Hassan Awadallah, Asli Celikyilmaz, Yang Liu, Xipeng Qiu, and Dragomir Radev. 2021b. QMSum: A new benchmark for query-based multi-domain meeting summarization. In *Proceedings of the 2021 Conference of the North American Chapter of the Association for Computational Linguistics: Human Language Technologies*, pages 5905–5921.

MUTE: A Multimodal Dataset for Detecting Hateful Memes

Eftekhar Hossain[$], **Omar Sharif**[Ψ] and **Mohammed Moshiul Hoque**[Ψ]
[$]Department of Electronics and Telecommunication Engineering
[Ψ]Department of Computer Science and Engineering
[$Ψ]Chittagong University of Engineering & Technology, Chattogram-4349, Bangladesh
{eftekhar.hossain,omar.sharif, moshiul_240}@cuet.ac.bd

Abstract

The exponential surge of social media has enabled information propagation at an unprecedented rate. However, it also led to the generation of a vast amount of malign content, such as hateful memes. To eradicate the detrimental impact of this content, over the last few years hateful memes detection problem has grabbed the attention of researchers. However, most past studies were conducted primarily for English memes, while memes on resource-constraint languages (i.e., Bengali) remain under-studied. Moreover, current research considers memes with a caption written in monolingual (either English or Bengali) form. However, memes might have code-mixed captions (English+Bangla), and the existing models can not provide accurate inference in such cases. Therefore, to facilitate research in this arena, this paper introduces a multimodal hate speech dataset (named ***MUTE***) consisting of 4158 memes having Bengali and code-mixed captions. A detailed annotation guideline is provided to aid the dataset creation in other resource-constraint languages. Additionally, extensive experiments have been carried out on MUTE, considering the only visual, only textual, and both modalities. The result demonstrates that joint evaluation of visual and textual features significantly improves ($\approx 3\%$) the hateful memes classification compared to the unimodal evaluation.

(a) Attack religious beliefs (b) Insult a person

Figure 1: Examples of hateful memes having (a) only Bengali caption (b) Code-mixed (Bengali + English) caption.

1 Introduction

With the advent of the Internet, social media platforms (i.e., Facebook, Twitter, Instagram) significantly impact people's day-to-day life. As a result, many users communicate by posting various content in these mediums. This content includes promulgating hate speech, misinformation, aggressive and offensive views. While some contents are beneficial and enrich our knowledge, they can also trigger human emotions that can be considered harmful. Among them, the propagation of hateful content can directly or indirectly attack social harmony based on race, gender, religion, nationality, political support, immigration status, and personal beliefs. In recent years, memes have become a popular form of circulating hate speech (Kiela et al., 2020). These memes on social media have a pernicious impact on societal polarization as they can instigate hateful crimes. Therefore, to restrain the interaction through hateful memes, an automated system is required to quickly flag this content and lessen the inflicted harm to the readers. Several works (Davidson et al., 2017; Waseem and Hovy, 2016) have accomplished hateful memes detection, most of which were for the English language. Unfortunately, no significant studies have been conducted on memes regarding low-resource languages, especially Bengali. In recent years an increasing trend has been observed among the people to use Bengali memes. As a result, it becomes monumental to identify the Bengali hateful memes to mitigate the spread of negativity. However, memes analysis is complicated as it requires a holistic understanding of visual and textual content to infer (Zhou et al., 2021). The visual content of the meme alone may not be harmful (Figure 1 (a)). However,

WARNING: This paper contains meme examples and words that are offensive in nature.

Proceedings of the AACL-IJCNLP 2022 Student Research Workshop, pages 32–39
November 20, 2022. ©2022 Association for Computational Linguistics

it becomes hateful with the incorporation of textual content as it directly attacks religious beliefs. A meme's caption can be written in a mixed language (written in both English and Bengali as in Figure 1 (b)), which can evade the surveillance engine in those cases. Developing a hateful meme detection system for such a scenario is complicated as no standard dataset is available. Moreover, developing an intelligent multimodal memes analysis system for Bengali is challenging due to the unavailability of benchmark corpus, lack of reliable NLP tools (such as OCR), and the complex morphological structure of the Bengali language. Therefore, this work aims to develop a multimodal dataset for Bangla hate speech detection and investigate various models for the task. The critical contributions of the work are summarized as follows:

- Created a multimodal hate speech dataset (MUTE) in Bengali consisting of 4158 memes annotated with Hate and Not-Hate labels.
- Performed extensive experiments with state-of-the-art visual and textual models and then integrate the features of both modalities using the early fusion approach.

2 Related Work

This section discusses the past studies on hate speech detection based on unimodal (i.e., image or text) and multimodal data.

Unimodal based hate speech detection: Hate speech detection is a prominent research issue among the researchers of different languages (Ross et al., 2016; Lekea and Karampelas, 2018). Most hate speech detection works were accomplished based on the text data. For example, both Davidson et al. (2017) and Waseem and Hovy (2016) developed hate speech datasets considering the Twitter posts. Similarly, De Gibert et al. (2018) constructs a dataset that considers the hate speech posted in a white supremacy forum. Some works were also accomplished concerning the low resource languages. For instance, Fortuna et al. (2019); Ousidhoum et al. (2019) introduced hate speech datasets for Portuguese and Arabic. A few works have also been done on Bengali hate speech detection (Romim et al., 2021; Mathew et al., 2021; Ishmam and Sharmin, 2019). Several architectures have been employed over the last few years to classify hateful texts. Earlier researchers widely used Recurrent Neural Network (Gröndahl et al., 2018), Long Short Term Memory (LSTM) Network (Badjatiya et al., 2017), and the combination of RNN and convolutional neural network (CNN) (Zhang et al., 2018b) based methods. Recently, Bidirectional Encoder Representations for Transformers or BERT-based models (Pamungkas and Patti, 2019; Fortuna et al., 2021) are applied and achieved superior performance compared to the deep learning-based methods.

Multimodal hate speech detection: In contrast to the text-based analysis, in recent years, few pieces of work considered multimodal information (i.e., image + text) for hate speech detection. For example, Kiela et al. (2020) introduced a multimodal memes dataset for detecting hate speech. Gomez et al. (2020) developed a large scale multimodal dataset (MMHS150k) for detecting hateful memes. In another work, Rana and Jha (2022) introduced a multimodal hate speech dataset concerning three modalities (i.e., image, text, and audio). However, few works have been accomplished on multimodal hate speech detection for resource constraint languages. Perifanos and Goutsos (2021) introduced a multimodal dataset for detecting hate speech in Greek social media. Likewise, Karim et al. (2022) developed a dataset for multimodal hate speech detection from Bengali memes. Several approaches were employed for detecting hate speech using multimodal learning. Some researchers exploited the different fusion (Sai et al., 2022; Perifanos and Goutsos, 2021) techniques (i.e., early and late fusion) to evaluate the image and textual features jointly. Others have employed bi-linear pooling (Chandra et al., 2021; Choi and Lee, 2019) and transformer-based methods (Kiela et al., 2020) such as MMBT, ViLBERT, and Visual-BERT. Despite having the state of the art multimodal transformer architectures, these models have only applied for high resource language (i.e., English).

Differences with existing researches: Though a considerable amount of work has been accomplished on multimodal hate speech detection, only a few works studied low-resource languages (i.e., Bengali). In our exploration, we found a work (Karim et al., 2022) that detects hate speech from multimodal memes for the Bengali language. However, they did not curate the social media memes for analysis; instead artificially created a memes dataset for Bengali by conjoining the hateful texts into various images. Moreover, the current works overlooked the memes containing captions written cross-lingually. Considering these drawbacks, the proposed research differs from the existing studies in three ways: *(i)* develops a multimodal hate speech dataset (i.e., MUTE) for Bengali considering the Internet memes, *(ii)* provides a detailed annotation guideline that can be followed for resource creation in other low resource languages, and *(iii)* consider the memes that contain code-mixed (English + Bangla) and code-switched (written Bengali dialects in English alphabets) caption.

3 MUTE: A New Benchmark Dataset

This work developed MUTE: a novel multimodal dataset for Bengali Hateful memes detection. The MUTE considered the memes with code-mixed and cod-switched captions. For developing the dataset, we follow the guidelines provided by Kiela et al. (2020). This section briefly describes the dataset development process with detailed statistics.

3.1 Data Accumulation

For dataset construction, we have manually collected memes from various social media platforms such as Facebook, Twitter, and Instagram. We search the memes using a set of keywords such as *Bengali Memes, Bangla Troll Memes, Bangla Celebrity Troll Memes, Bangla Funny Memes* etc. Besides, some popular public memes pages are also considered for the data collection, such as *Keu Amare Mairala, Ovodro Memes* etc. We accumulated 4210 memes from January 10, 2022, to April 15, 2022. During the data collection, some inappropriate memes are discarded by following the guidelines provided by Pramanick et al. (2021). The criteria for discarding data are: (i) memes contain only unimodal data, (ii) memes whose textual or visual information is unclear and (iii) memes contain cartoons. In this filtering process, 52 memes were removed and ended up with a dataset of **4158** memes. Afterwards, the caption of the memes is manually extracted as Bengali has no standard OCR. Finally, the memes and their corresponding captions are given to the annotators for annotation.

3.2 Dataset Annotation

The collected memes are manually labelled into two distinct categories: Hate and not-Hate. However, to ensure the dataset's quality, it is essential to follow a standard definition for segregating the two categories. After exploring some existing works on multimodal hate speech detection (Kiela et al., 2020; Gomez et al., 2020; Perifanos and Goutsos, 2021), we define the classes:

Hate: A meme is considered as Hateful if it intends to vilify, denigrate, bullying, insult, and mocking an entity based on the characteristics including gender, race, religion, caste, and organizational status etc.

Not-Hate: A meme is reckoned as not-Hateful if it does not express any inappropriate cogitation and conveys positive emotions (i.e., affection, gratitude, support, and motivation) explicitly or implicitly.

3.2.1 Process of Annotation

We instructed the annotators to follow the class definitions for performing the annotation. It also asked them to mention the reasons for assigning a meme to a particular class. This explanation will aid the expert in selecting the correct label during contradiction. Initially, we trained the annotators with some sample memes. Four annotators (computer science graduate students) performed the manual annotation process, and an expert (a Professor conducting NLP research for more than 20 years) verified the labels. Annotators were equally divided into two groups where each annotated a subset of memes. In case of disagreement, the expert decided on the final label. The expert ruled a total of 113 non-hateful and 217 hateful memes as hostile and non-hateful. An inter-annotator agreement was measured using Cohen (Cohen, 1960) Kappa Coefficient to ensure the data annotation quality. We achieved a mean Kappa score of 0.714, which indicates a moderate agreement between the annotators. Earlier, it is mentioned that this work is the very first attempt at multimodal hate speech detection that considers the social media memes of the Bengali language. Therefore, it requires more extensive scrutiny with more diverse data and a high level of annotator agreement to deploy the model trained on this dataset. The agreement score illustrates the difficulty in identifying the potential hateful memes by humans and brings a question of biases, thus limiting the broader impact of this work.

3.3 Dataset Statistics

For training and evaluation, the MUTE is split into the train (80%), test (10%), and validation (10%) set. Table 1 presents the class-wise distribution of the dataset. It is observed that the dataset is slightly imbalanced as the 'Not-Hate' class contains ≈60% data. Table 2 shows the statistics of the training

Class	Train	Test	Valid	Total
Hate	1275	159	152	1586
Not-Hate	2092	257	223	2572

Table 1: Number of instances in train, test and validation set for each class.

	Hate	Not-Hate
#Code-mixed texts	345	138
#Words	12854	22885
#Unique words	5781	8627
Max. caption length	51	87
Avg. #words/caption	10.08	10.94

Table 2: Training set statistics of the captions of the memes

set, which contains a total of 483 memes with code-mixed captions. Moreover, it is also illustrate that the 'Not-Hate' class has a higher number of words and unique words than the 'Hate' class. However, the average caption length is almost identical in both classes. Apart from this, we carried out a quantitative analysis using the Jaccard similarity index to figure out the fraction of overlapping words among the classes. We obtained a score of 0.391, indicating that some common words exist between the classes.

4 Methodology

Several computational models have been explored to identify hateful memes by considering the single modality (i.e., image, text) and the combination of both modalities (image and text). This section briefly discusses the methods and parameters utilized to construct the models.

4.1 Baselines for Visual Modality

This work employed convolutional neural networks (CNN) to classify hateful memes based on visual information. Initially, the images are resized into $150 \times 150 \times 3$ and then driven into the pre-trained CNN models. Specifically, we curated the VGG19, VGG16 (Simonyan and Zisserman, 2015), and ResNet50 (He et al., 2016) architectures that fine-tuned on MUTE dataset by using the transfer learning (Tan et al., 2018) approach. Before that, the top two layers of the models are replaced with a sigmoid layer for classification.

4.2 Baselines for Textual Modality

For text based hateful memes analysis, various deep learning models are employed including BiLSTM + CNN (Sharif et al., 2020), BiLSTM + Attention (Zhang et al., 2018a), and Transformers (Vaswani et al., 2017).

BiLSTM + CNN: At first, the word embedding (Mikolov et al., 2013) vectors are fed to a BiLSTM layer consisting of 64 hidden units. Following this, a convolution layer with 32 filters with kernel size two is added, followed by a max-pooling layer to extract the significant contextual features. Finally, a sigmoid layer is used for the classification. The final time steps output of the BiLSTM network provides the contextual information of the overall text.

BiLSTM + Attention: We applied the additive attention (Bahdanau et al., 2015) mechanism to the individual word representations of the BiLSTM cell. The CNN is replaced with an attention layer. The attention layer tries to give higher weight to the significant words for inferring a particular class.

Transformers: Pretrained transformer models have recently obtained remarkable performance in almost every NLP task (Naseem et al., 2020; Yang et al., 2020; Cao et al., 2020). As the *MUTE* contains cross-lingual text, this work employed three transformer models, namely Multilingual Bidirectional Encoder Representations for Transformer (M-BERT (Devlin et al., 2019)), Bangla-BERT (Sarker, 2020), and Cross-Lingual Representation Learner (XLM-R (Conneau et al., 2020)). All the models are downloaded from HuggingFace[1] transformer library. We follow their preprocessing [2] and encoding technique for preparing the texts. The transformer models provide a sentence representation vector of size 768. This vector is passed to a dense layer of 32 neurons, and then using the pre-trained weights, models are retrained on the developed dataset with a sigmoid layer.

4.3 Baselines for Multimodal Data

In recent years, joint evaluation of visual and textual data has proven superior in solving many complex NLP problems (Hori et al., 2017; Yang et al., 2019; Alam et al., 2021). This work investigates the joint learning of multimodal data for hateful memes

[1] https://huggingface.co/

[2] https://huggingface.co/docs/tokenizers/index

classification. For multimodal feature representation, we employed the feature fusion (Nojavanasghari et al., 2016) approach. In earlier experiments, all the visual and two textual (i.e., Bangla-BERT and XLM-R) models are used to construct the multimodal models. For the model construction, we added a dense layer of 100 neurons at both modality sides and then concatenated their outputs to make combined visual and textual data representations. Finally, this combined feature is passed to a dense layer of 32 neurons, followed by a sigmoid layer for the classification task.

5 MUTE: Benchmark Evaluation

The training set is used to train the models, whereas the validation set is for tweaking the hyperparameters. We have empirically tried several hyperparameters to obtain a better model's performance and reported the best one. The final evaluation of the models is done on the test set. This work selects the weighted f1-score (WF) as the primary metric for the evaluation due to the class imbalance nature of the dataset. Apart from this, we used the class weighting technique (Sun et al., 2009) to give equal priority to the minority class (hate) during the model training.

5.1 Results

Table 3 illustrates the outcome of the visual, textual, and multimodal models for hateful memes classification. In the case of the visual model, ResNet50 obtained the maximum WF of 0.641. For the text modality, the B-BERT model obtained the highest WF (0.649). The outcomes of the other textual models (i.e., BiLSTM + Attention, BiLSTM + CNN, and XLM-R) are not exhibited significant differences compared to the best model (B-BERT). On the other hand, with the multimodal information, the outcomes of the models are not improved. Almost all the models' WF lies around 0.60 except the VGG19 + B-BERT model (0.641). However, the VGG16 + B-BERT model outperformed all the models by achieving the highest weighted WF of 0.672, which is approximately 2% higher than the best unimodal model of B-BERT (0.649).

5.2 Error Analysis

We conducted a quantitative error analysis to investigate the model's mistakes across the two classes. To illustrate the errors, the number of misclassified instances is reported in Figure 2 for the best unimodal (ResNet50 and B-BERT) and multimodal (VGG19 + B-BERT) models. It is observed that the misclassification rate (MR) is increased ≈10% and decreased ≈9% from visual to textual model, respectively, for the 'Hate' and 'Not-Hate' classes. However, the joint evaluation of multimodal features significantly reduced the MR to 38% (from 44% and 54%) in the Hate class and thus improved the model's overall performance. Though the multimodal model showed superior performance compared to the unimodal models, there is still room for improvement. We point out several reasons behind the model's mistakes. Among them, identical words in different written formats (code-mixed, code-switched) made it difficult for the model to identify accurate labels. Moreover, the discrepancy between some memes' visual and textual information creates confusion for the multimodal model. Indeed, these are some significant factors that should be tackled to develop a more sophisticated model for Bengali hateful memes classification.

Approach	Models	P	R	WF
Visual	VGG19	0.594	0.579	0.584
	VGG16	0.636	0.644	0.638
	ResNet50	0.643	0.639	0.641
Textual	BiLSTM + CNN	0.617	0.663	0.608
	BiLSTM + Attention	0.647	0.653	0.642
	M-BERT	0.627	0.644	0.620
	B-BERT	0.645	0.658	0.649
	XLM-R	0.646	0.656	0.648
Multimodal	VGG19 + B-BERT	0.639	0.649	0.641
	VGG16 + B-BERT	0.676	0.670	**0.672**
	ResNet50 + B-BERT	0.606	0.620	0.609
	VGG16 + XLM-R	0.594	0.581	0.586
	VGG19 + XLM-R	0.515	0.605	0.489
	ResNet50 + XLM-R	0.651	0.600	0.604

Table 3: Performance comparison of the visual, textual, and multimodal models on the test set. Where P, R, WF denotes precision, recall and weighted f_1-score, respectively.

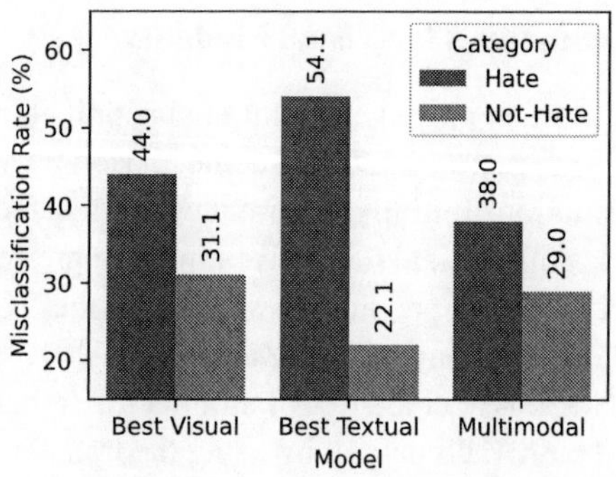

Figure 2: Miss-classification rate across two classes by different models.

6 Conclusion

This paper presented a multimodal framework for hateful memes classification and investigated its performance on a newly developed multimodal dataset (*MUTE*) having Bengali and code-mixed (Bangla + English) captions. For benchmarking the framework, this work exploited several computational models for detecting hateful content. The key finding of the experiment is that the joint evaluation of multimodal features is more effective than the memes' only visual or textual information. Moreover, the cross-lingual embeddings (XLM-R) did not provide the expected performance compared to the monolingual embeddings (Bangla-BERT) when jointly evaluated with the visual features. The error analysis reveals that the model's performance gets biased to a particular class due to the class imbalance. In future, we aim to alleviate this problem by extending the dataset to a large scale and framing it as a multi-class classification problem. Secondly, for robust inference, advanced fusion techniques (i.e., co-attention) and multitask learning approaches will be explored. Finally, future research will explore the impact of dataset sampling and do some ablation study (i.e., experimenting with only English, only Bangla, code-mixed, and code-switched text) to convey valuable insights about the models' performance.

References

Firoj Alam, Stefano Cresci, Tanmoy Chakraborty, Fabrizio Silvestri, Dimiter Dimitrov, Giovanni Da San Martino, Shaden Shaar, Hamed Firooz, and Preslav Nakov. 2021. A survey on multimodal disinformation detection. *arXiv preprint arXiv:2103.12541*.

Pinkesh Badjatiya, Shashank Gupta, Manish Gupta, and Vasudeva Varma. 2017. Deep learning for hate speech detection in tweets. In *Proceedings of the 26th international conference on World Wide Web companion*, pages 759–760.

Dzmitry Bahdanau, Kyung Hyun Cho, and Yoshua Bengio. 2015. Neural machine translation by jointly learning to align and translate. In *3rd International Conference on Learning Representations, ICLR 2015*.

Qingqing Cao, Harsh Trivedi, Aruna Balasubramanian, and Niranjan Balasubramanian. 2020. Deformer: Decomposing pre-trained transformers for faster question answering. In *Proceedings of the 58th Annual Meeting of the Association for Computational Linguistics*, pages 4487–4497.

Mohit Chandra, Dheeraj Pailla, Himanshu Bhatia, Aadilmehdi Sanchawala, Manish Gupta, Manish Shrivastava, and Ponnurangam Kumaraguru. 2021. "subverting the jewtocracy": Online antisemitism detection using multimodal deep learning. In *13th ACM Web Science Conference 2021*, pages 148–157.

Jun-Ho Choi and Jong-Seok Lee. 2019. Embracenet: A robust deep learning architecture for multimodal classification. *Information Fusion*, 51:259–270.

Jacob Cohen. 1960. A coefficient of agreement for nominal scales. *Educational and Psychological Measurement*, 20(1):37–46.

Alexis Conneau, Kartikay Khandelwal, Naman Goyal, Vishrav Chaudhary, Guillaume Wenzek, Francisco Guzmán, Edouard Grave, Myle Ott, Luke Zettlemoyer, and Veselin Stoyanov. 2020. Unsupervised cross-lingual representation learning at scale. In *ACL*.

Thomas Davidson, Dana Warmsley, Michael Macy, and Ingmar Weber. 2017. Automated hate speech detection and the problem of offensive language. In *Proceedings of the international AAAI conference on web and social media*, volume 11, pages 512–515.

Ona De Gibert, Naiara Perez, Aitor García-Pablos, and Montse Cuadros. 2018. Hate speech dataset from a white supremacy forum. *arXiv preprint arXiv:1809.04444*.

Jacob Devlin, Ming-Wei Chang, Kenton Lee, and Kristina Toutanova. 2019. BERT: Pre-training of deep bidirectional transformers for language understanding. In *Proceedings of the 2019 Conference of the North American Chapter of the Association for Computational Linguistics: Human Language Technologies, Volume 1 (Long and Short Papers)*, pages 4171–4186, Minneapolis, Minnesota. Association for Computational Linguistics.

Paula Fortuna, Joao Rocha da Silva, Leo Wanner, Sérgio Nunes, et al. 2019. A hierarchically-labeled portuguese hate speech dataset. In *Proceedings of the third workshop on abusive language online*, pages 94–104.

Paula Fortuna, Juan Soler-Company, and Leo Wanner. 2021. How well do hate speech, toxicity, abusive and offensive language classification models generalize across datasets? *Information Processing & Management*, 58(3):102524.

Raul Gomez, Jaume Gibert, Lluis Gomez, and Dimosthenis Karatzas. 2020. Exploring hate speech detection in multimodal publications. In *Proceedings of the IEEE/CVF winter conference on applications of computer vision*, pages 1470–1478.

Tommi Gröndahl, Luca Pajola, Mika Juuti, Mauro Conti, and N Asokan. 2018. All you need is" love" evading hate speech detection. In *Proceedings of the 11th ACM workshop on artificial intelligence and security*, pages 2–12.

Kaiming He, X. Zhang, Shaoqing Ren, and Jian Sun. 2016. Deep residual learning for image recognition. *2016 IEEE Conference on Computer Vision and Pattern Recognition (CVPR)*, pages 770–778.

Chiori Hori, Takaaki Hori, Teng-Yok Lee, Ziming Zhang, Bret Harsham, John R Hershey, Tim K Marks, and Kazuhiko Sumi. 2017. Attention-based multimodal fusion for video description. In *Proceedings of the IEEE international conference on computer vision*, pages 4193–4202.

Alvi Md Ishmam and Sadia Sharmin. 2019. Hateful speech detection in public facebook pages for the bengali language. In *2019 18th IEEE international conference on machine learning and applications (ICMLA)*, pages 555–560. IEEE.

Md Karim, Sumon Kanti Dey, Tanhim Islam, Bharathi Raja Chakravarthi, et al. 2022. Multimodal hate speech detection from bengali memes and texts. *arXiv preprint arXiv:2204.10196*.

Douwe Kiela, Hamed Firooz, Aravind Mohan, Vedanuj Goswami, Amanpreet Singh, Pratik Ringshia, and Davide Testuggine. 2020. The hateful memes challenge: Detecting hate speech in multimodal memes. *Advances in Neural Information Processing Systems*, 33:2611–2624.

Ioanna K Lekea and Panagiotis Karampelas. 2018. Detecting hate speech within the terrorist argument: a greek case. In *2018 IEEE/ACM International Conference on Advances in Social Networks Analysis and Mining (ASONAM)*, pages 1084–1091. IEEE.

Binny Mathew, Punyajoy Saha, Seid Muhie Yimam, Chris Biemann, Pawan Goyal, and Animesh Mukherjee. 2021. Hatexplain: A benchmark dataset for explainable hate speech detection. In *Proceedings of the AAAI Conference on Artificial Intelligence*, volume 35, pages 14867–14875.

Tomas Mikolov, Kai Chen, G. Corrado, and J. Dean. 2013. Efficient estimation of word representations in vector space. In *ICLR*.

Usman Naseem, Imran Razzak, Katarzyna Musial, and Muhammad Imran. 2020. Transformer based deep intelligent contextual embedding for twitter sentiment analysis. *Future Generation Computer Systems*, 113:58–69.

Behnaz Nojavanasghari, Deepak Gopinath, Jayanth Koushik, Tadas Baltrušaitis, and Louis-Philippe Morency. 2016. Deep multimodal fusion for persuasiveness prediction. In *Proceedings of the 18th ACM International Conference on Multimodal Interaction*, pages 284–288.

Nedjma Ousidhoum, Zizheng Lin, Hongming Zhang, Yangqiu Song, and Dit-Yan Yeung. 2019. Multilingual and multi-aspect hate speech analysis. In *Proceedings of the 2019 Conference on Empirical Methods in Natural Language Processing and the 9th International Joint Conference on Natural Language Processing (EMNLP-IJCNLP)*, pages 4675–4684.

Endang Wahyu Pamungkas and Viviana Patti. 2019. Cross-domain and cross-lingual abusive language detection: A hybrid approach with deep learning and a multilingual lexicon. In *Proceedings of the 57th Annual Meeting of the Association for Computational Linguistics: Student Research Workshop*, pages 363–370, Florence, Italy. Association for Computational Linguistics.

Konstantinos Perifanos and Dionysis Goutsos. 2021. Multimodal hate speech detection in greek social media. *Multimodal Technologies and Interaction*, 5(7):34.

Shraman Pramanick, Dimitar Dimitrov, Rituparna Mukherjee, Shivam Sharma, Md Shad Akhtar, Preslav Nakov, and Tanmoy Chakraborty. 2021. Detecting harmful memes and their targets. In *Findings of the Association for Computational Linguistics: ACL-IJCNLP 2021*, pages 2783–2796.

Aneri Rana and Sonali Jha. 2022. Emotion based hate speech detection using multimodal learning. *arXiv preprint arXiv:2202.06218*.

Nauros Romim, Mosahed Ahmed, Hriteshwar Talukder, Saiful Islam, et al. 2021. Hate speech detection in the bengali language: A dataset and its baseline evaluation. In *Proceedings of International Joint Conference on Advances in Computational Intelligence*, pages 457–468. Springer.

Bjorn Ross, Michael Rist, Guillermo Carbonell, Benjamin Cabrera, Nils Kurowsky, and Michael Wojatzki. 2016. Measuring the reliability of hate speech annotations: The case of the european refugee crisis. In *3rd Workshop on Natural Language Processing for Computer-Mediated Communication/Social Media*, pages 6–9. Ruhr-Universitat Bochum.

Siva Sai, Naman Deep Srivastava, and Yashvardhan Sharma. 2022. Explorative application of fusion techniques for multimodal hate speech detection. *SN Computer Science*, 3(2):1–13.

Sagor Sarker. 2020. Banglabert: Bengali mask language model for bengali language understading.

Omar Sharif, Eftekhar Hossain, and Mohammed Moshiul Hoque. 2020. TechTexC: Classification of technical texts using convolution and bidirectional long short term memory network. In *Proceedings of the 17th International Conference on Natural Language Processing (ICON): TechDOfication 2020 Shared Task*, pages 35–39, Patna, India. NLP Association of India (NLPAI).

K. Simonyan and Andrew Zisserman. 2015. Very deep convolutional networks for large-scale image recognition. *CoRR*, abs/1409.1556.

Yanmin Sun, Andrew KC Wong, and Mohamed S Kamel. 2009. Classification of imbalanced data: A review. *International journal of pattern recognition and artificial intelligence*, 23(04):687–719.

Chuanqi Tan, Fuchun Sun, Tao Kong, Wenchang Zhang, Chao Yang, and Chunfang Liu. 2018. A survey on deep transfer learning. In *International conference on artificial neural networks*, pages 270–279. Springer.

Ashish Vaswani, Noam M. Shazeer, Niki Parmar, Jakob Uszkoreit, Llion Jones, Aidan N. Gomez, Lukasz Kaiser, and Illia Polosukhin. 2017. Attention is all you need. *ArXiv*, abs/1706.03762.

Zeerak Waseem and Dirk Hovy. 2016. Hateful symbols or hateful people? predictive features for hate speech detection on twitter. In *Proceedings of the NAACL student research workshop*, pages 88–93.

Fan Yang, Xiaochang Peng, Gargi Ghosh, Reshef Shilon, Hao Ma, Eider Moore, and Goran Predovic. 2019. Exploring deep multimodal fusion of text and photo for hate speech classification. In *Proceedings of the third workshop on abusive language online*, pages 11–18.

Jiacheng Yang, Mingxuan Wang, Hao Zhou, Chengqi Zhao, Weinan Zhang, Yong Yu, and Lei Li. 2020. Towards making the most of bert in neural machine translation. In *Proceedings of the AAAI Conference on Artificial Intelligence*, volume 34, pages 9378–9385.

You Zhang, Jin Wang, and Xuejie Zhang. 2018a. Ynu-hpcc at semeval-2018 task 1: Bilstm with attention based sentiment analysis for affect in tweets. In *Proceedings of The 12th International Workshop on Semantic Evaluation*, pages 273–278.

Ziqi Zhang, David Robinson, and Jonathan Tepper. 2018b. Detecting hate speech on twitter using a convolution-gru based deep neural network. In *European semantic web conference*, pages 745–760. Springer.

Yi Zhou, Zhenhao Chen, and Huiyuan Yang. 2021. Multimodal learning for hateful memes detection. In *2021 IEEE International Conference on Multimedia & Expo Workshops (ICMEW)*, pages 1–6. IEEE.

A Simple and Fast Strategy for Handling Rare Words in Neural Machine Translation

Minh-Cong Nguyen-Hoang[1], **Thi-Vinh Ngo**[2], **Van-Vinh Nguyen**[1]

[1]*University of Engineering and Technology, VNU, Hanoi, Vietnam*
[2]*University of Information and Communication Technology, TNU, Thai Nguyen, Vietnam*
congnhm@vnu.edu.vn, ntvinh@ictu.edu.vn, vinhnv@vnu.edu.vn

Abstract

Neural Machine Translation (NMT) has currently obtained state-of-the-art in machine translation systems. However, dealing with rare words is still a big challenge in translation systems. The rare words are often translated using a manual dictionary or copied from the source to the target with original words. In this paper, we propose a simple and fast strategy for integrating constraints during the training and decoding process to improve the translation of rare words. The effectiveness of our proposal is demonstrated in both high and low resource translation tasks, including the language pairs: English → Vietnamese, Chinese → Vietnamese, Khmer → Vietnamese, and Lao → Vietnamese. We show the improvements of up to +1.8 BLEU scores over the baseline systems.

1 Introduction

Neural Machine Translation (NMT) (Cho et al., 2014; Sutskever et al., 2014; Vaswani et al., 2017) has recently shown impressive results compared to Statistical Machine Translation (SMT) (Wu et al., 2016; Klein et al., 2017). However, NMT systems still have great challenges (Koehn and Knowles, 2017), in that, addressing rare words is one of them. Due to NMT that has tended to bias in high-frequency words, low-frequency words have little chance of being considered in the inference process. To tackle this problem, some previous works have proposed various strategies to augment translation of low-frequency words. Typically, Luong et al. (2015a) demonstrate the effectiveness of NMT systems by replacing rare words by special symbols such as $unk_1, unk_2, ..., unk_i$ in the sentence. They use an aligned dictionary to map between an unk_i in the source sentence and an other unk_j in the target sentence. This approach tends to raise ambiguity in context of sentence as shown in (Sennrich et al., 2016). In addition, Sennrich et al. (2016) suggest for applying Byte Pair Encoding (BPE) (Gage, 1994) to NMT systems. This technique significantly reduces the vocabulary size and shows substantial improvements on performance translation, and it is widely applied for almost all translation systems nowadays. Following this approach, a rare word will be split into sub-words and the sentence context is still preserved, nevertheless, other new rare words can be also generated. Moreover, this segmentation could make it more difficult to discover original rare words from their sub-words.

To overcome this issue, Vinyals et al. (2015) propose *pointer networks* which automatically copy rare-words from the source sentence into the target sentence. To achieve this aim, they integrate a copy probability to the output distribution with a copy coefficient learnt during the training process. There are also some other variances of these networks such as (Gulcehre et al., 2016; Pham et al., 2018; Song et al., 2019). However, these techniques often copy only a part of rare words when they are separated into sub-words, and we find that they do not have benefit in the data sparsity situation.

Inspired by above *pointer networks*, we propose a simple and fast idea for representing the output probability distribution, though our strategy does not require learning any additional weights. Besides, we leverage neighboring words to identify the suitable position of translation in the source side that corresponds to a rare word in the target side when it has the wrong attention. The proposal is only performed during the inference process, therefore, it does not affect the training. Our experiments show the improvements overcoming the baseline systems.

The background of NMT is shown in 2. The detail of our method is described in section 3, experiments and results are shown in section 4. Finally, the related work is presented in section 5.

Proceedings of the AACL-IJCNLP 2022 Student Research Workshop, pages 40–46
November 20, 2022. ©2022 Association for Computational Linguistics

2 Neural machine translation

The goal of NMT systems is to translate a source sentence $x = x_1, ..., x_{|x|}$ to a target sentence $y = y_1, ..., y_{|y|}$. NMT has suggested in (Cho et al., 2014; Sutskever et al., 2014) with recurrent neural networks (RNNs) which use GRU (Gated Recurrent Unit) or LSTM (Long Short Term Memory) for handling the memory context of long sentences. However, these networks face the difficulty of parallel computations during the training process. Vaswani et al. (2017) presents the Transformer model to overcome this issue, which has shown the state-of-the-art in current NMT systems. The probability P (y|x, $\boldsymbol{\theta}$) indicate a NMT model (Vaswani et al., 2017) parameterized by $\boldsymbol{\theta}$. During the training process, parameters are optimized by minimizing the maximum likelihood of the sentence pairs:

$$L(y|x, \boldsymbol{\theta}) = \frac{1}{|y|} \sum_{k=1}^{|y|} logP(y_t|y_{<t}, x, \boldsymbol{\theta}), \quad (1)$$

in there, $y_{<t}$ is a partial translation.

Self-Attention In the Transformer architecture, both Encoder and Decoder are stacks of I identical layers, each layer contains number heads of self-attention to learn context representations.

$$\text{attn}(Q, K, V) = \text{softmax}(\frac{QK^T}{\sqrt{d}})V, \quad (2)$$

where K (key), Q (query), V (value) are vectors which present the hidden states of tokens in the input sequences and d is the size of hidden states.

Attention mechanism in Transformer between the source sentence and the target sentence is a variance of the attention proposed by Luong et al. (2015b). Its presentation is the same as in 2, however, keys and values are representations of the source sentence while queries are those of the target sentence.

3 Rare words Translation

This section will present details of steps in our method to enhance the translation system.

Tagging data In the first place, we use Giza++[1] to align between source and target sentences. Secondly, a dictionary will be generated from the alignment table. Finally, We tag a special token for rare words in both source and target sentences as in the Figure 1. In our experiments, words that have a frequency below 4 are considered as rare words. Each rare words is inside a pair of "#". We hope that these tokens will help translation systems detect rare words during the training and decoding process.

Inference Inspired by the *pointer network* (Vinyals et al., 2015)

$$P_{output}(y|x, \boldsymbol{\theta}) = \alpha * P_g + (1 - \alpha) * P_c, \quad (3)$$

where, α is a copy factor which is learnt during the training, P_g is the normal output distribution of the model while P_c is the copy distribution which presents the target-to-source attention weights to indicate which tokens will be copied from the source sentences to the target sentence. There are also some variants of P_c in previous works (Vinyals et al., 2015; Gulcehre et al., 2016; Song et al., 2019; Pham et al., 2018). However, because the copy factor α is automatically learnt in the training, therefore, it may be not good enough in data sparsity situations to perform the given aim, and this may lead to wrong predictions for both rare words and non rare words.

To address this issue, we fix the copy factor α to constants during the inference process. Base on tagged labels as mentioned above to the detection rare words, we set α to 1 after detecting the token *"#"* that mark the start position of each rare word in the step i^{th}, otherwise, it is set to 0 when the other stop token *"#"* is discovered.

Heuristic Due to the systems that could attend to the translation of a rare word in the target side to the wrong translation in the source side may contain many rare words. In this issue, around words are also used to support the inference process discovering the best suitable position of the corresponding translation in the source sentence. To implement this idea, we define a heuristic function $score_{ij}$ to estimate alignment weight between each rare word i^{th} in the target side and the rare word j^{th} in the source side during the inference process as in the formula 4.

$$score_{ij} = \beta * \sum P_{sw_{kj}} + \gamma * \sum P_{\#_{mj}} + \epsilon * \sum P_{a_{lj}} \quad (4)$$

where $P_{sw_{kj}}$ is the attention weight between the sub-word k^{th} of the rare word i^{th} in the target side and the rare word j^{th} in the source side. Similarly, $P_{\#_{mj}}$ is the attention weight of the token *"#"* m^{th}

[1] `https://github.com/moses-smt/giza-pp`

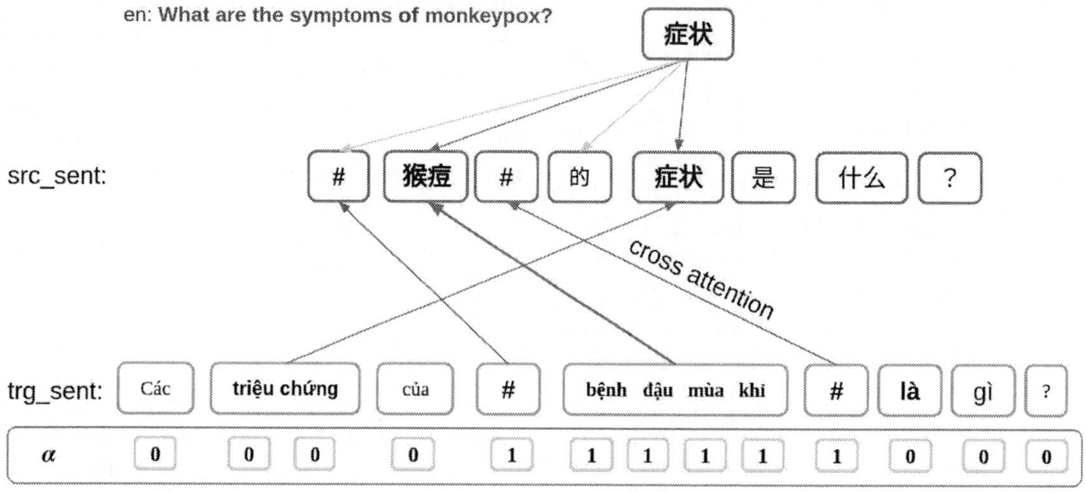

Figure 1: A illustration of our method: the rare word "bệnh đậu mùa khỉ (猴痘)" is put on a pair of "#", the non rare word "triệu trứng" is used to support the inference process detecting the suitable position of translation in the source side. The α is a copy factor which is described in the formula 3

.

that starts or ends the rare word i^{th}, and $P_{a_{lj}}$ is the attention weight of the around word l^{th} of the rare word i^{th}. In the experiment, we only consider two content words that are nearest to the rare word i^{th}, in which, one word before and another one after the the rare word i. $P_{sw_{kj}}$, $P_{\#_{mj}}$, and $P_{a_{lj}}$ will assigned to 1 if they attend to the rare word j^{th} in the source side, otherwise, they are 0. Besides, β, γ and ϵ are constants, in our experiments, both β and γ are the same value and they are assigned to 0.4 while ϵ is 0.2.

The rare word j^{th} in the source side that has the highest score corresponding to the rare word i^{th} in the target side will be chosen as the its best translation. Our algorithm is detailed in the Algorithm 1.

Thus, at each step n^{th}, the cross attention weights will be computed for each target token. We utilize head 0 with layer 0 in order to evaluate these attentions .To save time, we employ *"Cache Maintenance"* strategy inspired by (Yan et al., 2021) to archive Q_t, K_t, V_t, and $attn_t$ in beam search.

4 Experiments

This section presents our implementation of the translation systems. Our method show the efficiency of both bilingual and multilingual translation systems. The SacreBLEU score (Post, 2018)[2] is employed to evaluate the quality translation.

[2]https://github.com/mjpost/sacrebleu

4.1 Datasets and Training System

Datasets and Pre-processing We use different datasets from KC4.0 UET (Nguyen et al., 2022), Hugging Face[3], and Asian Language Treebank[4] (ALT) corpus. For all parallel corpus collected from Hugging Face, we filter and remove poor quality sentence pairs using LASER[5].

For all experiments, the development and test sets from the Asian Language Treebank (ALT) corpus are utilized for early stop and evaluate the efficiency of our strategy. The development set includes 1000 sentence pairs while the test set contains 1018 other ones.

To generate alignment dictionaries for tagging rare words, we use various segmentation tool for each language: pkuseg[6] for Chinese texts, laoNLP[7] for Laos texts, khmernltk[8] for Khmer texts, and moses[9] tokenizer for English and Vietnamese texts.

[3]https://huggingface.co

[4]https://www2.nict.go.jp/astrec-att/member/mutiyama/ALT/

[5]https://github.com/facebookresearch/LASER

[6]https://github.com/lancopku/pkuseg-python

[7]https://github.com/wannaphong/LaoNLP

[8]https://github.com/VietHoang1512/khmer-nltk

[9]https://github.com/moses-smt/mosesdecoder/tree/master/scripts

Algorithm 1: Finding the suitable position in the source sentence for a target rare word

Input :
attn_cache contains cross attentions,
marked_src_sent: marks the position of the rare word,
word_query: the translation of the rare word in target sentence including special token "#".
Output : The best candidate correspond to rare word

```
P_swkj, P_#mj, P_alj = {0} // Initial with 0 and their size is number of the rare words.
p_words = spm(word_query)  // the number of sub words of word query.
/* Compute P_swkj :                                  */
for i ← 0 to n − 1 do
    piece = p_words[i]
    attn_pos = arg_max(attn_cache[piece])
    rare_word = marked_src_sent[attn_pos]
    if rare_word is not equal 0 then
        P_swkj[rare_word-1] += 1
    end
end
/* Compute P_#mj :                                   */
for i ← 0 to 2 do
    // Two "#" nearest the rare word
    attn_pos = arg_max(attn_cache[#_i])
    rare_word = marked_src_sent[attn_pos]
    if rare_word is not equal 0 then
        P_#mj[rare_word-1] += 1
    end
end
/* Compute P_alj :                                   */
neighbor_word = get_neighbor(word_query)
    // get two nearest neighbor words
while neighbor_word ≠ None do
    pos = attn_cache[neighbor_word_i]
    attn_pos = arg_max(pos)
    rare_word = find_nearest(attn_pos)
        // Find the nearest rare word from attention position
    if rare_word is not equal 0 then
        P_alj[rare_word-1] += 1
    end
end
score_ij = β ∗ P_swkj + γ ∗ P_#mj + ϵ ∗ P_alj
rare_word = arg_max(score_ij)
return rare_word
```

No.	Lang	Size	Source
1	**Zh-Vi**	500k	KC4.0 UET
		2M	HuggingFace
		18k	ALT
2	**Lo-Vi**	150k	KC4.0 UET
		18k	ALT
3	**Km-Vi**	150k	KC4.0 UET
		18k	ALT
4	**En-Vi**	2.6M	HuggingFace

Table 1: The statistics of parallel datasets are used in our experiments.

For bilingual systems, we apply sentencePiece[10] (Kudo and Richardson, 2018) with split-digit option and 32K joint merge operations for the original texts in all languages. We estimate our proposed in the Chinese → Vietnamese pair including 150K sentence pairs which extracted from KC4.0 UET corpus in the low-resource issue and 2.5M which are concatenated from Hugging Face and KC4.0 UET corpus in the higher resource situation.

For the multilingual system, we mix all the parallel corpus as described in table 1 and gain approximately 5M5 sentence pairs. The texts from the baseline systems are tagged for rare words as described in the section 3.

System and training We implement our baseline NMT systems using the framework ViNMT[11] (Quan et al., 2021). All settings are the same for both bilingual and multilingual systems. The training system includes 6 layers for both encoder and decoder, the sizes of hidden states and embedding is 512, the number of heads are 8. The Adam Optimizer is used to optimize parameters of the whole model with the initial learning rate is 1e-3. The size of each mini-batch is 64 sentence pairs. The other settings are the defaults of ViNMT.

To apply our ideas to the NMT system, we modify the baseline architecture following the steps in the section 3. Besides, the baseline architecture is also reformed as in Song et al. (2019) for comparison purpose.

All systems are trained until they gain convergence on the development set. The best model in terms of unigram accuracy on the validation set is used to translate the test set with beam size of 4.

[10] https://github.com/google/sentencepiece

[11] https://github.com/KCDichDaNgu/KC4.0_MultilingualNMT

4.2 Results

The practical results are presented in Table 2 and Table 3.

Bilingual systems Our baseline systems have achieved 18.1 and 28.1 BLEU scores on two datasets. To estimate the efficiency of our method, the other strategy for dealing with the rare words in Song et al. (2019) are performed in our experiments. Our proposal overcomes both the baseline system and Song's system Song et al. (2019), and they have gained improvements of +0.2 and +1.0 BLEU scores in both two datasets.

No.	Systems	150K	2.5M
1	Baseline	18.1	28.1
3	Song et al. (2019)	17.5	28.0
4	Our proposal	**18.3**	**29.1**

Table 2: BLEU scores on ALT test set for bilingual systems for the Chinese → Vietnamese translation task when applying our method.

Multilingual system To further investigate the efficiency of our proposal, we train a multilingual system "many to one" from English (En), Chinese (Zh), Laos (Lo), and Khmer (Km) to Vietnamese. The result is shown in the Table 3.

No.	Lang	Baseline	Our proposal
1	En-Vi	32.4	**34.0** (+1.6)
2	Zh-Vi	28.0	**29.8** (+1.8)
3	Lo-Vi	24.4	**25.1** (+0.7)
4	Km-Vi	28.9	**29.2** (+0.3)

Table 3: The BLEU scores for the multilingual translation system

Our method has achieved significant improvements on almost translation tasks. In particular, it gains +1.6 BLEU scores for English → Vietnamese translation, and + 1.8 BLEU points for Chinese → Vietnamese translation. The translation task Laos → Vietnamese obtains +0.7 BLEU scores while it only acquires +0.3 BLEU points for the Khmer → Vietnamese translation task.

5 Related Work

Dealing with rare words has investigated by many previous works in machine translation. Tsvetkov and Dyer (2015) employed a model of lexical borrowing to enhance SMT systems. However, this approach claim extraction of complex features such as phonetic and semantic features, or pre-trained SMT systems, and it is difficult to apply to NMT systems. Jean et al. (2015) used a large vocabulary to solve the rare words but this increases parameters and leads to augmentation the size of models and rare words still exist. Some other works require additional resources to tackle rare words such as Trieu (2016) exploited word similarity, or Ngo et al. (2019) utilize synonyms to advance translation systems. Luong et al. (2015a) employed special symbols to present rare words or unknown words but this tend to increase the ambiguous of sentence context. Sennrich et al. (2016) applied BPE algorithm to separate rare words into sub-words, however, new sub-words are again generated. Furthermore, Vinyals et al. (2015) suggested point networks allow to copy automatically rare words from source side to the target side with learning supplemental parameters, and in some case, it has only a part of rare words (sub-words) are copied. This approach is also considered in recent studies Gulcehre et al. (2016); Song et al. (2019); Pham et al. (2018).

Our proposal also relies on the idea of point networks, nevertheless, we fix the copy factor to a constant. Besides, we leverage neighbouring words to specify the best position of the rare word in the source side that corresponds to the one in the target side.

6 Conclusion

In this work, we propose a simple and fast method to improve the translation quality for rare words. Our technique does not require training supplemental parameters, and this strategy is only performed in the inference process, therefore, the training time does not change. In the future, we would like to consider more neighbouring words around rare words for selecting position to improve the quality of translation tasks.

Acknowledgments

This work is supported by Ministry of Science and Technology of Vietnam under Program KC 4.0, No. KC-4.0.12/19-25.

References

Kyunghyun Cho, Bart van Merriënboer, Caglar Gulcehre, Dzmitry Bahdanau, Fethi Bougares, Holger Schwenk, and Yoshua Bengio. 2014. Learning phrase representations using RNN encoder–decoder for statistical machine translation. In *Proceedings*

Source (zh)	至少 11 人在 # 巴西里约 # 热内 # 卢[illegible] # 比街区 " # morro da Mineira # " （# 矿山 #）棚户区毒贩之间的帮派地盘争夺战中丧生。
Reference	Ít nhất 11 người đã thiệt trong các cuộc ẩu đả tranh giành địa bàn giữa các nhóm buôn lậu thuốc phiện ở khu ổ chuột "morro da Mineira" (Đồi Mỏ) thuộc địa phận Catumbi lân cận Rio de Janeiro, Brazil.
Meaning	At least 11 people have been killed in a gang turf war between drug dealers in the shantytown of "morro da Mineira" (The Mine) in Rio de Janeiro's Catumbi neighborhood.
Baseline	Ít nhất 11 người đã thiệt mạng trong cuộc tranh giành địa bàn giữa những kẻ buôn ma túy trong khu nhà lều ở Rio de Janeiro, Brazil.
Our Method	Ít nhất 11 người đã thiệt mạng trong cuộc chiến giữa các băng đảng buôn ma túy ở khu ổ chuột "morro da Mineira" (矿山) ở bang Rio de Janeiro, Brazil.
Source (lo)	ອີງຕາມ # [illegible] # [illegible] , [illegible] # [illegible] # ມີຈຳນວນ 626 ກໍລະນີ[illegible] , # [illegible] # ໄດ້ຊີ້ແຈງ 193 ກໍລະນີ[illegible]
Reference	Theo VKSND Tối cao, danh sách thu giữ tại Đại học Đông Đô, có tổng số 626 trường hợp được cấp văn bằng 2 tiếng Anh, CQDT đã làm rõ 193 trường hợp được cấp bằng không qua đào tạo.
Meaning	According to the VKSND Office, the list of names seized at Dong Do University has a total of 626 cases that received English degrees. CQDT explained 193 cases of obtaining a degree without training.
Baseline	Theo Viện Kiểm sát Nhân dân Tối cao, danh sách chiếm đoạt tại Trường ĐH Đông Đô có 626 trường hợp được cấp bằng tiếng Anh, cướp ngân hàng đã làm rõ 193 trường hợp được cấp bằng không qua đào tạo.
Our Method	Theo VKSND tối cao, danh sách thu giữ tại Đại học Đông Đô có 626 trường hợp được cấp bằng tiếng Anh, CQDT đã làm rõ 193 trường hợp được cấp bằng mà không cần đào tạo.
Source (km)	គូស្នេហ៍ # [illegible] # គឺ # Oliver Noteware # អាយុ ៣៤ ឆ្នាំ និង # Kathryn Adkins # អាយុ ៣៣ ឆ្នាំ។
Reference	Một cặp đôi khác là Oliver Noteware, 34 tuổi và Kathryn Adkins, 33 tuổi.
Meaning	The other couple is Oliver Noteware, 34, and Kathryn Adkins, 33.
Baseline	Một đối thủ khác là Oliver Neteware, 34 tuổi và Kathryn Adkins, 33 tuổi.
Our Method	Một cặp đôi khác là Oliver Noteware, 34 tuổi và Kathryn Adkins, 33 tuổi.

Figure 2: Examples of outputs from our multilingual translation systems with the proposed methods compare to the baseline systems for Zh → Vi, Lo → Vi, and Km → Vi translation tasks.

of the 2014 Conference on Empirical Methods in Natural Language Processing (EMNLP)*, pages 1724–1734, Doha, Qatar. Association for Computational Linguistics.

Philip Gage. 1994. A new algorithm for data compression. In *C Users J., 12(2):23–38, February*.

Caglar Gulcehre, Sungjin Ahn, Ramesh Nallapati, Bowen Zhou, and Yoshua Bengio. 2016. Pointing the unknown words.

S'ebastien Jean, Kyunghyun Cho, Roland Memisevic, and Yoshua Bengio. 2015. On using very large target vocabulary for neural machine translation. In *Proceedings of the 53rd Annual Meeting of the Association for Computational Linguistics and the 7th International Joint Conference on Natural Language Processing*, pages 1–10. Association for Computational Linguistics.

Guillaume Klein, Yoon Kim, Yuntian Deng, Jean Senellart, and Alexander M. Rush. 2017. Opennmt: Open-source toolkit for neural machine translation.

Philipp Koehn and Rebecca Knowles. 2017. Six challenges for neural machine translation.

Taku Kudo and John Richardson. 2018. Sentencepiece: A simple and language independent subword tokenizer and detokenizer for neural text processing.

Minh-Thang Luong, Ilya Sutskever, Quoc V. Le, Oriol Vinyals, and Wojciech Zaremba. 2015a. Addressing the rare word problem in neural machine translation.

Thang Luong, Hieu Pham, and Christopher D. Manning. 2015b. Effective approaches to attention-based neural machine translation. In *Proceedings of the 2015 Conference on Empirical Methods in Natural Language Processing*, pages 1412–1421, Lisbon, Portugal. Association for Computational Linguistics.

Thi-Vinh Ngo, Thanh-Le Ha, Phuong-Thai Nguyen, and Le-Minh Nguyen. 2019. Overcoming the rare word problem for low-resource language pairs in neural machine translation. *Proceedings of the 6th Workshop on Asian Translation*.

Van-Vinh Nguyen, Ha Nguyen-Tien, Huong Le-Thanh, Phuong-Thai Nguyen, Van-Tan Bui, Nghia-Luan Pham, Tuan-Anh Phan, Minh-Cong Nguyen Hoang, Hong-Viet Tran, and Huu-Anh Tran. 2022. Kc4mt: A high-quality corpus for multilingual machine translation.

Ngoc-Quan Pham, Jan Niehues, and Alexander Waibel. 2018. Towards one-shot learning for rare-word translation with external experts. In *Proceedings of the 2nd Workshop on Neural Machine Translation and Generation*, pages 100–109, Melbourne, Australia. Association for Computational Linguistics.

Matt Post. 2018. A call for clarity in reporting BLEU scores. In *Proceedings of the Third Conference on*

Machine Translation: Research Papers, pages 186–191, Brussels, Belgium. Association for Computational Linguistics.

Nguyen Hoang Quan, Nguyen Thanh Dat, Minh Cong Nguyen Hoang, Nguyen Van Vinh, Ngo Thi Vinh, Nguyen Phuong Thai, and Tran Hong Viet. 2021. Vinmt: Neural machine translation tookit. *CoRR*, abs/2112.15272.

Rico Sennrich, Barry Haddow, and Alexandra Birch. 2016. Neural machine translation of rare words with subword units.

Kai Song, Yue Zhang, Heng Yu, Weihua Luo, Kun Wang, and Min Zhang. 2019. Code-switching for enhancing NMT with pre-specified translation. In *Proceedings of the 2019 Conference of the North American Chapter of the Association for Computational Linguistics: Human Language Technologies, Volume 1 (Long and Short Papers)*, pages 449–459, Minneapolis, Minnesota. Association for Computational Linguistics.

Ilya Sutskever, Oriol Vinyals, and Quoc V. Le. 2014. Sequence to sequence learning with neural networks. *CoRR*, abs/1409.3215.

Nguyen L. M. Nguyen P. T. Trieu, H. L. 2016. Dealing with out-of-vocabulary problem in sentence alignment using word similarity. In *Proceedings of the 30th Pacific Asia Conference on Language, Information and Computation: Oral Papers (pp. 259-266).*

Yulia Tsvetkov and Chris Dyer. 2015. Lexicon stratification for translating out-of-vocabulary words. In *Proceedings of the 53rd Annual Meeting of the Association for Computational Linguistics and the 7th International Joint Conference on Natural Language Processing (Volume 2: Short Papers)*, pages 125–131, Beijing, China. Association for Computational Linguistics.

Ashish Vaswani, Noam Shazeer, Niki Parmar, Jakob Uszkoreit, Llion Jones, Aidan N. Gomez, Lukasz Kaiser, and Illia Polosukhin. 2017. Attention is all you need.

Oriol Vinyals, Meire Fortunato, and Navdeep Jaitly. 2015. Pointer networks. In *Advances in Neural Information Processing Systems*, volume 28. Curran Associates, Inc.

Yonghui Wu, Mike Schuster, Zhifeng Chen, Quoc V. Le, Mohammad Norouzi, Wolfgang Macherey, Maxim Krikun, Yuan Cao, Qin Gao, Klaus Macherey, Jeff Klingner, Apurva Shah, Melvin Johnson, Xiaobing Liu, Łukasz Kaiser, Stephan Gouws, Yoshikiyo Kato, Taku Kudo, Hideto Kazawa, Keith Stevens, George Kurian, Nishant Patil, Wei Wang, Cliff Young, Jason Smith, Jason Riesa, Alex Rudnick, Oriol Vinyals, Greg Corrado, Macduff Hughes, and Jeffrey Dean. 2016. Google's neural machine translation system: Bridging the gap between human and machine translation.

Yu Yan, Fei Hu, Jiusheng Chen, Nikhil Bhendawade, Ting Ye, Yeyun Gong, Nan Duan, Desheng Cui, Bingyu Chi, and Ruofei Zhang. 2021. FastSeq: Make sequence generation faster. In *Proceedings of the 59th Annual Meeting of the Association for Computational Linguistics and the 11th International Joint Conference on Natural Language Processing: System Demonstrations*, pages 218–226, Online. Association for Computational Linguistics.

C3PO: A Lightweight Copying Mechanism for Translating Pseudocode to Code

Vishruth Veerendranath and **Vibha Masti** and **Prajwal Anagani** and **Mamatha HR**
Department of Computer Science and Engineering, PES University, Bangalore, India
{vishruth, vibha, prajwala}@pesu.pes.edu, mamathahr@pes.edu

Abstract

Writing computer programs is a skill that remains inaccessible to most due to the barrier of programming language (PL) syntax. While large language models (LLMs) have been proposed to translate natural language pseudocode to PL code, they are costly in terms of data and compute. We propose a lightweight alternative to LLMs that exploits the property of code wherein most tokens can be simply copied from the pseudocode. We divide the problem into three phases: Copy, Generate, and Combine. In the Copy Phase, a binary classifier is employed to determine and mask the pseudocode tokens that can be directly copied into the code. In the Generate Phase, a Sequence-to-Sequence model is used to generate the masked PL code equivalent. In the Combine Phase, the generated sequence is combined with the tokens that the Copy Phase had masked. We show that our C3PO models achieve similar performance to non-C3PO models while reducing the computational cost of training as well as the vocabulary sizes.

1 Introduction

In recent years, computer programs have found applications in almost every field, from scientific to artistic fields. The demand and cost for programmers have gone up because writing code is a specialised skill. Although people may be able to describe the functionality of the required code, the syntax of a programming language serves as a barrier to writing code (Denny et al., 2011). Recently there has been an increase in Low-Code applications that only require the functionality of code to be specified as pseudocode in Natural Language (NL), which is then translated to source code in a Programming Language (PL). Pseudocode enables people unfamiliar with a PL's syntax to write the functionality of the required code in NL, and allows programmers to write PL-independent code, which emphasizes functionality over syntax.

Translating pseudocode to code is cumbersome due to the complex structures of programs that result from their syntax, semantics and logic. Existing state-of-the-art Pseudocode-to-Code translators, like Codex (Chen et al., 2021), which is used to power GitHub Copilot (GitHub, 2021), and CodeT5 (Wang et al., 2021), are being powered by complex transformer LLMs like GPT-3 (Brown et al., 2020) and T5 (Raffel et al., 2020) respectively. They are pre-trained on very large code datasets like CodeSearchNet (Husain et al., 2019) and CodeXGLUE (Lu et al., 2021). While these transformer architectures are good at generalizing to many downstream PL-related tasks, they require high-performance computational resources, large amounts of data, and significant time to train.

Our contributions are as follows: we propose C3PO (**C**omputationally efficient **C**opying mechanism for **C**onversion from **P**seudocode to c**O**de), a lightweight alternative to the current translators. We exploit the property of code wherein a large number of tokens (like identifiers and variable names) are present in both pseudocode and its corresponding PL code. These tokens can therefore be simply copied into the resultant PL code translation. The remaining tokens can then be generated based on PL syntax. We divide the task of pseudocode to code translation into three phases: the Copy Phase, Generate Phase and the Combine Phase.

In the Copy Phase, we use a Decision Tree Classifier to decide whether each token in the pseudocode needs to be copied or translated. In the Generate Phase, a Sequence-to-Sequence (Seq2Seq) model takes in a pseudocode sequence, in which the tokens that can be copied are masked, and generates a masked PL sequence. In the Combine Phase, the generated masked PL code is unmasked with the appropriate true pseudocode tokens. C3PO has been trained on the SPoC dataset (Kulal et al., 2019), which consists of human-written pseudocode lines in English with their corresponding C++ code lines.

Proceedings of the AACL-IJCNLP 2022 Student Research Workshop, pages 47–53
November 20, 2022.

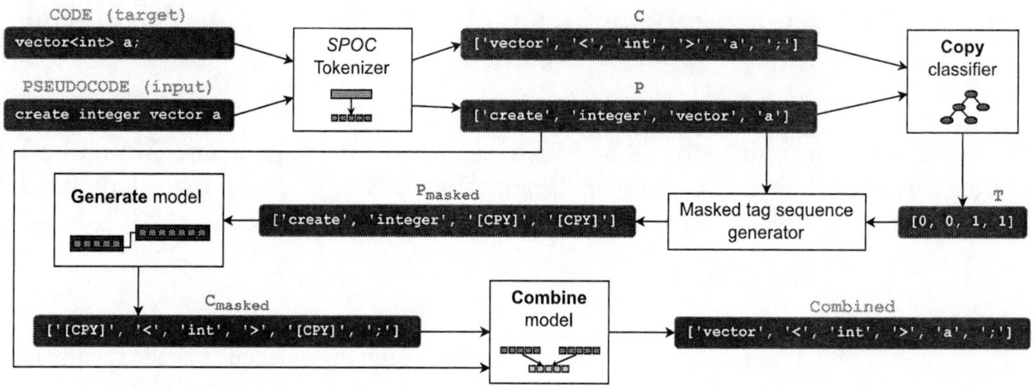

Figure 1: **An illustrative example of pseudocode being translated to C++ code during training**. The pseudocode and code are tokenized (P and C) and preprocessed together to get the truth-label for training the Copy Classifier. The binary tag sequence (T) is used to mask the tokens (P_{masked}) and generate the masked code sequence (C_{masked}). This is finally combined with the copied tokens from the input P, to result in the translation $Combined$.

2 Related Work

2.1 Pseudocode to Code translation

There have been many approaches taken to translate natural language input into a programmatic context. Some of the earlier works like Seq2SQL (Zhong et al., 2017) focused on the simpler task of generating SQL queries, where the query was segmented into its constituent parts (like `SELECT`, `WHERE`) with separate objectives for each part.

Kulal et al. (2019) approached the task as a search-based line-by-line translation task using LSTM Seq2Seq. With the introduction of large corpora for code (Lu et al., 2021), transformer architectures like Code-T5 (Wang et al., 2021), Codex (Chen et al., 2021) and CodeGen (Nijkamp et al., 2022) have been pre-trained on various objectives to generalize to various code related downstream tasks such as Code Generation and Summarization. While these facilitate fine-tuning, they require a lot of computational resources for training as well as inference.

There have also been approaches to translating code using code search techniques rather than synthesising code (Feng et al., 2020), (Neelakantan et al., 2022). These approaches generate embeddings using a variation of the BERT encoder and then use similarity metrics to search for the most semantically similar code from a corpus of code such as CodeSearchNet (Husain et al., 2019). For another such BERT model (Norouzi et al., 2021), the authors also proposed two new evaluation metrics namely *copy accuracy* and *generation accuracy*, and maximise each of these separately.

2.2 Copying Mechanism

CopyNet (Gu et al., 2016) describes a copy mechanism for natural language text, where the decoder in a Seq2Seq model is modified to probabilistically predict words from either the *copy-mode* or *generate-mode*. A related methodology called Pointer Networks (Vinyals et al., 2015) uses the attention mechanism to create pointers to the input words. The deobfuscation objective in DOBF (Roziere et al., 2021) provides an alternative to masked language modelling (MLM) for identifier names during pre-training.

3 Problem Definition

As we handle the task on a line-by-line basis, the task can be formulated as follows: The input sentence consists of a sequence of m pseudocode tokens $P = P_1, P_2 ... P_m$, and the objective is to translate this into its corresponding sequence of n code tokens $C = C_1, C_2, ... C_n$. We additionally split the pseudocode tokens P into 2 sets of tokens — P_{cpy} and P_{gen} — where $P = P_{cpy} \cup P_{gen}$.

The main idea for the copying mechanism stems from the fact that a good number of the code tokens (identifier names, constants and keywords) in the code translation are also present in the pseudocode input. Since such tokens can be simply copied into the translation, generating them from a Seq2Seq model is not necessary. Such tokens are referred to as the set of *copied tokens* denoted by P_{cpy}. In the SPoC dataset, we observed that the mean ratio of copied tokens to sequence length in pseudocode was around 60%.

Pseudocode	Ground-Truth Code	Generated Code
`if x is even`	`if(x % 2 == 0)`	`if(x % 2 == 0)`
`n,b = integers with b=0`	`int n, b=0;`	`int n, b=0;`
`while read n`	`while(cin >> n)`	`while n cin >> ;`
`print "NO"`	`cout << "NO" << endl;`	`cout << "NO" << "\n";`

Table 1: Examples of pseudocode, corresponding true code and generated code (correct in green, wrong in red)

The tokens that are not common to the pseudocode and code, referred to as the set of *generated tokens* and denoted by P_{gen}, describe code functionality in natural language and would have to be generated by a Seq2Seq model. For instance the token `read` will correspond to `cin` in C++.

4 Methodology

We devise a three-stage solution, which we call *C3PO*, to the above-defined problem. The three phases – *Copy*, *Generate* and *Combine* – are defined in an attempt to reduce the complexity of the model. The stages of *C3PO* are illustrated with an example in Fig. 1.

4.1 Copy Phase

We use a *Binary Classifier* to determine which tokens in the pseudocode are present in the code. For each token P_i in the pseudocode input, the binary classifier would discriminate which type of token it is – whether the token can be copied into the code output ($P_i \in P_{cpy}$), or whether it would have to be generated by the Seq2Seq model ($P_i \in P_{gen}$).

The binary classifier acts as a *tagger* on the pseudocode, generating a tag sequence. We define two different representations for the tag sequence. The first, named *binary tag sequence* (T) is a binary array – 1s referring to copied tokens, and 0s referring to generated tokens. An example of the binary tag sequence is shown in the output of the Copy classifier in Fig. 1.

The second, named *masked tag sequence* (P_{masked}) is a processed form of the input pseudocode sequence P. To facilitate this masking, we assign a special token which we call the *Copy Mask Token*, represented as `[CPY]`. We mask all tokens that belong to set P_{cpy} by replacing such tokens with the `[CPY]` tag, before passing the sequence as input to the Seq2Seq model.

4.2 Generate Phase

The masked tag sequence (P_{masked}) is provided as input to a Seq2Seq model, which would generate the corresponding masked code output (C_{masked}). C_{masked} is also masked with `[CPY]` tags when the output corresponds to a token that was originally masked in the pseudocode. The Seq2Seq model would only influence the position of copied tokens in the output code, and not the token itself.

4.3 Combine Phase

The generated masked code output (C_{masked}) needs to be transformed into actual code (C). To simplify our model, we assume that the order in which the masked tokens appear in the true code is the same as the order in which they appear in the final code, although this might not be the case at all times. This is a fair assumption to make in most cases as shown in Section 7.1. We replace only the `[CPY]` tags in C_{masked} directly with the copied tokens in set P_{cpy} in their order of occurrence in P. This simple combination of the two previous two phases leads to the resultant translation.

5 Models and Experiments

5.1 Dataset

The SPoC dataset (Kulal et al., 2019) is used for our experiments. It contains 18,356 C++ programs and their human-authored pseudo-code in English language. The dataset covers a wide variety of programs with multiple programs for a single problem statement sourced from CodeForces contests.

5.2 Copy Model

For the copy phase, a decision tree is used to predict whether or not each token gets directly copied into the code. The decision tree was created using sklearn's (Buitinck et al., 2013) `DecisionTreeClassifier` API and was trained on *pseudocode (input)* sequence from the entire SPoC training dataset, as shown in Fig. 1. For every token in every sentence, the following explicit features were passed as input to the tree:

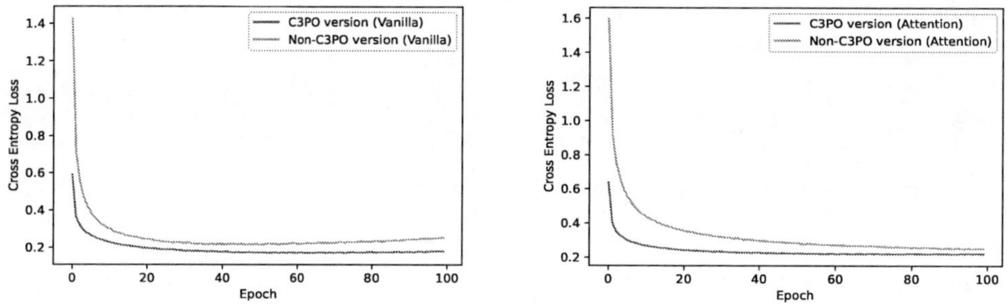

Figure 2: Average loss per epoch for the models and their 2 versions. (Left) Plot for Vanilla Seq2Seq versions, (Right) Plot for Attention Seq2Seq versions

- Token and its length
- If the token is numeric or alphabetical
- If the token is alphanumeric
- If the token is a punctuation mark
- The previous 2 tokens in that sentence
- The next 2 tokens in that sentence

The target or ground-truth prediction (0 or 1) for each token was generated by comparing the tokens of pseudocode sequence P and code sequence C, as a preprocessing step. If the current pseudocode token P_i also appeared in C, the target for binary tag sequence T_i would be 1. If it does not appear in C, the target would be 0. During inference, only the pseudocode sequence P is used and the features are passed as input to the decision tree.

5.3 Generate Model

To test the validity of the C3PO copy mechanism, it has been tested in conjunction with two different generate phase models – Vanilla Seq2Seq (Sutskever et al., 2014) and Attention Seq2Seq (Bahdanau et al., 2015). The models were built using PyTorch (Paszke et al., 2019). We will not review these popular architectures in detail.

For each generate model, two different versions have been trained. The first version, referred to as *non-C3PO version*, is trained on the non-masked input P with the target C. The second version, referred to as *C3PO version*, is trained with the masked tag sequence P_{masked} provided as input with target C_{masked}. The non-C3PO version provides a baseline to justify the C3PO version.

For the C3PO version, the input pseudocode vocabulary (denoted by $PVoc_{masked}$) is built after masking the copied tags, hence the copied tokens will not be included in the input vocabulary. This reduces the input vocabulary size to 30% of the original vocabulary size without masking (denoted by $PVoc$). Similarly, the output code vocabulary built after masking (denoted by $CVoc_{masked}$), also reduces the size to 20% of the original output vocabulary size without masking (denoted by $CVoc$) The vocabulary sizes are presented in Table 3

We additionally also experimented with *C3PO* and *non-C3PO* versions of a Vanilla Transformer model (Vaswani et al., 2017) trained from scratch.

5.4 Combine Model

To convert the C3PO model's output into the required code output, the masked tokens in the C_{masked} need to be unmasked. This is achieved by performing a one-to-one replacement of the masked tokens in their order of occurrence in P. If the model generates a `[CPY]` token, it is replaced with P_j which corresponds to one of the tokens in P that were masked ($P_j \in P_{cpy}$). If the model generated any other token, it is left as is.

$$Combined_i = \begin{cases} P_j & C_{masked_i} = \text{[CPY]} \\ C_{masked_i} & C_{masked_i} \text{ != [CPY]} \end{cases}$$

5.5 Experimental Setting

All our experiments were conducted using an NVIDIA GTX 1650 GPU with 4 GB of VRAM. The hyperparameters chosen for each Seq2Seq model for optimal performance on the GPU are as follows. For the Vanilla Seq2Seq models, an embedding size of 300, an LSTM hidden state size of 1024 and a batch size of 64 were chosen. For the Attention Seq2Seq models, an embedding size of 100, an LSTM hidden state size of 256 and a batch size of 32 were chosen. The hyperparameters were kept consistent across both versions (non-C3PO and C3PO) of each model. All models were trained

	Trainable Parameters		Training Time		BLEU	
Model (Version)	non-C3PO	C3PO	non-C3PO	C3PO	non-C3PO	C3PO
Vanilla Seq2Seq	20.3 M	**12.8 M**	21 h	**13 h**	0.44	**0.51**
Attention Seq2Seq	4.5 M	**2.5 M**	12 h	**7 h**	**0.75**	0.69
Vanilla Transformer	18.7 M	**11.7 M**	13 h	**10 h**	0.01	**0.19**

Table 2: Comparing non-C3PO and C3PO versions of the two models, in terms of the number of trainable parameters (in millions), training times (in hours) and BLEU score

for 100 epochs, using the Adam optimizer with a learning rate of 0.001, Cross-Entropy loss and teacher-forcing rate of 0.5.

For the Vanilla Transformer model, we used a batch size of 32, an embedding size of 512, 8 attention heads and 3 encoder and decoder layers each.

6 Results

BLEU-4 score (Papineni et al., 2002) is chosen as the evaluation metric and reported in Table 2, along with the model's training time and parameters. Some example translations generated by the C3PO model are demonstrated in Table 1.

The BLEU score for the non-C3PO version was 0.44 and for the C3PO was 0.51. Therefore we can say that using the C3PO mechanism, the model performed relatively better than the non-C3PO version. As for the Seq2Seq with Attention model, the BLEU score for the non-C3PO version is 0.75 and for the C3PO version is 0.69. In this case, the non-C3PO version performs better, but it comes at the cost of high training time and model size.

Further, we point out the significant difference in the number of parameters, and hence the training time, for both the versions in Table 2. The C3PO version has significantly fewer parameters owing to the decrease in vocabulary size. For the Vanilla Seq2Seq, this is a win on two counts; it achieved a higher BLEU score and it was more efficient.

The BLEU scores of the non-C3PO and C3PO Transformers are 0.01 and 0.19, respectively. Since transformers are data and compute-heavy architectures and we trained them on limited resources, they perform much worse than the RNN models.

In Fig 2, we can notice that in both Vanilla and Attention models, the C3PO version converges much faster than the non-C3PO version. This would lead us to believe that the C3PO versions would perform similarly, even if they were trained for lesser epochs than the non-C3PO version. It should also be noted that while the C3PO versions perform similarly, if not better, than the non-C3PO versions, they do so while using only 20% of the original vocabulary for both inputs and outputs, as shown in Table 3. This shows that the C3PO versions are both computationally efficient as well as data-efficient.

Version	Pseudocode	Code
non-C3PO version	6495	5647
C3PO version (ours)	**1984**	**1080**

Table 3: Input (pseudocode) and Output (code) vocabulary sizes in the two versions

7 Auxiliary Experiments

7.1 Numbered CPY tags

A possible problem with the C3PO is that the usage of the naive algorithm for combining in Section 5.4, assumes the order of copied tokens is the same in both pseudocode and code. To handle this, an attempt was made to use the Seq2Seq model itself to generate the CPY tags and put them in the right order. Instead of using a single `[CPY]` token, each unique variable was given a token `[CPY_n]`, where n is a unique number. For the example in Fig 1, the C_{masked} sequence would instead be `create integer [CPY1] [CPY2]`.

With numbered tags, the Vanilla Seq2Seq and Attention Seq2Seq obtained BLEU scores of **0.54** and **0.66** respectively. As this is only a marginal difference from the initial results, numbering the tags doesn't offer a significant benefit. However, it is interesting to note that the BLEU score increases for Vanilla Seq2Seq but reduces for Attention Seq2Seq when tags are numbered.

7.2 Pretrained CodeT5 model

A pretrained CodeT5 model was used on the text data (without CPY tags). It was fine-tuned on our data from 3 hours (4 epochs) using beam search. The results were encouraging, with a BLEU score of 0.85. The disadvantage of this approach lies only in its space and time complexity, which is suited for large datasets and high-performance compute. For computational efficient training on commodity hardware and a small amount of data, the C3PO versions of Attention and Vanilla Seq2Seq would be the best choice.

8 Conclusion and Future Work

We have introduced C3PO, a copying mechanism that emphasises computational and data efficiency. The methodology exploited the property of code where most tokens remain consistent across input and output. By masking such tokens, the vocabulary sizes are reduced significantly, which also reduced the training times. In future works, the method for filling masked tokens in output can be improved to fill the tokens while handling cases where the assumption that the order of masked tokens would remain consistent fails.

References

Dzmitry Bahdanau, Kyung Hyun Cho, and Yoshua Bengio. 2015. Neural machine translation by jointly learning to align and translate. In *3rd International Conference on Learning Representations, ICLR 2015*.

Tom Brown, Benjamin Mann, Nick Ryder, Melanie Subbiah, Jared D Kaplan, Prafulla Dhariwal, Arvind Neelakantan, Pranav Shyam, Girish Sastry, Amanda Askell, et al. 2020. Language models are few-shot learners. *Advances in neural information processing systems*, 33:1877–1901.

Lars Buitinck, Gilles Louppe, Mathieu Blondel, Fabian Pedregosa, Andreas Mueller, Olivier Grisel, Vlad Niculae, Peter Prettenhofer, Alexandre Gramfort, Jaques Grobler, Robert Layton, Jake VanderPlas, Arnaud Joly, Brian Holt, and Gaël Varoquaux. 2013. API design for machine learning software: experiences from the scikit-learn project. In *ECML PKDD Workshop: Languages for Data Mining and Machine Learning*, pages 108–122.

Mark Chen, Jerry Tworek, Heewoo Jun, Qiming Yuan, Henrique Ponde de Oliveira Pinto, Jared Kaplan, Harri Edwards, Yuri Burda, Nicholas Joseph, Greg Brockman, et al. 2021. Evaluating large language models trained on code. *arXiv preprint arXiv:2107.03374*.

Paul Denny, Andrew Luxton-Reilly, Ewan Tempero, and Jacob Hendrickx. 2011. Understanding the syntax barrier for novices. In *Proceedings of the 16th annual joint conference on Innovation and technology in computer science education*, pages 208–212.

Zhangyin Feng, Daya Guo, Duyu Tang, Nan Duan, Xiaocheng Feng, Ming Gong, Linjun Shou, Bing Qin, Ting Liu, Daxin Jiang, et al. 2020. Codebert: A pre-trained model for programming and natural languages. *arXiv preprint arXiv:2002.08155*.

GitHub. 2021. Github copilot. `https://github.com/features/copilot`. Accessed: 2022-09-06.

Jiatao Gu, Zhengdong Lu, Hang Li, and Victor O.K. Li. 2016. Incorporating copying mechanism in sequence-to-sequence learning. In *Proceedings of the 54th Annual Meeting of the Association for Computational Linguistics (Volume 1: Long Papers)*, pages 1631–1640, Berlin, Germany. Association for Computational Linguistics.

Hamel Husain, Ho-Hsiang Wu, Tiferet Gazit, Miltiadis Allamanis, and Marc Brockschmidt. 2019. Codesearchnet challenge: Evaluating the state of semantic code search. *arXiv preprint arXiv:1909.09436*.

Sumith Kulal, Panupong Pasupat, Kartik Chandra, Mina Lee, Oded Padon, Alex Aiken, and Percy S Liang. 2019. Spoc: Search-based pseudocode to code. *Advances in Neural Information Processing Systems*, 32.

Shuai Lu, Daya Guo, Shuo Ren, Junjie Huang, Alexey Svyatkovskiy, Ambrosio Blanco, Colin Clement, Dawn Drain, Daxin Jiang, Duyu Tang, et al. 2021. Codexglue: A machine learning benchmark dataset for code understanding and generation. *arXiv preprint arXiv:2102.04664*.

Arvind Neelakantan, Tao Xu, Raul Puri, Alec Radford, Jesse Michael Han, Jerry Tworek, Qiming Yuan, Nikolas Tezak, Jong Wook Kim, Chris Hallacy, et al. 2022. Text and code embeddings by contrastive pre-training. *arXiv preprint arXiv:2201.10005*.

Erik Nijkamp, Bo Pang, Hiroaki Hayashi, Lifu Tu, Huan Wang, Yingbo Zhou, Silvio Savarese, and Caiming Xiong. 2022. A conversational paradigm for program synthesis. *arXiv preprint arXiv:2203.13474*.

Sajad Norouzi, Keyi Tang, and Yanshuai Cao. 2021. Code generation from natural language with less prior knowledge and more monolingual data. In *Proceedings of the 59th Annual Meeting of the Association for Computational Linguistics and the 11th International Joint Conference on Natural Language Processing (Volume 2: Short Papers)*, pages 776–785, Online. Association for Computational Linguistics.

Kishore Papineni, Salim Roukos, Todd Ward, and Wei-Jing Zhu. 2002. Bleu: a method for automatic evaluation of machine translation. In *Proceedings of the 40th Annual Meeting of the Association for Computational Linguistics*, pages 311–318, Philadelphia, Pennsylvania, USA. Association for Computational Linguistics.

Adam Paszke, Sam Gross, Francisco Massa, Adam Lerer, James Bradbury, Gregory Chanan, Trevor Killeen, Zeming Lin, Natalia Gimelshein, Luca Antiga, Alban Desmaison, Andreas Kopf, Edward Yang, Zachary DeVito, Martin Raison, Alykhan Tejani, Sasank Chilamkurthy, Benoit Steiner, Lu Fang, Junjie Bai, and Soumith Chintala. 2019. Pytorch: An imperative style, high-performance deep learning library. In H. Wallach, H. Larochelle, A. Beygelzimer, F. d'Alché-Buc, E. Fox, and R. Garnett, editors, *Advances in Neural Information Processing Systems 32*, pages 8024–8035. Curran Associates, Inc.

Colin Raffel, Noam Shazeer, Adam Roberts, Katherine Lee, Sharan Narang, Michael Matena, Yanqi Zhou, Wei Li, Peter J Liu, et al. 2020. Exploring the limits of transfer learning with a unified text-to-text transformer. *J. Mach. Learn. Res.*, 21(140):1–67.

Baptiste Roziere, Marie-Anne Lachaux, Marc Szafraniec, and Guillaume Lample. 2021. Dobf: A deobfuscation pre-training objective for programming languages. *arXiv preprint arXiv:2102.07492*.

Ilya Sutskever, Oriol Vinyals, and Quoc V Le. 2014. Sequence to sequence learning with neural networks. *Advances in neural information processing systems*, 27.

Ashish Vaswani, Noam Shazeer, Niki Parmar, Jakob Uszkoreit, Llion Jones, Aidan N Gomez, Łukasz Kaiser, and Illia Polosukhin. 2017. Attention is all you need. *Advances in neural information processing systems*, 30.

Oriol Vinyals, Meire Fortunato, and Navdeep Jaitly. 2015. Pointer networks. *Advances in neural information processing systems*, 28.

Yue Wang, Weishi Wang, Shafiq Joty, and Steven CH Hoi. 2021. Codet5: Identifier-aware unified pre-trained encoder-decoder models for code understanding and generation. *arXiv preprint arXiv:2109.00859*.

Victor Zhong, Caiming Xiong, and Richard Socher. 2017. Seq2sql: Generating structured queries from natural language using reinforcement learning. *arXiv preprint arXiv:1709.00103*.

Outlier-Aware Training for Improving Group Accuracy Disparities

Li-Kuang Chen[1*] **Canasai Kruengkrai**[2] **Junichi Yamagishi**[2]
[1]National Tsing Hua University, Taiwan
lkchen@nlplab.cc
[2]National Institute of Informatics, Japan
{canasai,jyamagishi}@nii.ac.jp

Abstract

Methods addressing spurious correlations such as Just Train Twice (JTT, Liu et al. 2021) involve reweighting a subset of the training set to maximize the worst-group accuracy. However, the reweighted set of examples may potentially contain unlearnable examples that hamper the model's learning. We propose mitigating this by detecting outliers to the training set and removing them before reweighting. Our experiments show that our method achieves competitive or better accuracy compared with JTT and can detect and remove annotation errors in the subset being reweighted in JTT.[1]

1 Introduction

Machine learning models trained with empirical risk minimization (ERM, Vapnik 1992) can achieve a high average accuracy by minimizing the overall loss during training. Despite this, ERM models are also known to perform poorly on certain minority groups of examples. When specific attributes in a dataset frequently co-occur with a class label, ERM models often learn to correlate the co-occurring attributes and the label, using the attributes as "shortcuts" for classifying examples. These "shortcuts" are also called *spurious correlations*, because model performance can significantly decrease when the model encounters examples that belong to a minority group where the correlations between the attributes and class label do not hold.

More specifically, each class in a dataset can be divided by whether their examples contain such spurious attributes. Each set of examples with a class-attribute combination is called a "group". The worst group is characterized by having the poorest ERM model performance among other groups. As an example, Figure 1 shows accuracy disparities among groups in the FEVER dataset. The ERM-trained model can achieve close to perfect accuracy on the group with a spurious correlation (the REFUTES class with negation), but only half the accuracy on the worst group (the SUPPORTS class with negation).

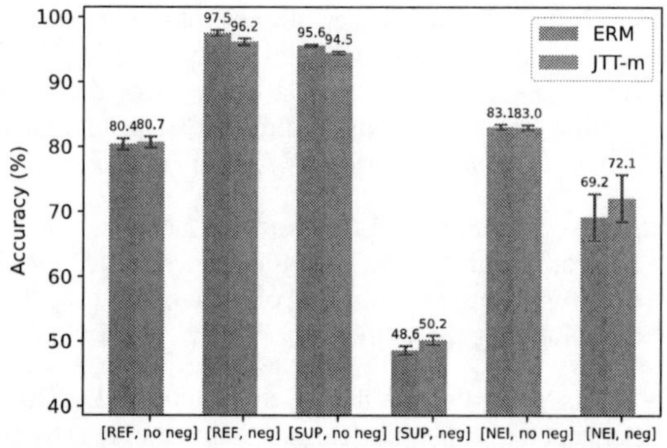

Figure 1: Results for the FEVER test set (Thorne et al., 2018; Schuster et al., 2021). The data are divided into six groups in accordance with *class-attribute* combinations, where class = {REFUTES (REF), SUPPORTS (SUP), NOT ENOUGH INFO (NEI)} and attribute = {no neg, neg}, indicating the presence of a negation word in the claim. Both methods perform well on groups with strong spurious correlations (e.g., [REF, neg]). Our proposed method (JTT-m) helps improve accuracies for groups where such spurious correlations do not appear (e.g., [SUP, neg] and [NEI, neg]).

Improving the worst-group performance of ERM models while maintaining the overall accuracy is an active topic of research that has applications in fair machine learning classifiers or robustness against adversarial examples (Słowik and Bottou, 2022). Methods aiming to maximize worst-group accuracy can be roughly categorized into two categories: those that utilize group information and those that do not. Group Distributionally Robust Optimization (Group DRO, Sagawa et al. 2020) uses attribute (and thus group) information during training to dynamically minimize the loss of each group. While Group DRO achieves a high worst-group and overall accuracy, it requires annotation

*This work was conducted during the author's internship under National Institute of Informatics, Japan.

[1]Our code is available at https://github.com/nii-yamagishilab/jtt-m.

Proceedings of the AACL-IJCNLP 2022 Student Research Workshop, pages 54–60
November 20, 2022.

on group information during training, which can be expensive to obtain and unavailable for less popular datasets. On the other hand, methods such as DRO with Conditional Value-at-Risk (CVaR DRO, Duchi et al. 2019; Levy et al. 2020), Learning from Failure (LfF, Nam et al. 2020), Predict then Interpolate (PI, Bao et al. 2021), Spectral Decoupling (SD, Pezeshki et al. 2021), Just Train Twice (JTT, Liu et al. 2021), and RWY and SUBY from (Idrissi et al., 2022) all aim to minimize worst-group loss without group information.

CVaR DRO minimizes worst-case loss over all subpopulations of a specific size and requires computing the worst-case loss at each step. LfF trains an intentionally biased model and upweights the minority examples. PI interpolates distributions of correct and incorrect predictions and can minimize worst-case loss over all interpolations. SD replaces the L_2 weight decay in the cross entropy loss function with logits. RWY reweights sampling probabilities so that mini-batches are class-balanced. SUBY subsamples large classes so that every class is the same size as the smallest class. JTT simply obtains misclassified examples (the *error set*) from the training set once and upweights the fixed set of erroneous examples. We focus on JTT due to its simplicity and relative effectiveness and because it does not require group information for improving worst-group accuracy. While Idrissi et al. (2022)'s SUBY and RWY also follow JTT in improving worst-group accuracies, their methods target only datasets with imbalanced classes, and are not applicable to class-balanced datasets such as MultiNLI (Williams et al., 2018).

We propose further enhancing JTT by removing outliers from the error set before upweighting it. The outliers might be examples that are difficult to learn, such as annotation errors. Keeping them from being upweighted allows the model to train on a cleaner error set and thus better show the intended effect of the original JTT. We focus on worst-group performance caused by the spurious correlations of negation words and evaluate on datasets susceptible to spurious correlations of this type. Our experiments on the FEVER and MultiNLI datasets show that our method can outperform JTT in terms of either the average or the worst-group accuracy while maintaining the same level of performance for the other groups.

Our contributions are as follows. We devise a method for improving worst-group accuracy without group information during training based on JTT (Section 3). We show that by removing outliers from the error set being upweighted, we can achieve similar or better overall and worst-group performance (Section 4.2). Our examination of the outliers being removed also suggests that the improvement may come from removing annotation errors in the upweighted error set (Section 4.3).

2 Background

Spurious correlations and minority groups

We investigate the spurious correlations occurring in two natural-language datasets: FEVER (Thorne et al., 2018) and MultiNLI (Williams et al., 2018). The task for FEVER involves retrieving documents related to a given *claim*, finding sentences to form *evidence* against the claim, and then classifying the claim on the basis of the evidence into three classes: SUPPORTS (SUP), REFUTES (REF), or NOT ENOUGH INFORMATION (NEI). We focus on improving the worst-group classification performance for the final part of the task. The task for MultiNLI is to classify whether the *hypothesis* is entailed by, neutral with, or contradicted by the *premise*. We use Schuster et al. (2021)'s preprocessing of both datasets, containing 178,059/11,620/11,710 training/dev/test examples for FEVER and 392,702/9,832 training/test examples for MultiNLI.

Attributes known to cause spurious correlations for these datasets are negation words (Gururangan et al., 2018) and verbs that suggest negating actions (Schuster et al., 2019). We merge these two sources of negation words into a single set: {*no, never, nothing, nobody, not, yet, refuse, refuses, refused, fail, fails, failed, only, incapable, unable, neither, none*}. Each class can be split into two groups based on whether each claim/hypothesis contains a spurious attribute (i.e., the negation words listed above). Models tend to perform well on groups where the attributes are highly correlated with the label. Groups where the correlation between the label and the attribute does not hold are called *minority groups* or *worst groups*, since models often fail to classify their examples correctly. For example, the claim "*Luis Fonsi does **not** go by his given name on stage.*", labeled SUPPORTS, belongs to the worst group [SUP, neg].

Table 1(a) shows that most claims containing negation are from the class REFUTES. The relatively small amount of examples from the groups

	No negation	Negation	
REF	27,575 (17.1%)	14,275 (86.3%)	41,850 (23.5%)
SUP	99,303 (61.5%)	1,267 (7.7%)	100,570 (56.5%)
NEI	34,633 (21.4%)	1,006 (6.0%)	35,639 (20.0%)

(a) FEVER

	No negation	Negation	
Contr	88,180 (27.3%)	42,723 (61.2%)	130,903 (33.3%)
Ent	118,554 (36.7%)	12,345 (17.7%)	130,899 (33.3%)
Neut	116,185 (36.0%)	14,715 (21.1%)	130,900 (33.3%)

(b) MultiNLI

Table 1: Class and group distributions for (a) FEVER and (b) MultiNLI training sets. Both datasets show a high spurious correlation between the REF (Contr) class and the attribute neg. Minority groups where the spurious correlation does not hold are [SUP (Ent), neg] and [NEI (Neut), neg].

(SUP, negation) and (NEI, negation) form the minority groups, where the ERM model performance fails. A similar trend can be seen in Table 1(b).

Empirical Risk Minimization (ERM)

Let $x \in \mathcal{X}$ be a training example and $y \in \mathcal{Y}$ be its label. Given a dataset $D = \{(x_i, y_i)\}_{i=1}^{N}$, ERM aims to minimize the average loss ("empirical risk"), defined as:

$$J_{\text{ERM}}(\theta) = \frac{1}{N} \sum_{(x,y) \in D} \ell(g_\theta(x), y), \quad (1)$$

where N is the number of training examples, $g_\theta(\cdot)$ is the model, and θ represents model parameters. We use cross-entropy loss as the loss function:

$$\ell(g_\theta(x), y) = -\sum_{y \in \mathcal{Y}} \mathbb{1}\{y = \hat{y}\} \log(p_\theta(\hat{y}|x)), \quad (2)$$

where $\mathbb{1}\{\cdot\}$ is the indicator function, x represents the input sentence pair (s_1, s_2), and $y \in \mathcal{Y} = \{$SUP, REF, NEI$\}$ ($\{$Ent, Contr, Neut$\}$ for MultiNLI). We first encode the input sentence pairs with BERT (Devlin et al., 2019) and feed the resulting embedding **e** into a multi-layer perceptron (MLP) followed by a softmax function for classification:

$$\begin{aligned} p_\theta(\hat{y}|x) &= \text{softmax}(\text{MLP}(\mathbf{e})), \\ \mathbf{e} &= \text{BERT}(s_1, s_2). \end{aligned} \quad (3)$$

Just Train Twice (JTT)

Liu et al. (2021) propose improving worst-group performance by simply training with an upweighted error set. During the first round of training, the set of incorrectly classified training examples is identified via an ERM model. The training error set E is then upweighted with a real and positive upweight factor $\lambda_{\text{up}} \in \mathbb{R}^+$, and a final model is trained on the reweighted objective:

$$\begin{aligned} &J_{\text{up}}(\theta, E) \\ &= \frac{1}{N_{\text{up}}} \Bigg(\lambda_{\text{up}} \sum_{\substack{(x,y) \\ \in E}} \ell(g_\theta(x), y) + \sum_{\substack{(x,y) \\ \notin E}} \ell(g_\theta(x), y) \Bigg), \end{aligned} \quad (4)$$

where λ_{up} is a hyperparameter, and N_{up} is the size of the training set after upweighting.

3 Proposed method

Even though the upweighted ERM error set can improve worst-group accuracy, it is possible that the error set contains *unlearnable* or *out-of-distribution* (OOD) examples, e.g., annotation errors. When upweighting the entire error set, these examples will get amplified along with the rest of the error set, lessening the overall benefits of upweighting and retraining.

We propose modifying the JTT algorithm by removing outliers in the ERM error set before training the second time. We adopt a similar approach from Lee et al. (2018) for detecting outliers. Let **x** be the output of the penultimate layer (i.e., the last layer before the logits) and belong to class y. First, we calculate the Mahalanobis distance for each **x** from the mean of each class y:

$$M(\mathbf{x}) = \sqrt{(\mathbf{x} - \boldsymbol{\mu}_y)^\top \boldsymbol{\Sigma}_y^{-1} (\mathbf{x} - \boldsymbol{\mu}_y)}, \quad (5)$$

where $\boldsymbol{\mu}_y$ and $\boldsymbol{\Sigma}_y$ are the class mean and covariance.[2] The greater the distance of **x** is from $\boldsymbol{\mu}_y$, the likelier it is to be an OOD example.

Then, we filter OOD examples by comparing the calculated Mahalanobis distance against a chi-squared distribution with a critical value α of 0.001 and a degree of freedom *df*:[3]

$$x_i \in \begin{cases} S_{\text{in}} & \text{if } p_i < \alpha, \\ S_{\text{out}} & \text{if } p_i \geq \alpha, \end{cases} \quad (6)$$

[2]We compute $\boldsymbol{\Sigma}_y$ using the standard covariance maximum likelihood estimate (MLE) implemented in scikit-learn.

[3]We select a value of *df* that yields the best worst-group accuracy on the dev set.

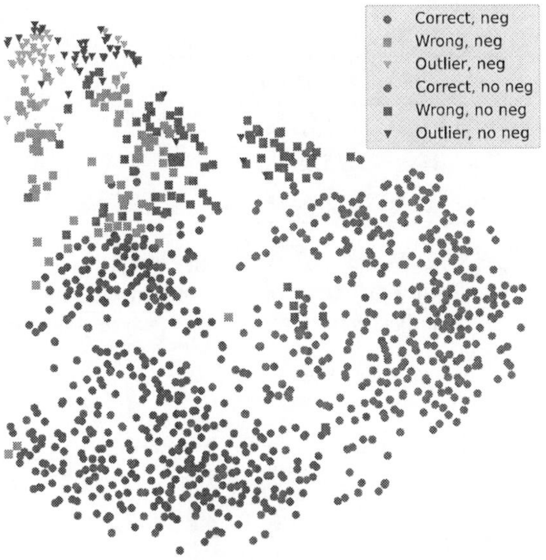

Figure 2: T-SNE visualization of samples from the class Entailment of the MultiNLI training set. Correct predictions of groups with and without negation (blue and red) are quite well separated. Wrong predictions lie at the top left, and outliers lie further away. Outliers are detected by their Mahalanobis scores.

where S_{in} and S_{out} are the sets of in-distribution and OOD training examples, and p_i is the p-value of the i-th example. We show the T-SNE visualization in Figure 2.

Once the OOD examples are identified, we remove the subset of misclassified OOD examples from the error set E, forming a new error set E_{in}:

$$E_{\text{in}} = \{(x_i, y_i) \text{ s.t. } \hat{y}_i \neq y_i \wedge x_i \notin S_{\text{out}})\}, \quad (7)$$

which is then upweighted as per JTT:

$$J_{\text{up-in}}(\theta, E_{\text{in}}) = \frac{1}{N_{\text{up}}}\left(\lambda_{\text{up}} \sum_{\substack{(x,y) \\ \in E_{\text{in}}}} \ell(g_\theta(x), y) + \sum_{\substack{(x,y) \\ \notin E_{\text{in}}}} \ell(g_\theta(x), y)\right), \quad (8)$$

4 Experiments

4.1 Training details

We follow Sagawa et al. (2020); Liu et al. (2021); Idrissi et al. (2022) in using different optimization settings for different training methods to maximize the validation accuracy. For ERM, we used the AdamW optimizer (Loshchilov and Hutter, 2019), linear learning rate decay, and a gradient clipping of 1. For the first training of JTT, we used the SGD optimizer without gradient clipping. The second training used the same settings as those of ERM.

We used HuggingFace's implementation (Wolf et al., 2020) of BERT-base with default parameter settings. For all methods, we used a batch size of 32, initial learning rate of 2e-5, and we trained them for 2 epochs. We tried $df \in \{4, 5, 6\}$ and $\lambda_{\text{up}} \in \{1, 2, 3, 4\}$ and selected the values yielding the best worst-group accuracy on the dev set. Since no dev set is provided for MultiNLI, we tuned the hyperparameters on FEVER and applied them to MultiNLI.

4.2 Results

We compared our proposed method (referred to as **JTT-m**, Eq. (8)) against two baselines: **ERM** (Eq. (1)) and **JTT** (Eq. (4)). Table 2 shows the results for the average and worst-group performances of various approaches.

As expected, **ERM** had the best average accuracy but performed poorly on the worst group across the two datasets. **JTT** and **JTT-m** had improved performance on the worst group with slightly decreased average accuracies on both datasets compared with **ERM**. On FEVER, **JTT-m** outperformed **JTT** in average accuracy while maintaining the same worst-group [SUP, neg] accuracy. On MultiNLI, **JTT-m** performed significantly better on the worst group [Neut, neg] and maintained the same average accuracy as **JTT**.

We also observed larger variations in the results for FEVER. This is likely due to the smaller group sizes in FEVER. The worst group of MultiNLI [Neut, neg] accounted for around 3.5% of the test set, while FEVER's [SUP, neg] was only 0.5% of the test set and was about 5 times lower than the smallest group in MultiNLI in absolute numbers. For the same reason, another minority group of FEVER, [NEI, neg], also displayed a higher variation.

In addition, **JTT-m** slightly reduced training time due to the smaller training set. Our Mahalanobis distance method detected 2,077 and 1,821 examples as outliers in the FEVER and MultiNLI error sets. By eliminating these examples, we could reduce the training time while achieving results similar to or better than **JTT**.

4.3 Discussion

The improvements for the MultiNLI worst group agree with our hypothesis: removing outliers from

Dataset	FEVER		MultiNLI	
	Avg. (%)	Worst (%)	Avg. (%)	Worst (%)
ERM	$87.8_{\pm 0.2}$	$48.6_{\pm 0.7}$	$84.9_{\pm 0.1}$	$72.0_{\pm 1.0}$
JTT	$86.8_{\pm 0.2}$	$50.5_{\pm 3.5}$	$83.0_{\pm 0.2}$	$75.5_{\pm 1.5}$
JTT-m	$87.4_{\pm 0.1^*}$	$50.2_{\pm 2.8}$	$83.0_{\pm 0.3}$	$77.3_{\pm 0.4^*}$

Table 2: Average and worst-group test accuracies for all methods. The "Worst" column indicates the worst-group accuracies on [SUP, neg] and [Neutr, neg] for FEVER and MultiNLI, respectively. We report mean and standard deviation computed across five runs using different random seeds. "$*$" indicates the statistical significance compared with JTT (paired t-test, $p < 0.05$).

Group	JTT	JTT-m
[REF, no neg]	$79.9_{\pm 0.5}$	$80.7_{\pm 0.3}$
[REF, neg]	$93.8_{\pm 0.6}$	$96.2_{\pm 0.6}^*$
[SUP, no neg]	$94.7_{\pm 0.2}$	$94.5_{\pm 0.1}$
[SUP, neg]	$50.5_{\pm 3.5}$	$50.2_{\pm 2.8}$
[NEI, no neg]	$82.5_{\pm 0.5}$	$83.0_{\pm 0.3}$
[NEI, neg]	$71.5_{\pm 0.9}$	$72.1_{\pm 3.3}$

(a) FEVER

Group	JTT	JTT-m
[Contr, no neg]	$82.8_{\pm 0.7}$	$82.8_{\pm 1.0}$
[Contr, neg]	$91.9_{\pm 0.1}$	$91.8_{\pm 0.6}$
[Ent, no neg]	$82.6_{\pm 0.2}$	$82.2_{\pm 1.1}$
[Ent, neg]	$79.5_{\pm 0.5}$	$78.9_{\pm 1.9}$
[Neut, no neg]	$81.2_{\pm 0.6}$	$81.7_{\pm 0.8}$
[Neut, neg]	$75.5_{\pm 1.5}$	$77.3_{\pm 0.4}^*$

(b) MultiNLI

Table 3: Accuracies and standard deviations for each group on (a) FEVER and (b) MultiNLI. "$*$" indicates statistical significance (paired t-test, $p < 0.05$).

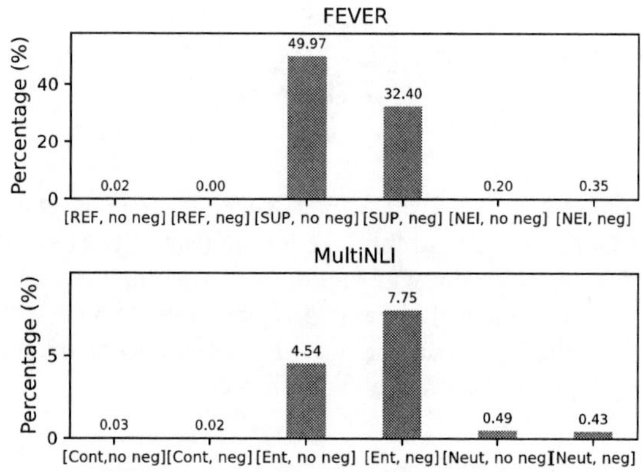

Figure 3: Percentage of OOD examples in the error set of each group. A large percentage of examples from classes SUP and Ent are regarded as outliers. FEVER's SUP has a much higher percentage removed compared with MultiNLI's Ent. All other groups contain only less than 1% of examples regarded as outliers.

the upweighted error set improves model performance. As seen in Table 3, all other groups of MultiNLI were either not affected by the removal of outliers or showed insignificant changes. On the other hand, removing outliers from the FEVER error set seemed to have a larger effect on groups other than the worst group [SUP, neg], especially on [REF, neg] and [NEI, neg].

We examined the group-wise percentage of the error-set OOD examples (i.e., the ones removed in **JTT-m**) to see how each group may be affected by the removal of their OOD examples (Figure 3). Despite the improvements in groups [REF, neg] and [Neut, neg], few to no examples from these groups were regarded as outliers by the Mahalanobis distance method. Instead, groups of classes SUP and Ent, whose performance does not improve when outliers are removed, contained the highest percentage of OOD examples. This suggests that these outliers can affect the model's decision boundaries among classes.

To investigate the properties of the OOD examples detected, we randomly sampled 100 examples from S_{in} and S_{out} for both FEVER and MultiNLI. For FEVER, we found 24 annotation errors in S_{out}, much higher than the 1 annotation error in S_{in}. For MultiNLI, S_{out} contained 10 annotation errors, whereas S_{in} contained 4. We show a sample of the annotation errors found in Table 4. This suggests that (1) the Mahalanobis distance method can detect at least a subset of annotation errors as outliers, and (2) the improvements in either the group or the overall performance may be partially due to the removal of these annotation errors.

Claim:	Nice & Slow was released in 1968.
Evidence:	"Nice & Slow" is a 1998 single from Usher's second album My Way.
Annotated label: SUPPORTS	
Predicted label: REFUTES	

(a) FEVER

Premise:	So far, no promising treatments exist according to Larry Gentilello.
Hypothesis:	Larry Gentilello asserted that effective treatments already exist, not just treatments that hold promise.
Annotated label: Entailment	
Predicted label: Contradiction	

(b) MultiNLI

Table 4: Example of annotation errors from (a) FEVER and (b) MultiNLI.

5 Conclusion

We have shown that the JTT algorithm can benefit from pruning the error set before upweighting and training a second time, improving worst-group accuracy or overall accuracy on two popular datasets. We also showed that annotation errors may occur in the error set, hampering JTT's effectiveness. These annotation errors can be mitigated by detecting and removing them with our Mahalanobis distance method. Investigating the effects of using other OOD-detection methods and finding a more effective way to tune the additional hyperparameters are directions for our future work.

Acknowledgments

This work is supported by JST CREST Grants (JPMJCR18A6 and JPMJCR20D3) and MEXT KAKENHI Grants (21H04906), Japan.

References

Yujia Bao, Shiyu Chang, and Regina Barzilay. 2021. Predict then interpolate: A simple algorithm to learn stable classifiers. In *Proceedings of the 38th International Conference on Machine Learning*, volume 139 of *Proceedings of Machine Learning Research*, pages 640–650. PMLR.

Jacob Devlin, Ming-Wei Chang, Kenton Lee, and Kristina Toutanova. 2019. BERT: Pre-training of deep bidirectional transformers for language understanding. In *Proceedings of the 2019 Conference of the North American Chapter of the Association for Computational Linguistics: Human Language Technologies, Volume 1 (Long and Short Papers)*, pages 4171–4186. Association for Computational Linguistics.

John Duchi, Tatsunori Hashimoto, and Hongseok Namkoong. 2019. Distributionally robust losses against mixture covariate shifts. `https://web.stanford.edu/~hnamk/papers/DuchiHaNa19.pdf`.

Suchin Gururangan, Swabha Swayamdipta, Omer Levy, Roy Schwartz, Samuel Bowman, and Noah A. Smith. 2018. Annotation artifacts in natural language inference data. In *Proceedings of the 2018 Conference of the North American Chapter of the Association for Computational Linguistics: Human Language Technologies, Volume 2 (Short Papers)*, pages 107–112, New Orleans, Louisiana. Association for Computational Linguistics.

Badr Youbi Idrissi, Martin Arjovsky, Mohammad Pezeshki, and David Lopez-Paz. 2022. Simple data balancing achieves competitive worst-group-accuracy. In *Proceedings of the First Conference on Causal Learning and Reasoning*, volume 177 of *Proceedings of Machine Learning Research*, pages 336–351. PMLR.

Kimin Lee, Kibok Lee, Honglak Lee, and Jinwoo Shin. 2018. A simple unified framework for detecting out-of-distribution samples and adversarial attacks. In *Advances in Neural Information Processing Systems*, volume 31. Curran Associates, Inc.

Daniel Levy, Yair Carmon, John C Duchi, and Aaron Sidford. 2020. Large-scale methods for distributionally robust optimization. In *Advances in Neural Information Processing Systems*, volume 33, pages 8847–8860. Curran Associates, Inc.

Evan Z Liu, Behzad Haghgoo, Annie S Chen, Aditi Raghunathan, Pang Wei Koh, Shiori Sagawa, Percy Liang, and Chelsea Finn. 2021. Just train twice: Improving group robustness without training group information. In *Proceedings of the 38th International Conference on Machine Learning*, volume 139 of *Proceedings of Machine Learning Research*, pages 6781–6792. PMLR.

Ilya Loshchilov and Frank Hutter. 2019. Decoupled weight decay regularization. In *International Conference on Learning Representations (ICLR)*.

Junhyun Nam, Hyuntak Cha, Sungsoo Ahn, Jaeho Lee, and Jinwoo Shin. 2020. Learning from failure: De-biasing classifier from biased classifier. In *Advances in Neural Information Processing Systems*, volume 33, pages 20673–20684. Curran Associates, Inc.

Mohammad Pezeshki, Oumar Kaba, Yoshua Bengio, Aaron C Courville, Doina Precup, and Guillaume Lajoie. 2021. Gradient starvation: A learning proclivity in neural networks. In *Advances in Neural Information Processing Systems*, volume 34, pages 1256–1272. Curran Associates, Inc.

Shiori Sagawa, Pang Wei Koh, Tatsunori B. Hashimoto, and Percy Liang. 2020. Distributionally robust neural networks. In *International Conference on Learning Representations (ICLR)*.

Tal Schuster, Adam Fisch, and Regina Barzilay. 2021. Get your vitamin C! robust fact verification with contrastive evidence. In *Proceedings of the 2021 Conference of the North American Chapter of the Association for Computational Linguistics: Human Language Technologies*, pages 624–643, Online. Association for Computational Linguistics.

Tal Schuster, Darsh Shah, Yun Jie Serene Yeo, Daniel Roberto Filizzola Ortiz, Enrico Santus, and Regina Barzilay. 2019. Towards debiasing fact verification models. In *Proceedings of the 2019 Conference on Empirical Methods in Natural Language Processing and the 9th International Joint Conference on Natural Language Processing (EMNLP-IJCNLP)*, pages 3419–3425. Association for Computational Linguistics.

Agnieszka Słowik and Leon Bottou. 2022. On distributionally robust optimization and data rebalancing. In *Proceedings of The 25th International Conference on Artificial Intelligence and Statistics*, volume 151 of *Proceedings of Machine Learning Research*, pages 1283–1297. PMLR.

James Thorne, Andreas Vlachos, Christos Christodoulopoulos, and Arpit Mittal. 2018. FEVER: a large-scale dataset for fact extraction and VERification. In *Proceedings of the 2018 Conference of the North American Chapter of the Association for Computational Linguistics: Human Language Technologies, Volume 1 (Long Papers)*, pages 809–819, New Orleans, Louisiana. Association for Computational Linguistics.

Vladimir Vapnik. 1992. Principles of risk minimization for learning theory. In *Advances in Neural Information Processing Systems*, volume 4. Morgan-Kaufmann.

Adina Williams, Nikita Nangia, and Samuel Bowman. 2018. A broad-coverage challenge corpus for sentence understanding through inference. In *Proceedings of the 2018 Conference of the North American Chapter of the Association for Computational Linguistics: Human Language Technologies, Volume 1 (Long Papers)*, pages 1112–1122. Association for Computational Linguistics.

Thomas Wolf, Lysandre Debut, Victor Sanh, Julien Chaumond, Clement Delangue, Anthony Moi, Pierric Cistac, Tim Rault, Remi Louf, Morgan Funtowicz, Joe Davison, Sam Shleifer, Patrick von Platen, Clara Ma, Yacine Jernite, Julien Plu, Canwen Xu, Teven Le Scao, Sylvain Gugger, Mariama Drame, Quentin Lhoest, and Alexander Rush. 2020. Transformers: State-of-the-art natural language processing. In *Proceedings of the 2020 Conference on Empirical Methods in Natural Language Processing: System Demonstrations*, pages 38–45, Online. Association for Computational Linguistics.

An Empirical Study on Topic Preservation in Multi-Document Summarization

Mong Yuan Sim and **Wei Emma Zhang** and **Congbo Ma**
University of Adelaide
Adelaide SA 5005
mongyuan.sim@student.adelaide.edu.au,
{wei.e.zhang, congbo.ma}@adelaide.edu.au

Abstract

Multi-document summarization (MDS) is a process of generating an informative and concise summary from multiple topic-related documents. Many studies have analyzed the quality of MDS dataset or models, however no work has been done from the perspective of topic preservation. In this work, we fill the gap by performing an empirical analysis on two MDS datasets and study topic preservation on generated summaries from 8 MDS models. Our key findings include i) Multi-News dataset has better gold summaries compared to Multi-XScience in terms of its topic distribution consistency and ii) Extractive approaches perform better than abstractive approaches in preserving topic information from source documents. We hope our findings could help develop a summarization model that can generate topic-focused summary and also give inspiration to researchers in creating dataset for such challenging task.

1 Introduction

Multi-document summarization (MDS) is a task to produce an informative and concise summary from multiple documents. In general, there are two different approaches to MDS, which are extractive and abstractive summarization (Ma et al., 2022). Extractive summarization refers to methods that select important sentences from input documents and produce a summary. These methods perform better at producing summary without grammatical errors. On the other hand, abstractive summarization refers to methods that have the ability to generate summaries with words that do not exist in input documents (Cui and Hu, 2021; Fabbri et al., 2019).

The development of text summarization model has been supported by the growing amount and quality of available dataset. The available dataset types vary from news articles (Fabbri et al., 2019) to scientific articles (Lu et al., 2020) and Wikipedia abstract (Perez-Beltrachini et al., 2019). However, information is not scarce in this era, but "valuable" information is. Many recent work (Cui and Hu, 2021; Zou et al., 2021; Zhu et al., 2021; Perez-Beltrachini et al., 2019) have been focusing on generating topic-guided summaries using one-size-fits-all dataset which are not meant for this kind of work, making it difficult to evaluate whether the model is performing better than "generic" model in terms of the quality of generated topic-focused summary. There are also work (Zhang et al., 2021; Tejaswin et al., 2021; Xu et al., 2020) focusing on the analysis of summarization models and datasets but none on topic-preservation. To the best of our knowledge, there is only one dataset (Bahrainian et al., 2022) created for topic-guided news summarization, but has been tailored for single document summarization. Therefore, it is essential to deep dive into current available MDS dataset, and investigate their suitability for developing topic-guided summarization models, and the pattern of high quality summaries in order to inspire future work in text summarization.

In this paper, we conducted several experiments in analyzing the relevance of input and output documents in automated summarization and the pattern of model-generated summaries. To sum up, our contributions are two-folds: i) for MDS dataset, we evaluated topic relation between source documents and gold summaries in widely used MDS dataset, inspiring future work on creating high quality dataset for topic-aware summarization model; ii) for MDS models, we investigated summaries generated from a wide range of state-of-the-art models in order to provide insights of how relevant it is to the source documents. Our observations could inspire research directions towards better topic-preserving MDS dataset and models.

2 Datasets and Models

In this work, we use two most commonly used multi-document summarization dataset Multi-

Proceedings of the AACL-IJCNLP 2022 Student Research Workshop, pages 61–67
November 20, 2022. ©2022 Association for Computational Linguistics

News and Multi-XScience in our experiments. We run 8 MDS models from non-deep learning based models to deep learning models including the recent Transformer-based state–of-the-art models. For fair comparison, training/validation and testing for all models are performed on a high performance computing cluster powered by NVIDIA V100.

2.1 MDS Datasets

2.1.1 Multi-News

Multi-News (Fabbri et al., 2019) is the first large-scale dataset constructed by collecting human-written articles which are summaries of multiple news article sources from newser.com. This dataset contains 44,972/5,622/5,622 instances for training, validation, and testing. Each instance has 2 to 10 source documents per summary.

Source documents and gold summaries for Multi-News are stored in different .txt files. In source documents file, documents used to generate one summary are separated by a token called "story_special_token_tag". We processed the dataset by removing the token to separate source document and unused words such as "<unk>" and "<blank>" before feeding them into topic model.

2.1.2 Multi-XScience

Multi-XScience (Lu et al., 2020) is a large-scale dataset created for extreme summarization task which is to write related-work section of a paper based on its abstract and the articles it references. Information is collected from arvix.org and Microsoft Academic Graph (MAG). This dataset contains 30,369/5,066/5,093 instances for training validation, and testing. Each instance has 10 to 20 references as input.

Multi-XScience dataset comes in as a JSON file. Each data instance contains a related work section which is the gold summary, along with multiple "ref_abstract" entries which act as source documents. The citation in the sources and targets are replaced by a common token "@cite". We process the dataset by storing them in a list, remove unused words and tokens such as "@cite".

2.2 MDS Models

In order to examine model generated summary, we generate summaries from 8 MDS models including both extractive and abstractive models. The overview of these models are as follows:

MMR (Goldstein and Carbonell, 1998) is an extractive approach that assigns scores to sentences and re-rank them to obtain relevant sentences.

Textrank (Mihalcea and Tarau, 2004) produces undirected weighted graph from input documents, focusing on keywords to find the most relevant sentences in text.

Lexrank (Erkan and Radev, 2004) is an extractive method that uses graph-based method to compute relative importance of documents.

PG (See et al., 2017) pointer-generator model extends the standard seq2seq framework with copy and coverage mechanism.

Transformer (Vaswani et al., 2017) captures cross-document relationships via attention mechanism.

CopyTransformer (Gehrmann et al., 2018) randomly chooses one of the attention heads of Transformer as the copy distribution.

Hi-Map (Fabbri et al., 2019) adapts a pointer-generator model with MMR to compute weights over multiple documents inputs.

SummPip (Zhao et al., 2020) converts documents to sentence graph, apply spectral clustering to obtain clusters of sentences.

3 Methods and Results

We compare and analyze topic-related patterns of source document, gold summaries (provided in MDS benchmark datasets), and the generated summaries (from 8 MDS models). Guided by topic modelling research, we adopt the topic related evaluation metrics in this work. We specifically study i) topic coherence, to identify the best settings; ii) number of documents in each topic, to study the overall topic distribution; iii) distances among topic distributions of summaries, to examine the document-level patterns; iv) topic words correlations in summaries, to analyze the word-level patterns.

3.1 Latent Dirichlet allocation (LDA)

Latent Dirichlet allocation (LDA) is a generative probabilistic topic model for which each document is represented as a random mixture of latent topics and each topic is represented as a distribution over fixed set of words (Onan et al., 2016). It aims to identify underlying latent topic structure based on observed data (Blei et al., 2003).

We make good use of information obtained from a LDA based topic model, which are topic distribution and word vector for each topic. Topic distribution is a vector contains N elements, where

N is number of topics. Each value represents the probability of a document falls into topic group n. Word vector shows the weight for each word in a topic:

$$\begin{aligned} doc_i &: [w_{tp1}, w_{tp2}, ..., w_{tpN}] \\ tp_j &: [w_{wd1}, w_{wd2}, ..., w_{wdM}], j \in [1, N] \end{aligned} \quad (1)$$

where w_{tpj} is the probability of the j-th topic in the i-th document, w_{wdq} is the probability of q-th word in j-th topic, M is the number of words to describe a topic. Both N and M are hyper-parameters.

We apply LDA topic modelling on the corpus containing all the source documents, gold summaries and generated summaries as they are in the same topic distribution space and we want to observe the topic patterns within.

3.2 Topic Coherence

Topic coherence is a qualitative measurement to measure the quality of topic modelling (Newman et al., 2010). The underlying idea is rooted in the distributional hypothesis of linguistics that consider words with similar meanings tend to occur in the similar contexts (Harris, 1954). If a topic's top K words have related meanings, the topic is considered to be coherent (Syed and Spruit, 2017).

In this study, we use topic coherence score to identify the best hyper-parameter settings for the topic model LDA, and use this setting for follow-up experiments. Particularly, we adopt the coherence measure proposed by Röder et al. (2015) (known as UMass-coherence) which is calculated based on co-occurrences of word pairs as follows:

$$C_{UMass}(T) = \sum_{m=2}^{M} \sum_{l=1}^{m-1} \log \frac{p(w_m, w_l) + \frac{1}{|D|}}{p(w_l)} \quad (2)$$

where $p(w_m, w_l)$ denotes the probability of the co-occurrence of words w_m and w_l in the corpus D. It is computed as the ratio of number of documents containing both words w_m and w_l and the total number of documents in D. M is the length of the word list.

Another commonly used topic coherence score is C_v score, which creates content vectors of words using word co-occurences and calculates the score using normalized pointwise mutual information (PMI) and cosine similarity.

We obtain topic distribution and word vector for each topic on both dataset, Multi-News and Multi-XScience from LDA. Then we identify the best topic coherence score for these two datasets in order to get the best topical setting. We compute the two types of coherence scores, namely u_mass and C_v score as discussed previously. The number of topics is set to 5, 10, 15, 20, 25 and 30. From the results shown in Figure 1, we observe that when the number of topics is 25, Multi-News dataset shows the highest coherence score. For Multi-XScience dataset, 5 topics achieves best coherence. We use these settings for the follow-up experiments.

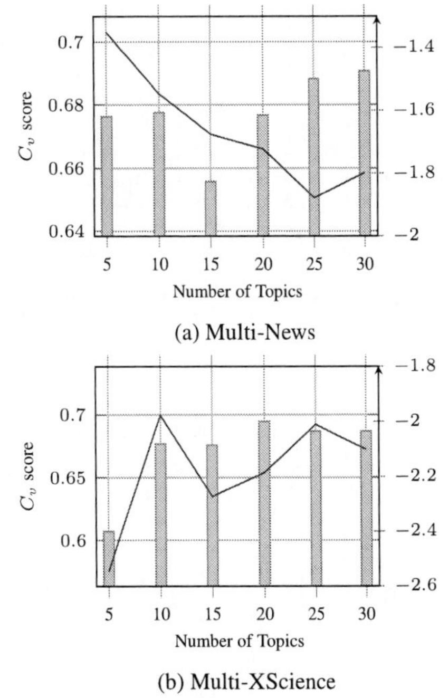

Figure 1: Topic coherence score for Multi-News and Multi-XScience datasets. The bar chart represents C_v score while line chart represents umass score.

3.3 Analyzing number of documents per topic

To discover the overall topic distribution of the dataset, we perform K-Means clustering on the topic distribution obtained from LDA model. We notice that in Figure 2a and 2b, Multi-News source documents are "heavy" in topic 9 while its gold documents mostly fall into topic 1, 2, 3, 8 and 12. For Multi-XScience, although it does not show domination by any topic, we can still see from Figure 2c and 2d that source documents and gold summaries do not follow the same topic distribution.

3.4 Distances of Topic Distributions

We measure the distances of document-topic distributions of source documents, gold summaries and the generated summaries, aiming to find document-level topical correlations.

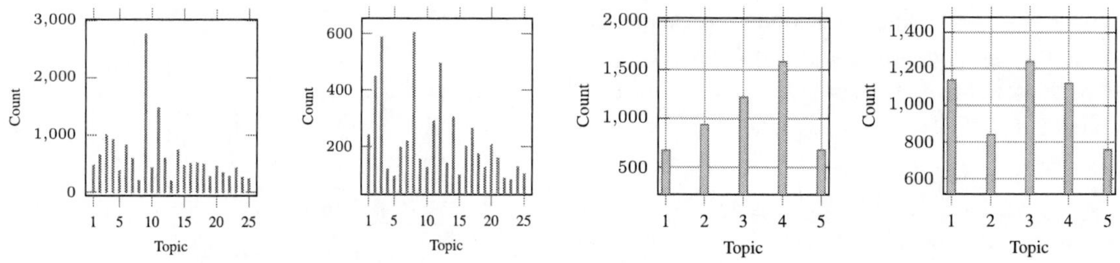

(a) Multi-News (Source) (b) Multi-News (Gold) (c) Multi-XScience (Source) (d) Multi-XScience (Gold)

Figure 2: Number of Documents per Topic for Multi-News and Multi-XScience.

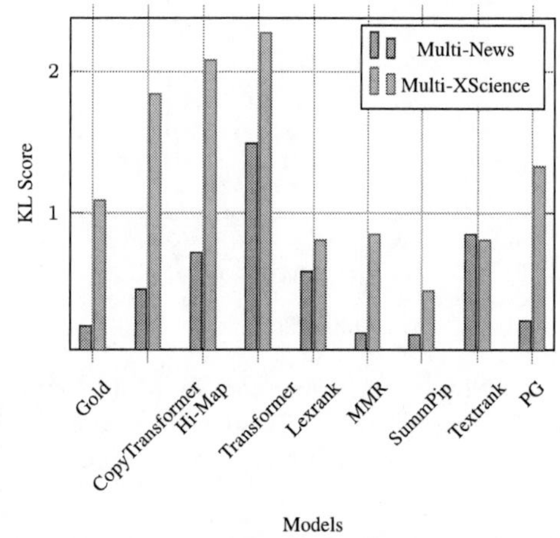

Figure 3: KL score for MultiNews and Multi-XScience. The first two bars shows the KL score between source documents and gold summaries. The rest of the bars show KL score between source documents and generated summaries as labeled.

We adopt Kullback-Leibler (KL) Divergence measure as the distance function. KL-divergence is a way to quantify the distances between two probability distributions (Shlens, 2014). Given two probability distribution density functions (PDFs), p and q, their KL divergence score, denoted as $KL(p \parallel q)$, is defined as :

$$KL(p \parallel q) = \int_{-\infty}^{+\infty} p(x) \log \frac{p(x)}{q(x)} dx \quad (3)$$

As we are focusing on multi-document summarization, the relationship between source document and summary is many to one. We first calculate the average topic distribution over all source documents, then compute KL divergence between source document and summary.

We present the document-level distances between source documents and summaries (gold and generated) in Figure 3. We can see that extractive models such as Lexrank, MMR, SummPip and Textrank tend to produce a summary where its topic distribution is closer to the source documents. On the other hand, the abstractive models which have proven to achieve higher ROUGE score, failed to produce a summary that is topic-relevant to the source documents. Transformer, one of the most popular trends in summarization has the highest KL score on both dataset which means summaries produced from this model are often "off-topic" in a sense that it fails to capture the underlying topic.

We also observe that Multi-News dataset provides gold summary that preserves topic information better than Multi-XScience. Overall, Multi-News has lower KL score in both gold and generated summaries compared to Multi-XScience.

3.5 Topic Words Correlation

As we want to explore the correlation between source documents and summaries, along with gold and model generated summaries, we compute a new weight of each word in a document by multiplying topic weight by word matrix for each topic. The resulting vector shows the weight for each word in a document. For example, the q-th word in the j-th topic of document i has weight $w_{tpj} * w_{wdq}$. Then we consider the correlation of words in two document as the euclidean distance of their weights.

We obtain the words' weights in a document by using their topical probabilities. We depict the word correlations between source documents, gold summaries and summaries generated from SummPip and Transformer in a heatmap. We selected SummPip and Transformer because they have the lowest and highest KL score respectively.

For visualisation purpose, we picked top-10 words from a topic and computed euclidean distance of each word in two vectors. If two documents are highly correlated,the heatmap will have a straight line from top left to bottom right.

From Figure 4, we can see that the result we obtain is very far away from best case scenario.

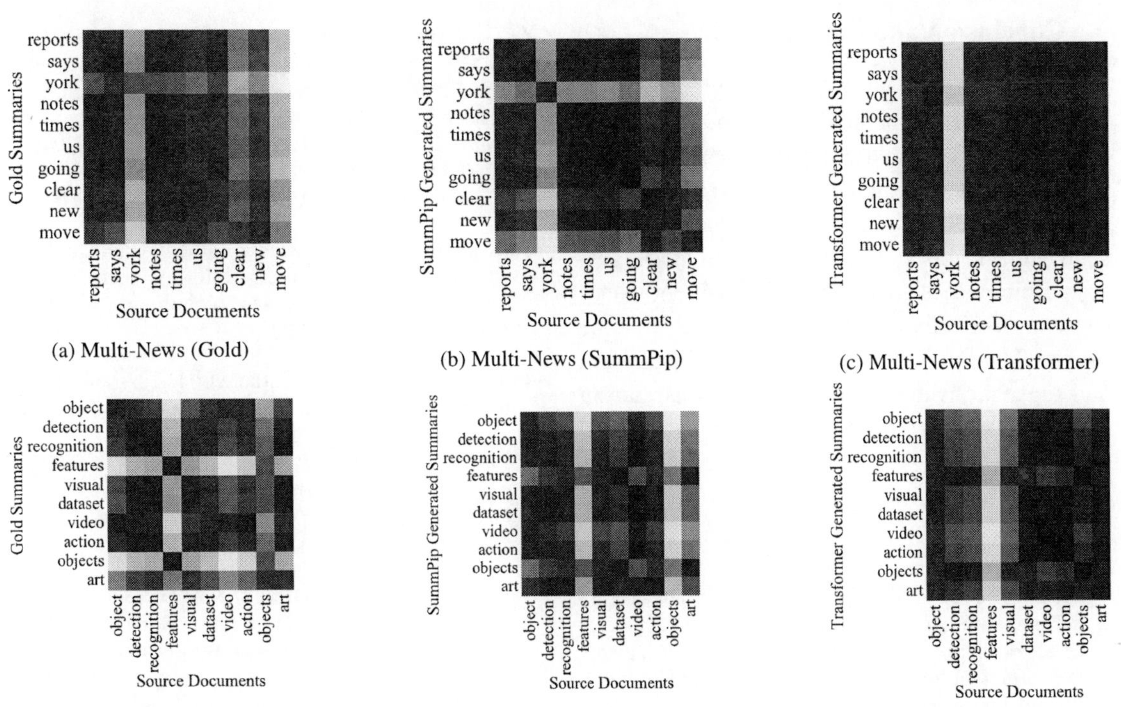

(a) Multi-News (Gold) (b) Multi-News (SummPip) (c) Multi-News (Transformer)

(d) Multi-XScience (Gold) (e) Multi-XScience (SummPip) (f) Multi-XScience (Transformer)

Figure 4: Word-level correlation for source documents and summaries for Multi-News and Multi-XScience dataset. We randomly select a topic and visualise the correlation between source documents and summaries with top-10 words for that topic. The higher the correlation, the darker the square is.

Instead, the words sparse across many different topics and are inconsistent. This means a model generated summary might be discussing about a very different topic than those in source documents.

4 Discussions

Our studies and observations raise the following questions that we believe need to be considered in the MDS research:

Is extractive MDS model better than abstractive MDS model in preserving topics? From results in Section 3.4, we find that in terms of topic preservation, extractive models work better than abstractive models. This could due to the "extract" nature of the former which shares the same vocabulary as the source document, resulting in higher word correlation between source documents and summaries. Future work could focus on analyzing word semantic similarities instead of relying on topic distribution similarities only as abstractive models use words that are different from source documents to generate a summary. To improve the topic preservation of abstractive models, we could consider select semantically similar words to the words in the source document during generation.

Whether gold summary follows source documents' topic distribution? From Section 3.4 we also find Multi-News's gold summaries topic distribution are well aligned with the topic distributions in its source document, however Multi-XScience does not perform well in this regard.This analysis could inspire future MDS dataset contributors to take topic preservation into consideration when preparing gold summaries such that source documents and gold summaries have similar topic distribution.

Whether the number of documents are similar across all topics? Dataset that is "heavy" on one topic can disadvantage summarization models in training as the vocabulary might be dominated by a specific topic causing topic information for other topics with less instances being discarded or normalised. This can be seen in Figure 2 where the document count per topic for source documents and gold summaries are inconsistent. Future dataset creation should focus on the topic distribution among all documents in data collected to make sure that the generation model captures equal information from all topics.

5 Conclusion and Future Work

In conclusion, we have systemically and empirically analyzed two popular multi-document summarization datasets and summaries generated from a variety of state-of-the-art summarization models. Our analysis over 100,000 documents reveals that source documents, gold summaries and model generated summaries are rarely topic coherent which cause the summary to be less informative for some usages. This analysis also lead to some inspiration and suggestions in creating better summarization models and dataset for real world application.

References

Seyed Ali Bahrainian, Sheridan Feucht, and Carsten Eickhoff. 2022. NEWTS: A corpus for news topic-focused summarization. In *Findings of the Association for Computational Linguistics: ACL 2022*, pages 493–503, Dublin, Ireland. Association for Computational Linguistics.

David M. Blei, Andrew Y. Ng, and Michael I. Jordan. 2003. Latent dirichlet allocation. *J. Mach. Learn. Res.*, 3(null):993–1022.

Peng Cui and Le Hu. 2021. Topic-guided abstractive multi-document summarization. In *Findings of the Association for Computational Linguistics: EMNLP 2021*, pages 1463–1472, Punta Cana, Dominican Republic. Association for Computational Linguistics.

Günes Erkan and Dragomir R. Radev. 2004. Lexrank: Graph-based lexical centrality as salience in text summarization. *J. Artif. Int. Res.*, 22(1):457–479.

Alexander Fabbri, Irene Li, Tianwei She, Suyi Li, and Dragomir Radev. 2019. Multi-news: A large-scale multi-document summarization dataset and abstractive hierarchical model. In *Proceedings of the 57th Annual Meeting of the Association for Computational Linguistics*, pages 1074–1084, Florence, Italy. Association for Computational Linguistics.

Sebastian Gehrmann, Yuntian Deng, and Alexander Rush. 2018. Bottom-up abstractive summarization. In *Proceedings of the 2018 Conference on Empirical Methods in Natural Language Processing*, pages 4098–4109, Brussels, Belgium. Association for Computational Linguistics.

Jade Goldstein and Jaime G. Carbonell. 1998. Summarization: (1) using MMR for diversity- based reranking and (2) evaluating summaries. In *TIPSTER TEXT PROGRAM PHASE III: Proceedings of a Workshop held at Baltimore, MD, USA, October 13-15, 1998*, pages 181–195. Morgan Kaufmann.

Zellig S. Harris. 1954. Distributional structure. *WORD*, 10(2-3):146–162.

Yao Lu, Yue Dong, and Laurent Charlin. 2020. Multi-xscience: A large-scale dataset for extreme multi-document summarization of scientific articles. In *Proceedings of the 2020 Conference on Empirical Methods in Natural Language Processing, EMNLP 2020, Online, November 16-20, 2020*, pages 8068–8074. Association for Computational Linguistics.

Congbo Ma, Wei Emma Zhang, Mingyu Guo, Hu Wang, and Quan Z. Sheng. 2022. Multi-document Summarization via Deep Learning Techniques: A Survey. Accepted at March 2022.

Rada Mihalcea and Paul Tarau. 2004. Textrank: Bringing order into text. In *Proceedings of the 2004 Conference on Empirical Methods in Natural Language Processing , EMNLP 2004, A meeting of SIGDAT, a Special Interest Group of the ACL, held in conjunction with ACL 2004, 25-26 July 2004, Barcelona, Spain*, pages 404–411. ACL.

David Newman, Jey Han Lau, Karl Grieser, and Timothy Baldwin. 2010. Automatic evaluation of topic coherence. In *Human Language Technologies: The 2010 Annual Conference of the North American Chapter of the Association for Computational Linguistics*, pages 100–108, Los Angeles, California. Association for Computational Linguistics.

Aytug Onan, Serdar Korukoglu, and Hasan Bulut. 2016. Lda-based topic modelling in text sentiment classification: An empirical analysis. *Int. J. Comput. Linguistics Appl.*, 7(1):101–119.

Laura Perez-Beltrachini, Yang Liu, and Mirella Lapata. 2019. Generating Summaries with Topic Templates and Structured Convolutional Decoders. In *Proceedings of the 57th Annual Meeting of the Association for Computational Linguistics*, pages 5107–5116, Florence, Italy. Association for Computational Linguistics.

Michael Röder, Andreas Both, and Alexander Hinneburg. 2015. Exploring the space of topic coherence measures. In *Proceedings of the Eighth ACM International Conference on Web Search and Data Mining, WSDM 2015, Shanghai, China, February 2-6, 2015*, pages 399–408. ACM.

Abigail See, Peter J. Liu, and Christopher D. Manning. 2017. Get to the point: Summarization with pointer-generator networks. In *Proceedings of the 55th Annual Meeting of the Association for Computational Linguistics (Volume 1: Long Papers)*, pages 1073–1083, Vancouver, Canada. Association for Computational Linguistics.

Jonathon Shlens. 2014. Notes on Kullback-Leibler Divergence and Likelihood. ArXiv:1404.2000 [cs, math].

Shaheen Syed and Marco Spruit. 2017. Full-Text or Abstract? Examining Topic Coherence Scores Using Latent Dirichlet Allocation. In *2017 IEEE International Conference on Data Science and Advanced Analytics (DSAA)*, pages 165–174, Tokyo, Japan. IEEE.

Priyam Tejaswin, Dhruv Naik, and Pengfei Liu. 2021. How well do you know your summarization datasets? In *Findings of the Association for Computational Linguistics: ACL/IJCNLP 2021, Online Event, August 1-6, 2021*, volume ACL/IJCNLP 2021 of *Findings of ACL*, pages 3436–3449. Association for Computational Linguistics.

Ashish Vaswani, Noam Shazeer, Niki Parmar, Jakob Uszkoreit, Llion Jones, Aidan N Gomez, Ł ukasz Kaiser, and Illia Polosukhin. 2017. Attention is all you need. In *Advances in Neural Information Processing Systems*, volume 30. Curran Associates, Inc.

Jiacheng Xu, Shrey Desai, and Greg Durrett. 2020. Understanding neural abstractive summarization models via uncertainty. In *Proceedings of the 2020 Conference on Empirical Methods in Natural Language Processing, EMNLP 2020, Online, November 16-20, 2020*, pages 6275–6281. Association for Computational Linguistics.

Yusen Zhang, Ansong Ni, Tao Yu, Rui Zhang, Chenguang Zhu, Budhaditya Deb, Asli Celikyilmaz, Ahmed Hassan Awadallah, and Dragomir R. Radev. 2021. An exploratory study on long dialogue summarization: What works and what's next. In *Findings of the Association for Computational Linguistics: EMNLP 2021, Virtual Event / Punta Cana, Dominican Republic, 16-20 November, 2021*, pages 4426–4433. Association for Computational Linguistics.

Jinming Zhao, Ming Liu, Longxiang Gao, Yuan Jin, Lan Du, He Zhao, He Zhang, and Gholamreza Haffari. 2020. Summpip: Unsupervised multi-document summarization with sentence graph compression. In *Proceedings of the 43rd International ACM SIGIR Conference on Research and Development in Information Retrieval*, SIGIR '20, page 1949–1952, New York, NY, USA. Association for Computing Machinery.

Fangwei Zhu, Shangqing Tu, Jiaxin Shi, Juanzi Li, Lei Hou, and Tong Cui. 2021. TWAG: A topic-guided Wikipedia abstract generator. In *Proceedings of the 59th Annual Meeting of the Association for Computational Linguistics and the 11th International Joint Conference on Natural Language Processing (Volume 1: Long Papers)*, pages 4623–4635, Online. Association for Computational Linguistics.

Yicheng Zou, Lujun Zhao, Yangyang Kang, Jun Lin, Minlong Peng, Zhuoren Jiang, Changlong Sun, Qi Zhang, Xuanjing Huang, and Xiaozhong Liu. 2021. Topic-oriented spoken dialogue summarization for customer service with saliency-aware topic modeling. In *Thirty-Fifth AAAI Conference on Artificial Intelligence, AAAI 2021, Thirty-Third Conference on Innovative Applications of Artificial Intelligence, IAAI 2021, The Eleventh Symposium on Educational Advances in Artificial Intelligence, EAAI 2021, Virtual Event, February 2-9, 2021*, pages 14665–14673. AAAI Press.

Detecting Urgency in Multilingual Medical SMS in Kenya

Narshion Ngao[◇] **Zeyu Wang**[†] **Lawrence Nderu**[◇]
Tobias Mwalili[◇] **Tal August**[†] **Keshet Ronen**[†]
[†]University of Washington, Seattle, WA, USA
[◇]Jomo Kenyatta University of Agriculture & Technology, Nairobi, Kenya

Abstract

Access to mobile phones in many low- and middle-income countries has increased exponentially over the last 20 years, providing an opportunity to connect patients with healthcare interventions through mobile phones (known as mobile health). A barrier to large-scale implementation of interactive mobile health interventions is the human effort needed to manage participant messages. In this study, we explore the use of natural language processing to improve healthcare workers' management of messages from pregnant and postpartum women in Kenya. Using multilingual, low-resource language text messages from the Mobile solutions for Women and Children's health (Mobile WACh NEO) study, we developed models to assess urgency of incoming messages. We evaluated models using a novel approach that focuses on clinical usefulness in either triaging or prioritizing messages. Our best-performing models did not reach the threshold for clinical usefulness we set, but have the potential to improve nurse workflow and responsiveness to urgent messages.

1 Introduction

In many low- and middle-income countries, access to healthcare is limited and unaffordable. Interactive short message service (SMS) communication with healthcare workers has shown great potential to promote access to care in such contexts by providing remote information and support (Hall et al., 2015; Rono et al., 2021).

One such system is the Mobile solutions for Women and Children's health (Mobile WACh) platform, an interactive semi-automated platform designed to connect pregnant and postpartum women to healthcare workers through SMS (Perrier et al., 2015; Unger et al., 2019, 2018; Harrington et al., 2019; Kinuthia et al., 2021; Ronen et al., 2021). Studies using this platform have reported significant impacts on health outcomes like breastfeeding and postpartum contraception (Unger et al., 2018; Harrington et al., 2019).

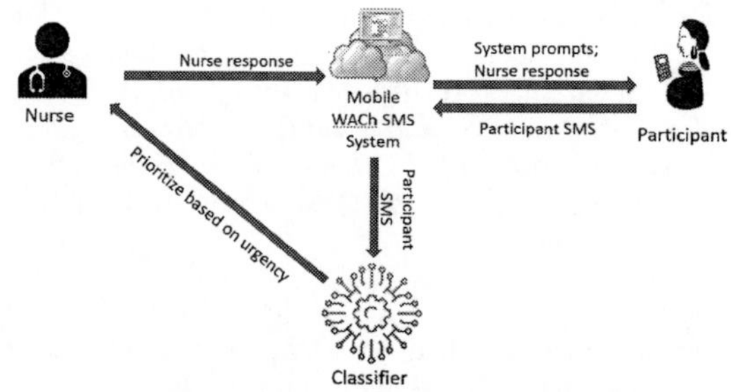

Figure 1: Task Definition Workflow

While promising, a major limitation of mobile health interventions is the human effort required to manage messages. Nurses involved in the Mobile WACh platform received hundreds of messages per day (Unger et al., 2019). Many of these messages did not require immediate responses; however, nurses couldn't distinguish between urgent and non-urgent messages without reading them.

Natural language processing (NLP) can potentially be used to automatically triage and prioritize incoming messages. This may significantly improve worker efficiency and improve reliability of the healthcare system in low-resource settings (Rono et al., 2021; Barron et al., 2017). In recent years, researchers have used NLP for content analysis of incoming messages in digital health interventions (Schwab-Reese et al., 2019; Klimis et al., 2021) and for analyzing messages in mental health discussions (Zhang and Danescu-Niculescu-Mizil, 2020; Althoff et al., 2016).

This paper explores the possibility of a clinically useful model to detect urgent participant messages in an interactive mobile health system in Kenya. Our study focuses on a dataset drawn from the Mobile WACh NEO studies (Unger et al., 2019; Ronen et al., 2021). The dataset contains real-world, informal messages in multiple low-resource languages

Proceedings of the AACL-IJCNLP 2022 Student Research Workshop, pages 68–75
November 20, 2022.

(Swahili, Luo and Sheng) and English. We explore methods for handling the unique challenges presented in our dataset, including additional pretraining (Gururangan et al., 2020) and adding prior conversation context. We tested several approaches to classifying urgency in labeled participant messages, with a focus on classifiers that could have clinical utility in improving healthcare worker workflow. Models based on mBERT can achieve performance levels close to our threshold of clinical usefulness, suggesting such systems could be useful to healthcare workers in the future. We discuss our findings and next steps for integrating such NLP models into real-world systems that could significantly improve global healthcare delivery.

2 Task Definition

We aim to introduce models that classify messages based on urgency as a way of prioritizing or triaging messages for nurses. Specifically, given a message, our task is to identify if the message requires immediate nurse attention (urgent) or can be looked at later (non-urgent). Figure 1 summarizes the Mobile WACh system and NLP task. Because of the sensitivity of all participant messages in this context, our task is not intended to replace nurses by filtering participant messages or generating responses.

3 Dataset

Our data consists of messages, from the Mobile WACh NEO pilot (messages sent between 05-12-2017 and 20-02-2019) (Unger et al., 2019) and Mobile WACh NEO RCT (messages sent between 09-09-2020 and 04-05-2022) studies (Ronen et al., 2021). Messages were exchanged between pregnant/postpartum women, nurses and the automated Mobile WACh system. The Mobile WACh NEO pilot dataset consists of a total of 58,834 messages that were exchanged between 800 participants, the automated system and 2 nurses. The Mobile WACh NEO RCT had a total of 161,735 messages that were exchanged between 1,724 participants, the automated system and 12 nurses. Therefore, the combined dataset consisted of 220,560 messages from 2,523 participants and 14 nurses (after cleaning). Automated messages were sent to participants weekly during pregnancy until 38 weeks gestation, then 2 messages daily for the first 2 weeks after delivery, and then every 2 days for 6 weeks follow-up post delivery. Participants could send messages to the system at any time. Nurses in the study manually replied to participant messages. These nurses had the same training and qualification as nurses in the public health facilities, however, they were employed by the study and did not have routine care provision responsibilities outside of study. A total of 112,220 (50.9%) messages were sent by the Mobile WACh system, 65,572 (29.7%) by participants and 42,768 (19.4%) by nurses (Table 1). Automated system messages were sent in English, Swahili (a Bantu language) or Luo (a Nilotic language) based on each participant's preference. Participant messages were sent in the participant's language of choice; about half (50.4%) were in English, 36.8% were in Swahili, 5.4% were in Luo, 4.5% were code-switched, and 2.9% were in a slang fusion known as Sheng (Table 2). To clean the dataset of any identifiable information, we removed standard salutation, and any location, nurse, or participant names. Automated messages used to validate participant registration in the SMS system were also removed. The total number of messages described here were the final dataset after the cleaning exercise.

Table 1: Messages By Source. Around a third of participant messages were less than 10 characters, suggesting many participant messages were short and depend on previous message context for detecting urgency.

Sent By	Total Messages	Messages with less than 10 characters	Mean number of characters in a message (std)
nurse	42768 (19.4%)	2500	97.9 (103.5)
participant	65572 (29.7%)	19769	36.5 (39.8)
system	112220 (50.9%)	0	257.3 (102.7)

The dataset we present here is typical of how language is used in Kenya (Bosire, 2006; Mondal et al., 2021). For instance, Swahili words used by participants in Nairobi may have different connotations from the same word in standard Swahili or Swahili used in Western Kenya. It is worth noting that this dataset also contains languages (Sheng and Luo) not commonly included in training for multilingual transformer-based models like mBERT (Devlin et al., 2019). Table 2 illustrates the breakdown of participant messages by language.

3.1 Urgency Labelling

Two nurses at the study clinics labelled a total of 11,129 messages from 772 participants. Of these, 30 participants were selected from the Mo-

Table 2: Labelled Participant Messages by language. While the majority of messages are in English, Swahili and Luo make up more than 40% of the total messages. Note that the total number of labelled messages was 11129.

Language	Total Messages	Percentage
english	5646	50.7%
swahili	3893	35.0%
sheng	572	5.1%
luo	566	5.1%
Code-Switched	452	4.1%
TOTAL	65572	100%

bile WACh NEO pilot study and had a total of 1,477 messages. The remaining 742 participants were from the Mobile WACh RCT study. Nurses labelled urgency based on how quickly a given participant message should be replied to by a nurse: 1) immediately, 2) within 2 hours, 3) before end of work day 4) by tomorrow 5) no need to reply. Nurses were instructed to use information from prior messages to inform assessment of the urgency of a given participant message. A sampled agreement between two raters had a Cohen Kappa score of 0.75, indicating high agreement. From the labelled data, we split the 5 urgency categories into a binary label of urgent (categories 1 and 2) and not urgent (categories 3, 4 and 5). The distribution of urgency labels was imbalanced (2,383 out of 11,129 were labelled as urgent, 21.4% of all labelled messages). This data represents the reality that in the context of the Mobile WACh studies, most messages received were not urgent. Because we are interested in a model than can eventually be useful in this real-world context, we leave the data imbalanced. Finally, the data was split into training 7,790 (70%), test 2,337(20%), and validation 1,002(10%) sets, having been stratified by label.

4 Classifying Urgency

We defined the task of predicting message urgency as a binary classification task. We tested two modeling approaches. Our first approach was a penalized logistic regression (penalty: l2, maximum iterations: 570) with bigram lexical features as input. The bigram features were extracted from uni- and bi-grams from the messages using Scikit-learn's count vectorizer (Pedregosa et al., 2011). In our second approach, we evaluated a fine-tuned multilingual BERT model (mBERT) (Devlin et al., 2019). mBERT was pretrained in 104 languages including English and Swahili. Linear models have been used as a baseline in mobile health classification tasks (Losada et al., 2020), and mBERT is a strong multi-lingual text classification model.

4.1 Adding Context

We observed that many participant messages are short (Table 1) and messages like "okay", "thank you", "no", and "yes" can have different meanings depending on the context of the conversation. Past work has found that including prior message context when analyzing SMS messages can be helpful for understanding conversation trajectory (Althoff et al., 2016) and appropriate responses (Zhang and Danescu-Niculescu-Mizil, 2020). We took inspiration from this work and evaluated whether adding preceding message context to participant messages would improve model performance.

We represented context by prepending the message preceding a participant message. We developed two versions of the dataset: one in which each participant message was prepended with the preceding system message (system context) and one in which each message was prepended with the preceding nurse message, or, in the event there was no nurse message, then the most recent system message (nurse context). Example messages are displayed in Table 3. We compared results for both the logistic regression with bigram features and mBERT using these approaches.

4.2 Additional Pretraining

It has been shown that additional in-domain and task-adaptive pretraining can improve model performance in a variety of settings (Gururangan et al., 2020). Since our dataset differs from the languages and domains used to pretrain mBERT, we reasoned this may be particularly impactful in our task.

We explored two versions of pretraining. In the first approach, we pretrained on all 49,786 participant messages that were not in the test or validation sets (this included both labelled and unlabelled data). Similar to our approach for fine-tuning data, we tested pretraining with participant messages that were prepended with system messages or nurse messages. In the second approach, we used the 11,129 labeled (both urgent and non-urgent) participant messages that were also prepended with system messages or nurse messages (Table 3). Note that in this second approach, we did not include the

Table 3: Sample messages with contexts

System Message	Nurse Message	Participant Message	Urgency Label
Make sure you come in for antenatal care even at the end of your pregnancy We check for any problems and help you prepare a birth plan Do you have any questions or concerns Are you feeling the baby move often	Am glad your OK have a nice day	You To	0
We are checking to see how you are doing How is your bleeding Do you have any pain in your lower abdomen Any fevers Please let us know if you feel unwell	Are you still having the headache	yeah	1
Regular strong stomach pains are a sign of labour If you feel this strong tightening regularly pains leaking of fluid or bleeding go to the facility Do you feel any contractions Do you have any concerns	Hello That is fine Please avoid strenuous activities at this point in your pregnancy	Its OK I willthanks for your concerns	0
Newborns sleep a lot but wont stay asleep for more than 24 hours at a time You may still be up several times at night to change feed and comfort your baby Take naps with your baby and try and interact with your baby during the day and keep things dark and quiet at night How is the baby sleeping	Hello there is no problem with topping up for the baby if the baby not satisfied Where are you getting the milk to top up What do you mean by yellow skin and which treatment is this for yellow skin that you are referring to	My baby had jodesyellow skin colour and was put on photo therapynow am asking can the baby suffer from the same problem a gain the Normal skin colour of the baby turning to yellow...	1

labels, only the text of the messages, for pretraining. We explore this method for mBERT.

We present the models in which pretraining and fine-tuning data are matched in terms of the context used (i.e., system, nurse, or no context) since we observed that this led to the largest increases in performance. We pretrained with masked language modelling with 15% of the text masked and used a batch size of 4, with a maximum input sequence size of 512. During fine tuning the models, we used default hyper parameters apart from batch size which was 16. The default parameters can be found at (huggingface.co).

5 Evaluation

While F1 score is a common classification evaluation metric, clinically useful systems may not require both high recall and high precision to improve healthcare worker workflow. We visualize the trade offs of models' precision and recall with precision-recall curves. We can use these PR curves to pick potential models that could be clinically useful by defining two regions in the graph: a triage region and a prioritize region.

A precision-recall curve shows the trade offs of models' precision and recall across a range of classification thresholds. This allows us to visualization of trade-offs of the results of the system between high precision and high recall. We can use models' precision-recall curves to visualization of trade-offs of high precision and high recall and pick potential models that could be clinically useful by defining two regions in the graph: one region for a triage model and the other for a prioritize model (see Figure 2).

We defined three potential model use cases and their evaluation criteria: 1) triage, 2) prioritize, or 3) combination. Most machine learning models for binary classification output a real number between 0 and 1 and use 0.5 as the default threshold for classification. While in most scenarios this threshold is sufficient, in our case it is helpful to examine the model performance with a range of thresholds which might be better suited for different scenarios (e.g., triaging or prioritizing messages).

Below we define the evaluations for these regions (§5.2 & 5.1) and their combination (§5.3).

5.1 Triage

An ideal triage model is aimed at reducing the number of messages that the healthcare staff need to read by ruling out messages that do not indicate urgency. A triage model needs to be able to reduce message volume enough to justify its implementation costs (e.g., debugging or training nurses to use the system) while also ensuring a minimal number of false negatives. Within the Mobile WACh studies, we choose the threshold of 30%. This means that the model should assign non-urgent (negative) to at least 30% of the messages while maintaining near-perfect recall. Knowing the number of samples in the dataset and the number of actual positive labels, we can get the relationship between precision and recall:

$$precision_{triage} \geq \frac{recall_{triage} \cdot actualpositives}{datasize \cdot 70\%}$$

We can take a high value for recall$_{triage}$ (95% in our case) and calculate a threshold for precision$_{triage}$. This creates a region in the precision-recall graph that a triage model's

Table 4: Performance of bigram and mBERT models with varying context. Bolded text indicates best-performing model in terms of F1.

Model	Pre Data	Pre Context	FT Context	Precision	Recall	F1
Bigrams	-	-	none	51	20	29
Bigrams	-	-	system	58	29	39
Bigrams	-	-	nurse	59	29	39
mBERT	-	-	none	46	34	39
mBERT	-	-	system	50	27	35
mBERT	-	-	nurse	52	38	44
mBERT	labelled	system	system	50	32	39
mBERT	**labelled**	**nurse**	**nurse**	**50**	**45**	**47**
mBERT	unlabelled	system	system	49	39	44
mBERT	unlabelled	nurse	nurse	48	38	42

precision-recall curve crosses (Figure 2).

5.2 Prioritize

An ideal prioritize model should identify urgent messages that should be replied to more quickly than other messages. This approach is helpful when the healthcare staff need guidance on which messages to read first. Since all the messages will eventually be reviewed, the focus is not on reducing false negatives, but false positives, since this will determine the trust of the healthcare staff in the system. This model should have a high precision and maintain a significant number of positive cases. We decide on a threshold of 10% here. This means the model should predict a message as urgent at least 10% of the time while maintaining a near-perfect precision. Similar to the triage region, we can calculate the relationship between precision and recall for a prioritize model:

$$recall_{prioritize} \geq \frac{precision_{prioritize} \cdot datasize \cdot 10\%}{actualpositives}$$

We can take a high precision$_{prioritize}$ (95% in our case) and calculate a threshold for recall$_{prioritize}$. This creates a region on the graph that a prioritize model's precision-recall curve crosses (Figure 2).

5.3 Combination

A combination model is one that is able to meet the targets of both triage and prioritize models. The model should have a high F1 score. When a model's precision-recall curve cuts across the overlapping region between the triage and prioritize regions, the model is a combination model.

6 Results

Table 4 summarizes the performance of our models. The best performing bigram model used participant messages with nurse context, outperforming the bigram model with system context by one precision point. The mBERT model using nurse context achieved an F1 score of 44, with 52 precision and 38 recall. While the precision is worse than the bigram model, the recall is higher by 8 points. The models incorporating nurse context messages performed better than system context. The effect of incorporating context on the performance of mBERT models is summarized in Table 5.

Table 5: Effect on mBERT model performance of prepending messages with context and additional pretraining. Pretraining here refers to pretraining on the labelled data with matched context (i.e., System + pretraining is pretraining on participant messages prepended with system messages, using labeled data only). Baseline model was with no pretraining and no context added to the messages.

Metric	Baseline	System	Nurse	Nurse + pretraining	System + pretraining
Precision	46	50 (+4)	52 (+6)	50 (+4)	50 (+4)
Recall	34	27 (-7)	38 (+4)	45 (+11)	32 (-2)
F1	39	35 (-4)	44 (+5)	47 (+8)	39 (+0)

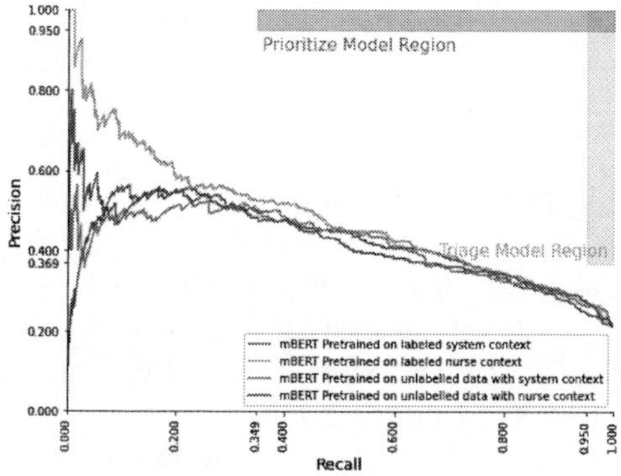

Figure 2: Performance of mBERT models with additional pre-training on varying data type

6.1 Additional Pretraining

Recall improved when the models were pretrained with nurse context messages. For system context models, only pretraining with unlabelled data increased recall. Table 5 details these results. The highest performing model was mBERT with nurse pretraining on labelled data. Figure 2 presents precision-recall curves for the above pretrained models. We found that the model pretrained and finetuned on labelled nurse context messages was the best model overall, though it did not pass into either the prioritize or triage region.

7 Related Work

NLP techniques for information extraction have been used in several SMS based mHealth applications. For example, Gupta et al. (2020) developed a virtual assistant health coach using text messages in English to help patients set physical activity goals. Lowres et al. (2020) developed NLP models to triage incoming English SMS text messages to reduce the burden of healthcare worker review. Fewer studies have applied these methods to low-resource languages and multilingual datasets. The MomConnect program from South Africa's National Department of Health is one such application where Engelhard et al. (2018) used multilingual data from the project to perform a feasibility study on triaging incoming messages of pregnant clients. Using data from the same program, Daniel et al. (2019) created an automated multilingual digital helpdesk service. Daniel et al. (2019) reported the challenges of this dataset as being multilingual, in low-resource languages, and with high prevalence of code-switching, spelling errors and abbreviations. Like the MomConnect data, Mobile WACh messages are in multiple low-resource languages, with code-switching, misspellings and abbreviations.

8 Discussion & Conclusion

Consistent with prior literature (Gururangan et al., 2020), our results showed that performing additional pretraining boosts performance. Our evaluations show that our modeling approaches have the potential to support healthcare workers in a unique low-resource and multilingual setting, though more work must be done to have the models achieve clinical usefulness based on our measures. Moving forward, to improve performance of these models, future studies could look into how to optimize the models when the dataset is skewed for non-urgent messages (as is the case currently). Another approach would be to explore models explicitly trained on the languages in our dataset, for example, models trained on Swahili datasets or code-switched languages from East Africa (Ogueji et al., 2021) and (flax community). We also plan to validate our highest-performing models with healthcare workers and implement a model in a pilot context similar to the Mobile WACh SMS system.

9 Ethical Considerations

The context of this study requires careful attention to preserving patient anonymity and the potential for unforeseen consequences. The Mobile WACh NEO pilot and RCT studies were approved by our institution's ethics and review board. All participants provided written informed consent for participation in the studies, including participation in the SMS intervention and use of data for secondary analyses. All patient data were made anonymous for our analyses. Because of the sensitive nature of the messages, the dataset will not be made publicly available, though researchers are welcome to contact the Mobile WACh study for anonymized data.

Deploying any system for triaging or prioritizing patient messages also must be piloted in real-world settings. While our analyses suggest that such systems are possible, ensuring that patient messages are not mislabeled is paramount. A single urgent message mislabelled could be catastrophic for a patient. Our evaluations aim to capture such considerations, but additional safegaurds are necessary. For example, all messages should be reviewed by nurses within a day regardless of model predictions, or patients should have a way of overriding model predictions if they have an urgent issue. We are excited to pilot models in real-world settings to see how they can support mobile health interventions.

References

Tim Althoff, Kevin Clark, and Jure Leskovec. 2016. Large-scale analysis of counseling conversations: An application of natural language processing to mental health. *Transactions of the Association for Computational Linguistics*, 4:463–476.

Peter Barron, Joanne Peter, Amnesty E. LeFevre, Jane Sebidi, Marcha Bekker, Robert Allen, Annie Neo Parsons, Peter Benjamin, and Yogan Pillay. 2017. Mobile health messaging service and helpdesk for south african mothers (momconnect): history, successes and challenges. *BMJ Glob Health*.

Mokaya Bosire. 2006. Hybrid languages: The case of sheng.

J. E. Daniel, Willie Brink, Ryan Eloff, and Charles Copley. 2019. Towards automating healthcare question answering in a noisy multilingual low-resource setting. In *ACL*.

Jacob Devlin, Ming-Wei Chang, Kenton Lee, and Kristina Toutanova. 2019. BERT: Pre-training of deep bidirectional transformers for language understanding. In *Proceedings of the 2019 Conference of the North American Chapter of the Association for Computational Linguistics: Human Language Technologies, Volume 1 (Long and Short Papers)*, pages

4171–4186, Minneapolis, Minnesota. Association for Computational Linguistics.

Matt Engelhard, Charles Copley, Jacqui Watson, Yogan Pillay, Peter Barron, and Amnesty E Lefevre. 2018. Optimising mhealth helpdesk responsiveness in south africa: towards automated message triage. *BMJ Global Health*, 3.

flax community. Gpt2 swahili.

Itika Gupta, Barbara Maria Di Eugenio, Brian D. Ziebart, Aiswarya Baiju, Bing Liu, Ben S. Gerber, Lisa Kay Sharp, Nadia Nabulsi, and Mary H. Smart. 2020. Human-human health coaching via text messages: Corpus, annotation, and analysis. In *SIGDIAL*.

Suchin Gururangan, Ana Marasović, Swabha Swayamdipta, Kyle Lo, Iz Beltagy, Doug Downey, and Noah A. Smith. 2020. Don't stop pretraining: Adapt language models to domains and tasks. In *Proceedings of the 58th Annual Meeting of the Association for Computational Linguistics*, pages 8342–8360, Online. Association for Computational Linguistics.

Amanda K. Hall, Heather J. Cole-Lewis, and Jay M. Bernhardt. 2015. Mobile text messaging for health: a systematic review of reviews. *Annual review of public health*, 36:393–415.

Elizabeth K. Harrington, Alison L. Drake, Daniel Matemo, Keshet Ronen, Alfred Osoti, Grace C John-Stewart, John Kinuthia, and Jennifer A. Unger. 2019. An mhealth sms intervention on postpartum contraceptive use among women and couples in kenya: A randomized controlled trial. *American Journal of Public Health*, 109:934–941.

huggingface.co. multilingual bert training arguments.

John Kinuthia, Keshet Ronen, Jennifer A. Unger, Wenwen Jiang, Daniel Matemo, Trevor Perrier, Lusi Osborn, Bhavna H Chohan, Alison L. Drake, Barbra A. Richardson, and Grace C John-Stewart. 2021. Sms messaging to improve retention and viral suppression in prevention of mother-to-child hiv transmission (pmtct) programs in kenya: A 3-arm randomized clinical trial. *PLoS Medicine*, 18.

Harry Klimis, Joel Nothman, Di Lu, Chao Sun, N Wah Cheung, Julie Redfern, Aravinda Thiagalingam, and Clara K Chow. 2021. Text message analysis using machine learning to assess predictors of engagement with mobile health chronic disease prevention programs: Content analysis. *JMIR Mhealth Uhealth*, 9(11):e27779.

David E. Losada, Fabio Crestani, and Javier Parapar. 2020. Overview of erisk 2020: Early risk prediction on the internet. In *Experimental IR Meets Multilinguality, Multimodality, and Interaction*, pages 272–287, Cham. Springer International Publishing.

Nicole Lowres, Andrew Duckworth, Julie Redfern, Aravinda Thiagalingam, and Clara K. Chow. 2020. Use of a machine learning program to correctly triage incoming text messaging replies from a cardiovascular text–based secondary prevention program: Feasibility study. *JMIR mHealth and uHealth*, 8.

Ishani Mondal, Kalika Bali, Mohit Jain, Monojit Choudhury, Ashish Sharma, Evans Gitau, Jacki O'Neill, Kagonya Awori, and Sarah Njeri Gitau. 2021. A linguistic annotation framework to study interactions in multilingual healthcare conversational forums. *Proceedings of The Joint 15th Linguistic Annotation Workshop (LAW) and 3rd Designing Meaning Representations (DMR) Workshop*.

Kelechi Ogueji, Yuxin Zhu, and Jimmy Lin. 2021. Small data? no problem! exploring the viability of pretrained multilingual language models for low-resourced languages. In *Proceedings of the 1st Workshop on Multilingual Representation Learning*, pages 116–126, Punta Cana, Dominican Republic. Association for Computational Linguistics.

F. Pedregosa, G. Varoquaux, A. Gramfort, V. Michel, B. Thirion, O. Grisel, M. Blondel, P. Prettenhofer, R. Weiss, V. Dubourg, J. Vanderplas, A. Passos, D. Cournapeau, M. Brucher, M. Perrot, and E. Duchesnay. 2011. Scikit-learn: Machine learning in Python. *Journal of Machine Learning Research*, 12:2825–2830.

T Perrier, N Dell, Brian DeRenzi, Anderson R, John Kinuthia, and Jennifer A. Unger. 2015. Engaging pregnant women in kenya with a hybrid computer-human sms communication system. proceedings of the 33rd annual acm conference on human factors in computing systems. *ACM Press*, CHI 15.

Keshet Ronen, Esther M Choo, Brenda Wandika, Jenna I Udren, Lusi Osborn, Peninah Kithao, Anna B Hedstrom, Millicent Masinde, Manasi Kumar, Dalton C. Wamalwa, Barbra A. Richardson, John Kinuthia, and Jennifer A. Unger. 2021. Evaluation of a two-way sms messaging strategy to reduce neonatal mortality: rationale, design and methods of the mobile wach neo randomised controlled trial in kenya. *BMJ Open*, 11.

Hillary Rono, Andrew Bastawrous, David Macleod, Ronald Mamboleo, Cosmas Bunywera, Emmanuel Wanjala, Stephen Gichuhi, and Matthew J. Burton. 2021. Effectiveness of an mhealth system on access to eye health services in kenya: a cluster-randomised controlled trial. *The Lancet. Digital Health*, 3:e414 – e424.

Laura Marie Schwab-Reese, Nitya Kanuri, and Scottye J. Cash. 2019. Child maltreatment disclosure to a text messaging–based crisis service: Content analysis. *JMIR mHealth and uHealth*, 7.

J Unger, Keshet Ronen, Trevor Perrier, Brian DeRenzi, Jennifer A. Slyker, AL Drake, Danstan O Mogaka, John Kinuthia, and Gc. John-Stewart. 2018. Short message service communication improves exclusive breastfeeding and early postpartum contraception in a low- to middle-income country setting: a randomised trial. *BJOG: An International Journal of Obstetrics & Gynaecology*, 125:1620 – 1629.

Jennifer Unger, Brenda Wandika, Keshet Ronen, Claire Rothschild, Jay Shih, Dalton Wamalwa, Wangui Muthigani, Maneesh Batra, John kinuthia, and Grace John-Stewart. 2019. Mobile wach neo: Engagement of pregnant and postpartum women with a two-way sms service to improve neonatal outcomes.

Justine Zhang and Cristian Danescu-Niculescu-Mizil. 2020. Balancing objectives in counseling conversations: Advancing forwards or looking backwards. In *Proceedings of ACL*.

Language over Labels: Contrastive Language Supervision Exceeds Purely Label-Supervised Classification Performance on Chest X-Rays

Anton Orell Wiehe[1,2], **Florian Schneider**[1], **Sebastian Blank**[2], **Xintong Wang**[1]
Hans-Peter Zorn[2], **Chris Biemann**[1]
[1]Universität Hamburg, 20146 Hamburg, Germany
[2]inovex GmbH, 75179 Pforzheim, Germany
antonwiehe@gmail.com
{florian.schneider,xintong.wang,christian.biemann}@uni-hamburg.de
{sebastian.blank,hzorn}@inovex.de

Abstract

The multi-modal foundation model CLIP computes representations from texts and images that achieved unprecedented performance on tasks such as zero-shot image classification. However, CLIP was pretrained on public internet data. Thus it lacks highly domain-specific knowledge. We investigate the adaptation of CLIP-based models to the chest radiography domain using the MIMIC-CXR dataset. We show that the features of the pretrained CLIP models do not transfer to this domain. We adapt CLIP to the chest radiography domain using contrastive language supervision and show that this approach yields a model that outperforms supervised learning on labels on the MIMIC-CXR dataset while also generalizing to the CheXpert and RSNA Pneumonia datasets. Furthermore, we do a detailed ablation study of the batch and dataset size. Finally, we show that language supervision allows for better explainability by using the multi-modal model to generate images from texts such that experts can inspect what the model has learned.

1 Introduction

Multi-modal models that understand text and images, as well as the relations between them, surged in performance due to the pioneering work of CLIP (Radford et al., 2021). Through a contrastive loss based on language supervision, the model embeds matching text-image pairs closely in latent space. This enables various applications, such as image classification (Radford et al., 2021), object detection (Alex Shonenkov, 2021), semantic segmentation, (Zhou et al., 2021; Rao et al., 2021), and text-to-image generation (Crowson et al., 2022).

As the CLIP models were trained on data scraped from the internet, they work remarkably well for data of the general domain and excel at tasks such as food (Bossard et al., 2014), car brand (Krause et al., 2013), or animal classification (Parkhi et al., 2012). However, for more specialized tasks such as satellite image (Helber et al., 2019, 2018) and cancer cell classification (Veeling et al., 2018), they do not perform much better than a random guess (Radford et al., 2021). To make these models work for these tasks, they require adaptation to the specific domain.

In this paper, we study the adaptation of CLIP models to the domain of chest x-ray images of the MIMIC-CXR (Johnson et al., 2019b; Goldberger et al., 2000; Johnson et al., 2019a,c) dataset. We show that the CLIP model pretrained on data scraped from the internet (Radford et al., 2021) does not transfer well to MIMIC-CXR. Furthermore, two approaches to adapting the model are compared: contrastive language supervision (CLS) and supervised fine-tuning (FT) on labels. We show that CLS combined with linear probing performs better than only using FT on labels. Furthermore, we show that the same language-supervised model can be used to achieve good performance with only a linear probe on other chest radiograph datasets without retraining.

Our first ablation study investigates the batch size, as the massive batch size of 32,768 used for the original CLIP training would impose an obstacle for any CLS fine-tuning. We show that a small batch size is sufficient to achieve good CLS performance. We also find that a batch size that is too large hurts performance, contrary to the findings of prior work (Chen et al., 2020; Grill et al., 2020; Radford et al., 2021).

Next to the large batch size, CLIP also used a large dataset of over 400 million image-text pairs. In a second ablation study, we investigate whether CLS needs a large dataset size to outperform supervised learning. We show that CLS can be superior to FT even with only 20,000 image-text pairs (10% of the MIMIC-CXR dataset).

In the last experiment, we display how to get

Proceedings of the AACL-IJCNLP 2022 Student Research Workshop, pages 76–83
November 20, 2022. ©2022 Association for Computational Linguistics

more interpretable neural network classifiers. The language-supervised model can compare the similarity of the features of a text and an image. Through the gradient of the similarity towards the image, an image can be generated purely from a text. This generation allows clinicians and machine learning scientists to visualize model representations. This approach, inspired by CLIP-based text-to-image approaches such as VQGAN-CLIP (Crowson et al., 2022) resembles the work of DeepDream (Mordvintsev et al., 2015). Instead of visualizing classes or neuron activations, it visualizes texts.

2 Related Work

In a closely related work named ConVirt, (Zhang et al., 2020) train a model using CLS on the image-text pairs of the MIMIC-CXR dataset and compare it to supervised learning on the labels. Their pioneering work partially inspired the creation of CLIP (Radford et al., 2021). Our work is complementary to their work by using the widely adapted architecture and simplified loss function of CLIP, evaluating the performance of the OpenAI-pretrained CLIP model on MIMIC-CXR, running ablation studies on the batch size and dataset size, and introducing the text-to-image visualization of diagnoses.

In CLIP-art (Conde and Turgutlu, 2021), CLIP was fine-tuned using CLS on a large dataset of museum artworks with descriptions. The features of the fine-tuned CLIP model do not lead to a significantly better classification performance than the features of the base CLIP model. More related to the approach of this paper is PubMedCLIP (Eslami et al., 2021). The authors fine-tune CLIP using the CLS objective on image-text pairs from medical papers. They show that the pretrained CLIP features improve visual question-answering performance over the current state-of-the-art baseline. The continued pretraining using CLS only slightly improves the performance over the base CLIP model.

A current preprint follows a similar approach as our paper. (Seibold et al., 2022) compare the zero-shot performance of a model trained using CLS-like loss functions to the performance of supervision on labels. Their work confirms the benefits of training using language supervision over labels. However, their work focuses on selecting training data and loss functions. In contrast, our work analyzes batch sizes, dataset sizes, and an explainability approach.

3 Background

This work investigates the effect of pretraining using CLS on text-image pairs before FT on labels. We are given a set of images S, corresponding texts T, and labels Y. For both the CLS and FT stages, a network (in this case, a Transformer (Vaswani et al., 2017) network from Radford et al., 2021) first transforms its input into an encoding, leading to the encodings e_{text} and e_{image}. In the CLS stage these encodings are improved by training the weights of both transformers using a contrastive loss, whereas the FT stage only uses the vision transformer and its encoding, followed by a linear layer. An overview of the two stages is given in Figure 1.

For FT, a prediction $\hat{y}_{ni}$ of the target label $n \in Y$ for image $s_i \in S$ is made by a network f: $f(s_i) = y_{ni}$. The binary cross entropy loss L_{BCE} is calculated per label y_n and then averaged over all N labels to get the supervised loss L_{SL}, as was done in previous work in multi-label settings (Liu et al., 2021; Nam et al., 2014).

The BCE loss L_{BCE} of label n is calculated using the ground truth y_{ni} and the prediction y_{ni} for sample i. It assigns a loss that is high initially and drops off logarithmically as the prediction approaches the ground truth:

$$\begin{aligned} L_{BCE_n}(y_{ni}, \hat{y}_{ni}) = \\ -1(y_{ni} \log(\hat{y}_{ni}) + (1 - y_{ni}) \log(1 - \hat{y}_{ni})) \end{aligned} \quad (1)$$

The pretraining stage of CLS utilizes text and image representations e_{text} and e_{image} computed by the text and image encoders of CLIP, respectively. During the later FT stage, the linear probe is trained based on the image encoding e_{image}, and the full fine-tuning also tunes the weights of the image encoder. During pretraining, a batch of size K image-text pairs is sampled and encoded. The loss is calculated by using every encoding of both modalities once as the anchor sample x_i. The matching positive sample x_i^+ is the paired encoded sample of the other modality and all other encodings from the other modality of the sampled batch are the negative samples X^-. For each anchor sample, the InfoNCE loss (Oord et al., 2018) is calculated with

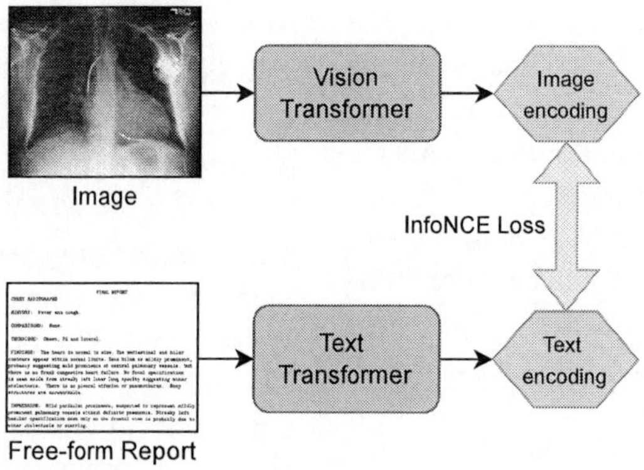

(a) Contrastive Language Supervision Stage (CLS)

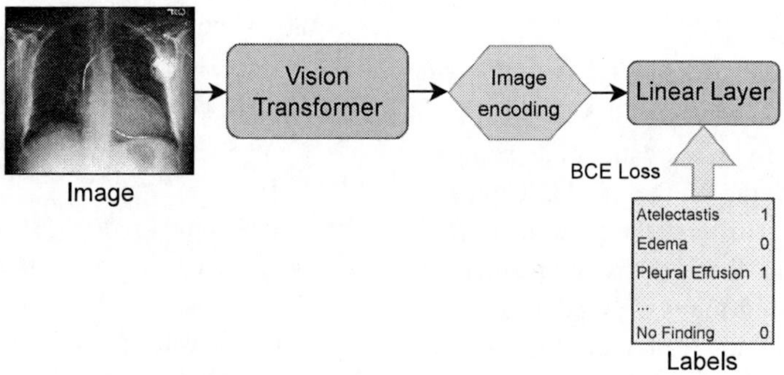

(b) Supervised Fine-tuning Stage (FT)

Figure 1: Loss calculation flowcharts for the different training stages. The Contrastive Language Supervision (CLS) stage is always followed by the Supervised Fine-tuning Stage (FT) to adapt the model to predict the labels. The FT stage either trains only a new linear layer head (linear probe via a logistic regression) or it also trains the weights of the vision transformer. Red rectangles are networks with trainable weights, green shadings indicate encodings, and yellow arrows indicate the gradient flow.

a similarity function $\text{sim}(x, y)$:

$$L_{\text{InfoNCE}}(x_i, x_i^+, X^-) = -\log \frac{\exp(\text{sim}(x_i, x_i^+))}{\sum_{j=0}^{K} \exp(\text{sim}(x_i, x_j^-))} \quad (2)$$

The total InfoNCE loss is the average of all individual losses of the samples from the batch. We use the cosine similarity as a similarity function, as in the original CLIP paper.

4 Methods

The code for training and evaluating is available online [1]. All models were evaluated using the macro average of the area under the receiver-operator curve (ROC-AUC or AUC) (Bradley, 1997) averaged over all labels of the dataset. This metric was used to enable a comparison with prior work. For a clinical evaluation, the sensitivity and specificity should be studied in more detail.

[1]https://github.com/NotNANtoN/master_thesis

4.1 MIMIC-CXR dataset

The MIMIC-CXR dataset contains 227,827 studies of chest radiographs with a written report by expert radiologists. There are one or multiple radiography images present for each study, leading to 377,095 total image-text pairs. The labels were extracted by the automatic labeler from the CheXpert dataset (Irvin et al., 2019). For each report, 14 diagnoses can appear individually and in conjunction. The official validation and test splits were used. No images were excluded. Examples for images and extracts of reports can be seen in Figure 2.

We marked all labels which are either not contained in a report or contained with an uncertainty quantifier as negative. All others were marked as positive. The report text was cleaned for language

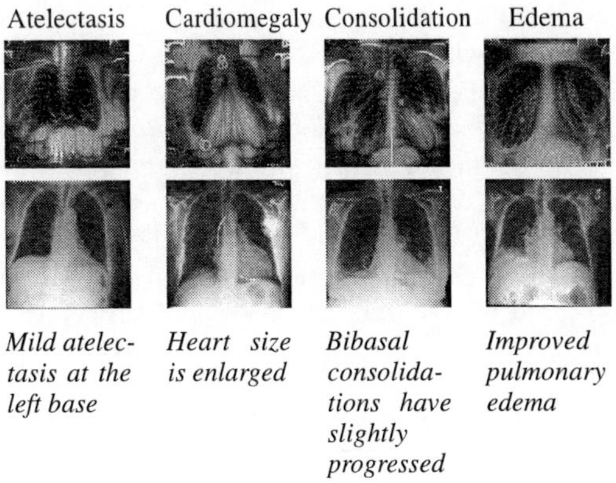

Figure 2: Text-to-image generations for a subset of four diagnoses: atelectasis, cardiomegaly, consolidation, and edema. The first row shows the generated images. The second row shows real radiography images of MIMIC-CXR with the sentence of the report relevant to the labeling of the diagnosis.

supervision by filtering repetitive headers, censored personal information, newlines, and other unnecessary characters. The images were resized such that the smaller side has a length of 256 pixels.

4.2 External Test Datasets

The RSNA Pneumonia (Wang et al., 2017; Shih et al., 2019) and cheXpert (Irvin et al., 2019) datasets were used to evaluate if the model pretrained on MIMIC-CXR generalizes to data from other hospitals with other labels. Linear probes were trained on the features of the pretrained models to predict the labels of the external datasets. The cheXpert dataset contains 223,648 images labeled with the same diagnoses as MIMIC-CXR. The official validation split was used as our test set. The RSNA dataset contains 30,227 images of which 9,555 are annotated with the pneumonia diagnosis, forming a single-class, single-label classification task. A random subset of 10% of the data was used as a test set, the rest was used for training.

4.3 Model training

In preliminary FT experiments, the CLIP models RN50, RN50x4, ViT-B/32, ViT-B/16, and ViT-L/14 were investigated. The ViT-B/32 model was chosen as it is the fastest model and as the performances of all models were nearly equal. The aim of this paper is not the best performance but rather a comparison of the training procedure.

The training setup follows the setup of the original CLIP paper (Radford et al., 2021), using Adam (Kingma and Ba, 2015) with a weight decay (Loshchilov and Hutter, 2019) of 0.2, β_1 value of 0.9, and β_2 value of 0.98 for training all models. A learning rate schedule with a linear warmup from zero to the maximum learning rate was used during the first 5% of training and a cosine decay schedule for the rest of the training. During training, the images were augmented by rotating them randomly by up to 45 degrees, shifting them randomly in the x and y-axis by up to 15% of the image length, and zooming into and out of the image by up to 10% of the image size.

All model runs used the pretrained weights from Radford et al., 2021. The FT models were trained for 10 epochs with a batch size of 256. The learning rates $\{1e{-}6, 3e{-}5, 1e{-}5, 3e{-}5, 1e{-}4\}$ were evaluated, of which $1e{-}5$ performed best on the validation set. The CLS model was trained for 10 epochs with a batch size of 196. The sentences of each report text were randomly shuffled during training to avoid always truncating the final part of the report if it is longer than 75 tokens (tokenized with the pretrained CLIP tokenizer). The learning rate for the CLS stage was tuned with the same set of learning rates as above. The best learning rate for a linear probe on the validation set was again $1e{-}5$. After the CLS stage, the model was continued to be trained on the labels with either a linear probe using logistic regression or with the FT setup from above.

4.4 Ablation Studies

The first ablation study varied the batch size while keeping other parameters constant. It measures the impact of the number of negative samples in CLS, which is dependent on the batch size. We varied the batch size from 6 to 1,536. The maximum batch size for a single GPU with 12 GB of VRAM is 192. Training runs with batch sizes below 192 accumulate the gradients for as many steps to match the number of update steps done with a batch size of 192. To accommodate the reduction in update steps due to the increased batch size, we tested scaling the learning rate linearly proportional to the batch size and compared it to keeping the learning rate constant.

The second ablation study varied the dataset size to a minimum of 1% to understand whether CLS is performant on smaller datasets. We trained once for 10 and 50 epochs for each dataset size. Training for more epochs increases the training duration. Therefore it balances the effect of having fewer batches in an epoch for smaller dataset sizes. The learning rate and other hyperparameters stayed unchanged.

4.5 Text-to-Image Generation

In the text-to-image generation approach, a language-supervised model was used after only 3 epochs of training to avoid any overfitting. To generate an image from a text, first, the text of a diagnosis is encoded into a text feature vector. The image is randomly initialized as a single-channel tensor of size 224x224, randomly sampled from a normal distribution with a mean of 0.5 and a standard deviation of 0.25. The gradient of the cosine similarity between the image's features and the diagnosis's features towards the image is applied repeatedly to the image to iteratively increase the similarity to the text. Optimization was done with Adam (Kingma and Ba, 2015) with a learning rate of 0.03 and a weight decay (Loshchilov and Hutter, 2019) of 0.1.

Directly optimizing the pixels without any regularization creates adversarial examples (Crowson et al., 2022). The generated image is augmented before encoding it with CLIP to avoid this . We use the augmentation pipeline proposed by (Crowson et al., 2022).

Multiple images of different resolutions overlaying each other are optimized simultaneously to increase image quality. Images of pixel sizes [224, 112, 61, 30, 15] are randomly initialized and optimised. During the iterative generation process, the images are resized to 224x224 pixels and then averaged. The images of smaller resolutions learn general shapes, and the higher resolution ones focus on the details. The average of all resized images forms the generated image. The augmentations are applied to this image. The loss to be optimized is the cosine similarity between the features of this image and the features of the target text.

5 Results

5.1 Language Supervision Compared to Supervised Learning

The results of the comparison between FT and CLS are shown in Table 1. The CLIP ViT-B/32 model performs worst when using randomly initialized weights with a linear probe. The improvement when using pretrained weights is only marginal, showing that the features of the general CLIP model do not transfer to the chest radiographs of MIMIC-CXR. Training the model using FT increases the AUC significantly from 0.66 to 0.77. CLS beats this score by a slight margin. CLS with only a linear probe is competitive with and slightly superior to pure FT.

The comparison with the results of prior work shows that similar performance has been reached for all datasets. For both external datasets, CLS with a linear probe reaches competitive performance, which displays the generality of the learned features.

Table 1: Table comparing the results of CLS and SL, set into context with prior work. CLS stands for contrastive language supervision, FT for supervised fine-tuning, ZS for zero-shot, and LP for linear probe. *Rand.* indicates that the weights of the network were randomly initialized - in all other cases the pretrained weights from Radford et al., 2021 are used. *AUC* stands for the macro ROC-AUC, averaged over all labels and multiplied by 100 for legibility. *Ours* stands for the CLIP ViT-B/32 model.

(a) MIMIC-CXR (Johnson et al., 2019c)

Model	Type	AUC
Nunes et al., 2019	FT	65.6
Seibold et al., 2022	ZS	79.4
Ours	Rand. + LP	66.5
Ours	LP	66.7
Ours	FT	77.2
Ours	CLS + LP	77.8
Ours	CLS + FT	77.3

(b) CheXpert (Irvin et al., 2019)

Model	Type	AUC
Seibold et al., 2022	ZS	78.9
Zhang et al., 2020	CLS + LP	87.3
Zhang et al., 2020	CLS + FT	88.1
Azizi et al., 2021	FT	77.0
Ours	CLS + LP	87.2

(c) RSNA (Wang et al., 2017; Shih et al., 2019)

Model	Type	AUC
Zhang et al., 2020	CLS + LP	92.1
Zhang et al., 2020	CLS + LP	92.7
Han et al., 2021	FT	92.3
Ours	CLS + LP	90.7

5.2 Batch Size Ablation

The results of the batch size ablation experiment can be seen in Figure 3. For smaller batch sizes, the performance drops but stays above 0.75. Notably, the best batch size is 576. The AUC drops for larger

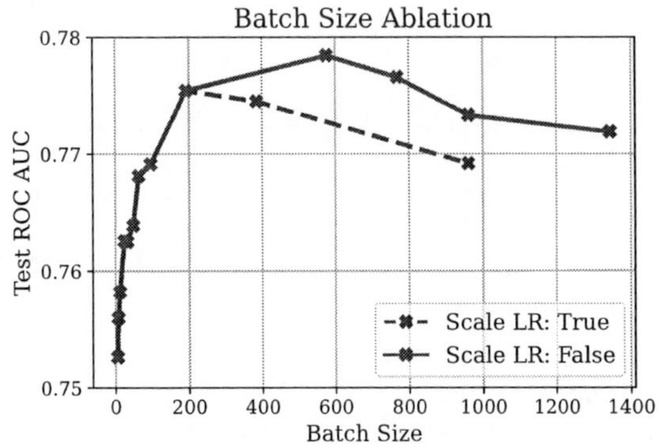

Figure 3: The batch size plotted against the test ROC AUC score. The batch size is varied to investigate whether a larger pool of negative samples is necessary for CLS. The optimal batch size peaks at 576. *Scale LR* indicates whether the learning rate is scaled linearly with the batch size for batch sizes beyond 196.

batch sizes independent of the learning rate scaling method. This drop demonstrates an upper limit of the optimal batch size for our model and dataset.

5.3 Dataset Size Ablation

The results of the dataset size ablation study in Figure 4 show that the main results hold at varying dataset sizes. Pretraining using CLS on the whole dataset, followed by fine-tuning on a fraction of the labels consistently performs best. CLS with a linear probe outperforms FT for all dataset sizes greater or equal than 10% (around 20,000 image-text pairs) when trained for 50 epochs. With only 10% of the dataset, CLS nearly matches the performance of applying it to the full dataset. The difference between the performance of the 10 and 50 epoch runs is large for the CLS runs that use at least 10% of the dataset size and small lower dataset sizes. This discrepancy could indicate that a critical dataset size of around 10% of the total dataset size exists that CLS requires to learn good representations.

5.4 Explainability via Text-to-image Generation

The interpretability results are shown in the top row of Figure 2. Qualitatively, one can observe that the generated images display a lung and a heart. They also greatly differ depending on which text they are conditioned on. We consulted two radiologists from a local clinic who both were able to assign 2 out of 4 diagnoses correctly to the generated images. These qualitative analyses open the door

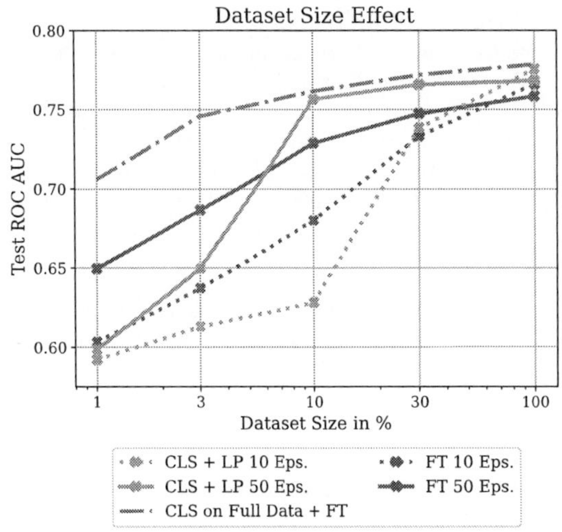

Figure 4: The dataset size plotted against the test ROC AUC score for FT and CLS. *FT* stands for supervised fine-tuning, *CLS* for contrastive language supervision. *CLS + FT* is the two-stage approach of first applying CLS to text-image pairs, followed by full fine-tuning via labels. *CLS + LP* is CLS followed by a linear probe. The *CLS on Full Data + FT* approach uses all data for CLS and a reduced dataset size for FT.

for further empirical studies.

6 Conclusion

We show that CLS with a simple linear probe outperforms FT on the MIMIC-CXR dataset, even when using small batch sizes on a single GPU. Models trained using CLS generalize to datasets of the same domain. CLS outperforms FT for all dataset sizes down to 20,000 image-text pairs.

The optimal batch size in our experiments was 576. Furthermore, CLS stopped being performant when using fewer than 20,000 training pairs. Future work could investigate how the optimum batch size changes depending on the dataset size and if this critical dataset size is replicable for other datasets.

Acknowledgments

This research was partially funded by the German Research Foundation – "DFG Transregio SFB 169: Crossmodal Learning" and by inovex GmbH.

References

Denis Karachev Alex Shonenkov, Sergey Shtekhin. 2021. CLIP ODS: CLIP object detection & segmentation. `https://github.com/shonenkov/CLIP-ODS`.

Shekoofeh Azizi, Basil Mustafa, Fiona Ryan, Zachary Beaver, Jan Freyberg, Jonathan Deaton, Aaron Loh, Alan Karthikesalingam, Simon Kornblith, Ting Chen, Vivek Natarajan, and Mohammad Norouzi. 2021. Big self-supervised models advance medical image classification. In *2021 IEEE/CVF International Conference on Computer Vision, ICCV 2021, Montreal, QC, Canada, October 10-17, 2021*, pages 3458–3468. IEEE.

Lukas Bossard, Matthieu Guillaumin, and Luc Van Gool. 2014. Food-101 - mining discriminative components with random forests. In *Computer Vision - ECCV 2014 - 13th European Conference, Zurich, Switzerland, September 6-12, 2014, Proceedings, Part VI*, volume 8694 of *Lecture Notes in Computer Science*, pages 446–461. Springer.

Andrew P. Bradley. 1997. The use of the area under the ROC curve in the evaluation of machine learning algorithms. *Pattern Recognit.*, 30(7):1145–1159.

Ting Chen, Simon Kornblith, Mohammad Norouzi, and Geoffrey E. Hinton. 2020. A simple framework for contrastive learning of visual representations. In *Proceedings of the 37th International Conference on Machine Learning, ICML 2020, 13-18 July 2020, Virtual Event*, volume 119 of *Proceedings of Machine Learning Research*, pages 1597–1607. PMLR.

Marcos V. Conde and Kerem Turgutlu. 2021. Clip-art: Contrastive pre-training for fine-grained art classification. In *IEEE Conference on Computer Vision and Pattern Recognition Workshops, CVPR Workshops 2021, virtual, June 19-25, 2021*, pages 3956–3960. Computer Vision Foundation / IEEE.

Katherine Crowson, Stella Biderman, Daniel Kornis, Dashiell Stander, Eric Hallahan, Louis Castricato, and Edward Raff. 2022. VQGAN-CLIP: Open domain image generation and editing with natural language guidance. *arXiv preprint arXiv:2204.08583*.

Sedigheh Eslami, Gerard de Melo, and Christoph Meinel. 2021. Does CLIP benefit visual question answering in the medical domain as much as it does in the general domain? *arXiv preprint arXiv:2112.13906*.

Ary L. Goldberger, Luis A. Nunes Amaral, L Glass, Jeffrey M. Hausdorff, Plamen Ch. Ivanov, Roger G. Mark, Joseph E. Mietus, George B. Moody, Chung-Kang Peng, and Harry Eugene Stanley. 2000. PhysioBank, PhysioToolkit, and PhysioNet: components of a new research resource for complex physiologic signals. *Circulation*, 101 23:E215–20.

Jean-Bastien Grill, Florian Strub, Florent Altché, Corentin Tallec, Pierre H. Richemond, Elena Buchatskaya, Carl Doersch, Bernardo Ávila Pires, Zhaohan Guo, Mohammad Gheshlaghi Azar, Bilal Piot, Koray Kavukcuoglu, Rémi Munos, and Michal Valko. 2020. Bootstrap your own latent - A new approach to self-supervised learning. In *Advances in Neural Information Processing Systems 33: Annual Conference on Neural Information Processing Systems 2020, NeurIPS 2020, December 6-12, 2020, virtual.*

Yan Han, Chongyan Chen, Ahmed H. Tewfik, Ying Ding, and Yifan Peng. 2021. Pneumonia detection on chest x-ray using radiomic features and contrastive learning. In *18th IEEE International Symposium on Biomedical Imaging, ISBI 2021, Nice, France, April 13-16, 2021*, pages 247–251. IEEE.

Patrick Helber, Benjamin Bischke, Andreas Dengel, and Damian Borth. 2018. Introducing eurosat: A novel dataset and deep learning benchmark for land use and land cover classification. In *2018 IEEE International Geoscience and Remote Sensing Symposium, IGARSS 2018, Valencia, Spain, July 22-27, 2018*, pages 204–207. IEEE.

Patrick Helber, Benjamin Bischke, Andreas Dengel, and Damian Borth. 2019. Eurosat: A novel dataset and deep learning benchmark for land use and land cover classification. *IEEE J. Sel. Top. Appl. Earth Obs. Remote. Sens.*, 12(7):2217–2226.

Jeremy Irvin, Pranav Rajpurkar, Michael Ko, Yifan Yu, Silviana Ciurea-Ilcus, Chris Chute, Henrik Marklund, Behzad Haghgoo, Robyn L. Ball, Katie S. Shpanskaya, Jayne Seekins, David A. Mong, Safwan S. Halabi, Jesse K. Sandberg, Ricky Jones, David B. Larson, Curtis P. Langlotz, Bhavik N. Patel, Matthew P. Lungren, and Andrew Y. Ng. 2019. Chexpert: A large chest radiograph dataset with uncertainty labels and expert comparison. In *The Thirty-Third AAAI Conference on Artificial Intelligence, AAAI 2019, The Thirty-First Innovative Applications of Artificial Intelligence Conference, IAAI 2019, The Ninth AAAI Symposium on Educational Advances in Artificial Intelligence, EAAI 2019, Honolulu, Hawaii, USA, January 27 - February 1, 2019*, pages 590–597. AAAI Press.

Alistair E. W. Johnson, Tom J. Pollard, Seth J. Berkowitz, Nathaniel R. Greenbaum, Matthew P. Lungren, Chih-ying Deng, Roger G. Mark, and Steven Horng. 2019a. MIMIC-CXR, a de-identified publicly available database of chest radiographs with free-text reports. *Scientific Data*, 6(1):317.

Alistair E. W. Johnson, Tom J. Pollard, Nathaniel R. Greenbaum, Matthew P. Lungren, Chih-ying Deng, Yifan Peng, Zhiyong Lu, Roger G. Mark, Seth J. Berkowitz, and Steven Horng. 2019b. MIMIC-CXR-JPG, a large publicly available database of labeled chest radiographs. *arXiv preprint arXiv:1901.07042*.

Alistair E. W. Johnson, Tom J. Pollard, Roger G. Mark, Seth J. Berkowitz, and Steven Horng. 2019c. MIMIC-CXR database (version 2.0.0). *PhysioNet*.

Diederik P. Kingma and Jimmy Ba. 2015. Adam: A method for stochastic optimization. *arXiv preprint arXiv:1412.6980*.

Jonathan Krause, Michael Stark, Jia Deng, and Li Fei-Fei. 2013. 3D object representations for fine-grained categorization. In *2013 IEEE International Conference on Computer Vision Workshops, ICCV Workshops 2013, Sydney, Australia, December 1-8, 2013*, pages 554–561. IEEE Computer Society.

Weiwei Liu, Haobo Wang, Xiaobo Shen, and Ivor Tsang. 2021. The emerging trends of multi-label learning. *IEEE transactions on pattern analysis and machine intelligence*.

Ilya Loshchilov and Frank Hutter. 2019. Decoupled weight decay regularization. In *7th International Conference on Learning Representations, ICLR 2019, New Orleans, LA, USA, May 6-9, 2019*. OpenReview.net.

A. Mordvintsev, Christopher Olah, and Mike Tyka. 2015. Inceptionism: Going deeper into neural networks. *Blog Article*.

Jinseok Nam, Jungi Kim, Eneldo Loza Mencía, Iryna Gurevych, and Johannes Fürnkranz. 2014. Large-scale multi-label text classification — revisiting neural networks. In *Machine Learning and Knowledge Discovery in Databases*, pages 437–452. Springer Berlin Heidelberg.

Nelson Nunes, Bruno Martins, Nuno André da Silva, Francisca Pais Leite, and Mário J. Silva. 2019. A multi-modal deep learning method for classifying chest radiology exams. In *Progress in Artificial Intelligence - 19th EPIA Conference on Artificial Intelligence, EPIA 2019, Vila Real, Portugal, September 3-6, 2019, Proceedings, Part I*, volume 11804 of *Lecture Notes in Computer Science*, pages 323–335. Springer.

Aaron van den Oord, Yazhe Li, and Oriol Vinyals. 2018. Representation learning with contrastive predictive coding. *arXiv preprint arXiv:1807.03748*.

Omkar M Parkhi, Andrea Vedaldi, Andrew Zisserman, and C. V. Jawahar. 2012. Cats and dogs. In *2012 IEEE Conference on Computer Vision and Pattern Recognition*, pages 3498–3505.

Alec Radford, Jong Wook Kim, Chris Hallacy, Aditya Ramesh, Gabriel Goh, Sandhini Agarwal, Girish Sastry, Amanda Askell, Pamela Mishkin, Jack Clark, Gretchen Krueger, and Ilya Sutskever. 2021. Learning transferable visual models from natural language supervision. In *Proceedings of the 38th International Conference on Machine Learning, ICML 2021, 18-24 July 2021, Virtual Event*, volume 139 of *Proceedings of Machine Learning Research*, pages 8748–8763. PMLR.

Yongming Rao, Wenliang Zhao, Guangyi Chen, Yansong Tang, Zheng Zhu, Guan Huang, Jie Zhou, and Jiwen Lu. 2021. DenseCLIP: Language-guided dense prediction with context-aware prompting. *arXiv preprint arXiv:2112.01518*.

Constantin Seibold, Simon Reiß, M. Saquib Sarfraz, Rainer Stiefelhagen, and Jens Kleesiek. 2022. Breaking with fixed set pathology recognition through report-guided contrastive training. *arXiv preprint arXiv:2205.07139*.

George Shih, Carol C. Wu, Safwan S. Halabi, Marc D. Kohli, Luciano M. Prevedello, Tessa S. Cook, Arjun Sharma, Judith K. Amorosa, Veronica Arteaga, Maya Galperin-Aizenberg, Ritu R. Gill, Myrna C.B. Godoy, Stephen Hobbs, Jean Jeudy, Archana Laroia, Palmi N. Shah, Dharshan Vummidi, Kavitha Yaddanapudi, and Anouk Stein. 2019. Augmenting the national institutes of health chest radiograph dataset with expert annotations of possible pneumonia. *Radiology: Artificial Intelligence*, 1(1):e180041. PMID: 33937785.

Ashish Vaswani, Noam Shazeer, Niki Parmar, Jakob Uszkoreit, Llion Jones, Aidan N Gomez, Łukasz Kaiser, and Illia Polosukhin. 2017. Attention is all you need. *Advances in neural information processing systems*, 30.

Bastiaan S. Veeling, Jasper Linmans, Jim Winkens, Taco Cohen, and Max Welling. 2018. Rotation equivariant cnns for digital pathology. In *Medical Image Computing and Computer Assisted Intervention - MICCAI 2018 - 21st International Conference, Granada, Spain, September 16-20, 2018, Proceedings, Part II*, volume 11071 of *Lecture Notes in Computer Science*, pages 210–218. Springer.

Xiaosong Wang, Yifan Peng, Le Lu, Zhiyong Lu, Mohammadhadi Bagheri, and Ronald M. Summers. 2017. Chestx-ray8: Hospital-scale chest x-ray database and benchmarks on weakly-supervised classification and localization of common thorax diseases. In *2017 IEEE Conference on Computer Vision and Pattern Recognition, CVPR 2017, Honolulu, HI, USA, July 21-26, 2017*, pages 3462–3471. IEEE Computer Society.

Yuhao Zhang, Hang Jiang, Yasuhide Miura, Christopher D. Manning, and Curtis P. Langlotz. 2020. Contrastive learning of medical visual representations from paired images and text. *arXiv preprint arXiv:2010.00747*.

Chong Zhou, Chen Change Loy, and Bo Dai. 2021. DenseCLIP: Extract free dense labels from CLIP. *arXiv preprint arXiv:2112.01071*.

Dynamic Topic Modeling by Clustering Embeddings from Pretrained Language Models: A Research Proposal

Anton Eklund
Umeå University
Adlede AB
Umeå, Sweden
anton.eklund@cs.umu.se

Mona Forsman
Adlede AB
Umeå, Sweden
mona.forsman@adlede.com

Frank Drewes
Umeå University
Umeå, Sweden
drewes@cs.umu.se

Abstract

A new trend in topic modeling research is to do Neural Topic Modeling by Clustering document Embeddings (NTM-CE) created with a pretrained language model. Studies have evaluated static NTM-CE models and found them performing comparably to, or even better than other topic models. An important extension of static topic modeling is making the models dynamic, allowing the study of topic evolution over time, as well as detecting emerging and disappearing topics. In this research proposal, we present two research questions to understand dynamic topic modeling with NTM-CE theoretically and practically. To answer these, we propose four phases with the aim of establishing evaluation methods for dynamic topic modeling, finding NTM-CE-specific properties, and creating a framework for dynamic NTM-CE. For evaluation, we propose to use both quantitative measurements of coherence and human evaluation supported by our recently developed tool.

1 Introduction

The ever-accelerating pace at which online documents, and specifically text documents, are published creates a need for methods able to analyze text documents in large quantities, something topic models were created to do. In this paper, the term *document* refers to a sequence of words in natural language, such as a tweet or a news article. The topic model analyzes a collection of documents to discover the major topics appearing in it. Then, each document is related to the discovered topics. Successful topic modeling applications cover a wide range of fields, such as studying historical documents (Newman and Block, 2006), discovering gender bias in datasets (Devinney et al., 2020), and catching new trends on social networks (Cataldi et al., 2010).

Topic models that do not consider the temporal dimension of a document collection are called *static* topic models. However, an important aspect missed by such models is the evolution of topics or different temporal contexts a document can be situated in. For example, a topic centered around diabetes will have a different discussion before and after the discovery of insulin, and the topics surrounding *Ukraine* have shifted rather dramatically during 2022. Models that consider the temporal dimension are called *dynamic* topic models (DTMs). This paper proposes an extensive study on how to efficiently create DTMs based on neural topic models.

Neural Topic Models (NTMs) are topic models that are created with the help of neural networks (Zhao et al., 2021). They became competitive with the advances in language modeling in the previous decade. An NTM with an incorporated pretrained language model (PLM) is called NTM-PLM. A pretrained language model, such as BERT (Devlin et al., 2019), is capable of embedding words or documents into a vector representation that reflects aspects of the meaning of the text and thus its relation to other texts. We define a document embedding to be a mapping of the document collection to a vector space in such a way that the vector representing a given document captures some sort of information about the document. The information should largely be obtained using the PLM, but can also blend with other information if there is extra input such as timestamps. Since each two embedding vectors are at a certain well-defined distance from each other in the vector space, the conceptually most straightforward approach to do topic modeling is to apply a distance-based clustering algorithm to the embeddings. In this paper, we call this procedure *Neural Topic Modeling by Clustering Embeddings (from pretrained language models)*, NTM-CE.

The distinction between our definition of NTM-CE and other models within the NTM-PLM sphere is how the topics are formed. For a model to be an

Proceedings of the AACL-IJCNLP 2022 Student Research Workshop, pages 84–91
November 20, 2022. ©2022 Association for Computational Linguistics

NTM-CE, the topics must be formed by applying a distance-based clustering algorithm to the embeddings that were created by the PLM. We define the core pipeline of NTM-CE as *vectorization* $\rightarrow$ *transformation* $\rightarrow$ *clustering*. The most common NTM-CE methods that we are aware of use a dimension reduction technique as a vector transformation before clustering. However, we also consider other transformations that could be applied to enhance the vector space to discover meaningful topics. Belonging to our definition of NTM-CE models are CETopic (Zhang et al., 2022) and BERTopic (Grootendorst, 2022), but not models such as *Embedding Topic Model* (ETM) (Dieng et al., 2020) or ZeroShotTM (Bianchi et al., 2021b) since the latter do not directly cluster the embeddings. NTM-CE models have shown promising performance (Sia et al., 2020; Thompson and Mimno, 2020; Zhang et al., 2022) when compared to classic generative methods such as *Latent Dirichlet Allocation* (LDA, Blei et al. (2003)).

Moreover, NTM-CE are gaining traction due to their conceptual simplicity and modularity. Early studies compare the topic coherence of NTM-CE with other established models to legitimize its use. However, an understudied part of these new topic models is their ability to do dynamic topic modeling. Having a conceptually simple DTM which improves with advancements in language modeling is attractive for many research communities and industries whose data tends to end up consisting of large unstructured sets of documents collected over time. Dynamic topic modeling may, for instance, enable a company to discover and react to trends before they become mainstream.

An important aspect of research on DTMs is how to evaluate such models. For the evaluation of static models, there has been substantial research on how different quantitative measurements relate to topic quality and human judgment (Chang et al., 2009; Lau et al., 2014). In contrast, little research has been devoted to the fair comparison of DTMs. Therefore, we suggest to develop a framework to make such comparisons. In this proposal, we present some potential ways in which such a comparative evaluation of DTMs could be done.

While NTM-CE is a promising technique, there is little research on adding a temporal dimension to NTM-CE and how to fairly compare DTMs. Therefore, we propose the following research questions in an attempt to thoroughly investigate the prospect of using NTM-CE for dynamic topic modeling.

RQ1: What requirements exist for a dynamic topic modeling system and how can NTM-CE properties respond to those requirements?

RQ2: How viable is dynamic topic modeling with NTM-CE in practice?

With RQ1 we aim to lay a theoretical foundation that will lead to knowledge that remains valid beyond the current state of the art in language modeling. The goal is to create a general framework and to thoroughly address the strengths and weaknesses of NTM-CE from a dynamic perspective. RQ2 puts theoretical knowledge into practice and will reveal insights and limitations of dynamic NTM-CE. Here, we strive to create functional models that can solve problems of practical relevance for academia and industry.

2 Literature Review

Topic modeling is a field within text mining whose objective is to find topics that best describe a collection of documents and then assign the documents to these topics. Models from the stochastic school use Latent Dirichlet Allocation (LDA) (Blei et al., 2003) and its variants to fulfill this objective using probabilistic distributions to discover topics. The field of dynamic topic modeling (DTM[1]) is the study of topics evolving over time. Discrete DTM such as Discrete LDA (d-LDA) (Blei and Lafferty, 2006) divides a topic into batches of discrete time steps where the next time step in a topic evolves from the previous. Continuous DTM (c-DTM) as introduced by Wang et al. (2008) borrowed the concept of Brownian motion from physics, which makes it possible to view the evolution of topics in continuous time. Another model that works continuously is *Topics Over Time* (TOT) by Wang and McCallum (2006) which associates each topic with a beta distribution representing the temporal dimension. In our project, we wish to study how to create a continuous-time topic model with NTM-CE as its basis. In addition, we want to use the dynamic models mentioned above for benchmarking future models.

With the introduction of Word2Vec (Mikolov et al., 2013), topic modeling saw a new era of models that make use of embeddings. The surveys by Zhao et al. (2021) and Churchill and Singh

[1]We use the abbreviation DTM for both the modeling techniques and the resulting models.

(2021) describe how topic modeling meets neural networks in the modern era. They also describe many models that incorporate PLMs. Dieng et al. (2020) proposed a model called *Embedded Topic Model* (ETM) that merges LDA and Word2Vec into the same vector space. This makes it possible to extract more meaningful topics. The dynamic version of this model (d-ETM, Dieng et al. (2019)) similarly merges d-LDA with Word2Vec. Bianchi et al. (2021b) and Bianchi et al. (2021a) describe other examples of models that incorporate embeddings created by PLM (e.g. S-BERT, Reimers and Gurevych (2019)) to a traditional topic modeling structure, but without using a distance-based clustering algorithm to determine topics.

Models that directly cluster vectors in the vector space created by a PLM are what we call NTM-CE. The popularity of this approach increased after the release of BERT (Devlin et al., 2019), and most models since then have used BERT or a BERT variant. Sia et al. (2020) used BERT, principle component analysis (PCA) (Pearson, 1901; Hotelling, 1933), and K-Means clustering (Lloyd, 1982) and found the NTM-CE pipeline to perform similarly to LDA. Thompson and Mimno (2020) compared different flavors of BERT and GPT-2 (Radford et al., 2019) in combination with PCA and K-Means, also concluding that the technique performs better than LDA. Using more recent libraries, Grootendorst (2022) proposed BERTopic, which uses BERT, UMAP (McInnes et al., 2018), and HDBSCAN (Campello et al., 2013; McInnes and Healy, 2017) together with a novel term-weighting procedure c-TF-IDF to discover topics in news data. Similarly, Zhang et al. (2022) use BERT, UMAP, and K-Means together with term weighting and conclude that the model outperforms all previous models. While all of these models use PLM embeddings, there is no consensus as to which embeddings to cluster. Sia et al. (2020) clusters vocabulary-level embeddings, Thompson and Mimno (2020) clusters token-level embeddings and Grootendorst (2022) clusters sentence-level embeddings. Part of the current proposal is to investigate differences in properties between different embedding choices and to study whether one of them is preferable for NTM-CE.

Taking another perspective, Meng et al. (2022) jointly train the dimension reduction and clustering components to obtain a vector space with high clusterability in the sense of (Ackerman and Ben-David, 2009). Their model TopClus was highly successful and thus an interesting testament to what can be done when combining components. However, to limit the research plan described here, we will initially focus on approaches with separately trained components, saving jointly trained ones for later.

3 Proposed work

In this section, we present the proposed work to seek answers to the research questions posed in Section 1. The research is divided into four phases, expected to correspond to 1–2 papers each. The work is to be done over two years. Before explaining the phases, an outline of a potential system that is supposed to accompany the theoretical work is given.

3.1 Topic Modeling System

The preliminary framework for a dynamic NTM-CE is shown in Figure 1. As previously mentioned, the core of an NTM-CE model is *vectorization* $\rightarrow$ *transformation* $\rightarrow$ *clustering*. To make it a dynamic topic model, the component *temporalization* is added. The temporal functionality is loosely defined as the part of the system that adds the dynamic aspect to the topic model. For the discrete case, this could be the binning of the documents depending on their timestamps. For the continuous case, this could be relating the documents to a time function. Deciding how the temporalization should be designed and where it should be placed in the system is a core part of the research to be done.

In terms of limitations, systems for topic modeling usually have an additional component that roughly describes each of the topics in a human-readable format. This description usually takes the form of keywords. However, the exploration of topic descriptions is considered to be outside the scope of this research proposal as the aim of the project is to study the dynamic aspect. Another limitation of NTM-CE is that the topics need to be created by a distance-based clustering algorithm. This means that the system will have freedom in how to create and manipulate vectors, but that the vectors in the end must be susceptible to mentioned clustering algorithms.

3.2 Phases

Phase I: An intuitive NTM-CE model in discrete time that can be compared with other DTMs will be implemented. The previously mentioned experi-

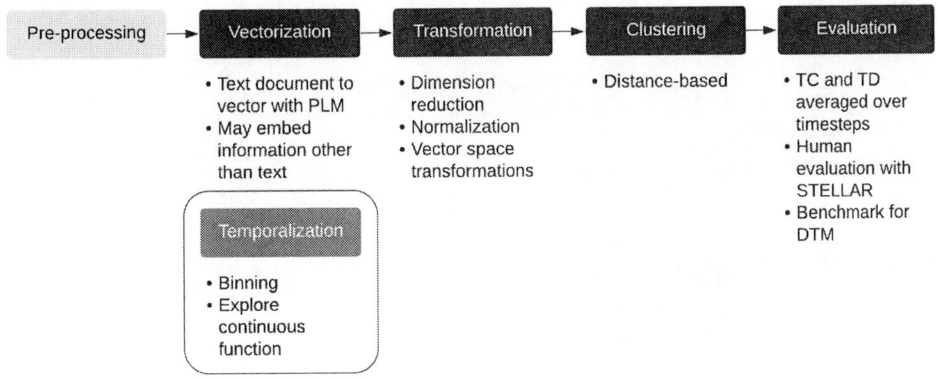

Figure 1: A preliminary framework in which to build dynamic topic models. The temporalization component is loosely defined as the part that adds functionality for making the topic modeling system dynamic. This includes binning documents to different timesteps and also a more explorative continuous function for NTM-CE. TC=Topic Coherence. TD=Topic Diversity.

ments by Grootendorst (2022) compared a binned BERTopic with d-LDA on the averaged topic coherence and topic diversity over a number of timesteps. However, we want to compare more models binned in this way, as well as models such as TOT and c-DTM. This work will establish a baseline for the comparison of dynamic topic models. Phase I will include the work to develop a code base for the comparison and evaluation of dynamic topic models. The evaluation, discussed further in Section 4, will combine automatic quantitative metrics and human evaluation. Moreover, familiarization with the strengths and weaknesses of existing models is crucial for continued research.

Phase II: An exploration of general NTM-CE properties is needed to work towards RQ1. Properties are often revealed in the vector space as patterns or structures that could be exploited. The requirements an ideal dynamic topic modeling would put on a system will be used to guide which properties to look for and to extract from NTM-CE. Properties could originate from any of the components described in Section 3.1, or a combination of them. A topic model based on the properties found will be developed. This model would likely compete with the state-of-the-art models or showcase some other features that are unique to dynamic NTM-CE.

Phase III: After developing a model in Phase II, the model will be generalized into a framework that is robust to future changes in components. A natural start is to generalize the framework to include Word2Vec-based models. With that, we can see if the properties found for transformations are general enough for different PLMs or if we need to reconsider. The desired outcome of this phase is a framework that not only works for the specific components available today, such as current transformer-based models, but would allow replacing components in the pipeline with future, more advanced ones.

Phase IV: The last step after developing a framework will be to expand the evaluation and study further application areas. The project has an industry partner and will therefore have the unique opportunity to perform real-world evaluations on industry datasets of news articles, considering applications more relevant to those outside of academia. A planned study is to look at the news cycle spanning over at least two years to analyze events that reoccur, and events that emerge and then disappear. Another ongoing related project at our home university looks at the detection of formal narrative structures in news articles with the aim to use it in longitudinal studies of reporting. Moreover, our home university does extensive work in gender studies which opens up for similar studies around gender bias. For example, the dynamic topic model can be used to identify changes in the use of stereotypical gender roles in language, and, in extension, that understanding may help the debiasing of datasets used in NLP.

4 Evaluation

Evaluation of topic models is not trivial as the lack of an objective ground truth makes it hard

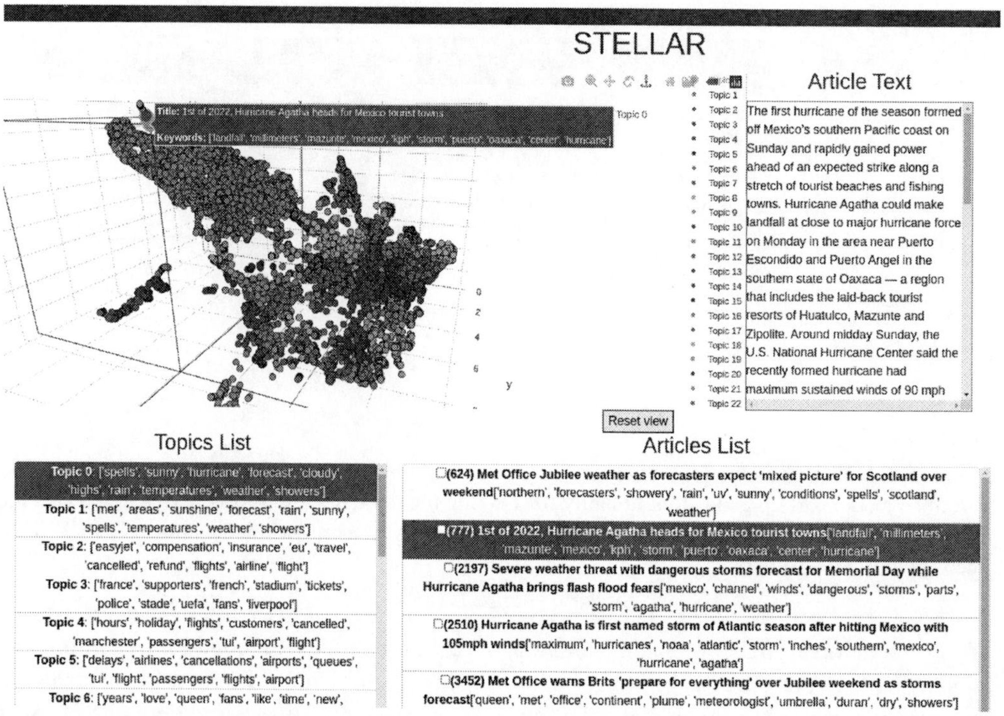

Figure 2: The topic browser that can be used for quick human evaluation of topics. The main functions are the 3D graph which shows a reduced version of the vector space, the list of topics with keywords, the list of articles in a topic, and the article text of a selected article.

to achieve a consensus on the number and nature of topics. Automatic measurements for evaluating topic models are topic coherence and topic diversity. While there are many approaches, topic coherence is usually automatically measured using normalized point-wise mutual information (NPMI, Bouma (2009)) and is considered by some to mimic human judgment (Lau et al., 2014). Topic diversity measures in different ways how diverse the top words in a topic are to each other (Bischof and Airoldi, 2012; Dieng et al., 2020; Bianchi et al., 2021a). There are tools like OCTIS (Terragni et al., 2021) that make it easy to compare static topic models. We plan to extend OCTIS or use similar ideas to facilitate fair comparisons between DTMs. As a first step, an OCTIS extension may average topic coherence and topic diversity over the time steps as has been done by Grootendorst (2022) and Dieng et al. (2019). Furthermore, part of the work in Phase I will be to assess how to measure aspects more specific to dynamic modeling requirements. This could, e.g., result in the requirement to develop an initial benchmark dataset for topic change over time, or to find a way to quantitatively assess topic change without a ground truth.

The importance of automatic measurements that correlate with human judgment has been known (Chang et al., 2009) and NPMI was adopted after showing such a correlation. However, a recent study by Hoyle et al. (2021) argues that automatic coherence measurements, including the prevailing topic model evaluation standard NPMI, should not be considered equivalent to human judgment. Therefore, we plan to complement automatic measurements with human evaluation when resource allocation is justified, for example, when a core pillar of the work needs to be validated. Qualitatively, we assume that a human can look at a sample of topics produced by a topic model and decide if they think the topics are coherent and also which documents should not be considered to belong to the topic. We use this assumption to develop a tool for rapid human evaluation of topics, which we intend to make use of to validate automatic measurements. This tool is described further in Section 5

5 Preliminary Work

STELLAR[2] (Systematic Topic Evaluation Leveraging Lists of ARticles) (Eklund and Forsman, 2022) was developed as a tool for rapid human

[2]https://github.com/antoneklund/STELLAR

evaluation; see Figure 2. The idea behind it is that the coherence of a topic can be more confidently assessed if an evaluator reads the actual titles and text of the articles rather than only a few describing keywords. By having the evaluator systematically go through all topics, we can get a score for how well the model performs from a human perspective. This requires expert evaluators who can contextualize a given number of articles and then also mark articles that do not belong to the topic.

STELLAR is supposed to aid the evaluation process and make it faster. The core functionalities are a topic list, an article list from the chosen topic, a box for reading the article text body, and a 3D visualization of the document vector space. In the article list, the articles can be marked as not belonging to the topic. The tool will be extended to make it easier to analyze dynamic topic models. The extension could add functionality like selecting articles within different time periods, visualizing the varying size of topics over time, or visualizing changes in the topic description over time. The functions and statistics that are needed we expect to become clear over the course of working with this project.

6 Impact

In the current information era, there are obvious benefits to having fast and trusted topic models which can process large corpora of documents. We have seen that there is a wide range of applications such as analyzing historical documents, social media, or news articles. Research on NTM-CE is particularly interesting because of the modularity of the different components, especially to isolate the language model in the system. This allows for exchanging parts of the system when new and better components are developed, meaning that this type of topic modeling will continue to improve even after the popular language model at the time is superseded by a better one. Developing a solid framework for dynamic topic modeling with this modularity will ensure that NTM-CE models are as flexible as LDA-based models in their applications.

7 Summary

This paper presented an outline to explore the dynamic topic modeling in detail with NTM-CE. We proposed two research questions in an attempt to cover both the theoretical framework and practical application of dynamic topic modeling with NTM-CE. We propose four phases in which the work will be done and where the main contributions will be: 1) a codebase for evaluating dynamic topic models, 2) a general framework for how to efficiently create dynamic topic models with NTM-CE, and 3) insights from practical application of the framework to various datasets. The research questions and phases were developed to the best of our ability with our current understanding. However, we see them as constantly evolving as we learn more. Therefore, we highly welcome all types of input from the research community to make this project as relevant and impactful as it can be.

Acknowledgements

This Ph.D. student is funded by the Swedish Foundation for Strategic Research, project id ID19-0055.

References

Margareta Ackerman and Shai Ben-David. 2009. Clusterability: A theoretical study. In *Artificial intelligence and statistics*, pages 1–8. PMLR.

Federico Bianchi, Silvia Terragni, and Dirk Hovy. 2021a. Pre-training is a hot topic: Contextualized document embeddings improve topic coherence. In *Proceedings of the 59th Annual Meeting of the Association for Computational Linguistics and the 11th International Joint Conference on Natural Language Processing (Volume 2: Short Papers)*, pages 759–766, Online. Association for Computational Linguistics.

Federico Bianchi, Silvia Terragni, Dirk Hovy, Debora Nozza, and Elisabetta Fersini. 2021b. Cross-lingual contextualized topic models with zero-shot learning. In *Proceedings of the 16th Conference of the European Chapter of the Association for Computational Linguistics: Main Volume*, pages 1676–1683, Online. Association for Computational Linguistics.

Jonathan Bischof and Edoardo M Airoldi. 2012. Summarizing topical content with word frequency and exclusivity. In *Proceedings of the 29th International Conference on Machine Learning (ICML-12)*, pages 201–208.

David M. Blei and John D. Lafferty. 2006. Dynamic topic models. In *ICML '06: Proceedings of the 23rd international conference on Machine learning*, pages 113–120.

David M Blei, Andrew Y Ng, and Michael I Jordan. 2003. Latent dirichlet allocation. *Journal of machine Learning research*, 3(Jan):993–1022.

Gerlof Bouma. 2009. Normalized (pointwise) mutual information in collocation extraction. *Proceedings of the Biennial GSCL Conference*.

Ricardo J. G. B. Campello, Davoud Moulavi, and Joerg Sander. 2013. Density-based clustering based on hierarchical density estimates. In *Advances in Knowledge Discovery and Data Mining*, pages 160–172, Berlin, Heidelberg. Springer Berlin Heidelberg.

Mario Cataldi, Luigi Di Caro, and Claudio Schifanella. 2010. Emerging topic detection on twitter based on temporal and social terms evaluation. In *Proceedings of the tenth international workshop on multimedia data mining*, pages 1–10.

Jonathan Chang, Sean Gerrish, Chong Wang, Jordan Boyd-Graber, and David Blei. 2009. Reading tea leaves: How humans interpret topic models. *Advances in neural information processing systems*, 22.

Rob Churchill and Lisa Singh. 2021. The evolution of topic modeling. *ACM Comput. Surv.* Just Accepted.

Hannah Devinney, Jenny Björklund, and Henrik Björklund. 2020. Semi-supervised topic modeling for gender bias discovery in English and Swedish. In *Proceedings of the Second Workshop on Gender Bias in Natural Language Processing*, pages 79–92, Barcelona, Spain (Online). Association for Computational Linguistics.

Jacob Devlin, Ming-Wei Chang, Kenton Lee, and Kristina Toutanova. 2019. BERT: Pre-training of deep bidirectional transformers for language understanding. In *Proceedings of the 2019 Conference of the North American Chapter of the Association for Computational Linguistics: Human Language Technologies, Volume 1 (Long and Short Papers)*, pages 4171–4186, Minneapolis, Minnesota. Association for Computational Linguistics.

Adji B. Dieng, Francisco J. R. Ruiz, and David M. Blei. 2019. The dynamic embedded topic model. *arXiv preprint arXiv:1907.05545*.

Adji B. Dieng, Francisco J. R. Ruiz, and David M. Blei. 2020. Topic modeling in embedding spaces. *Transactions of the Association for Computational Linguistics*, 8:439–453.

Anton Eklund and Mona Forsman. 2022. Topic modeling by clustering language model embeddings: Human validation on an industry dataset. In *Proceedings of the 2022 Conference on Empirical Methods in Natural Language Processing: Industry Papers*. Just accepted.

Maarten Grootendorst. 2022. BERTopic: Neural topic modeling with a class-based TF-IDF procedure. *arXiv preprint arXiv:2203.05794*.

Harold Hotelling. 1933. Analysis of a complex of statistical variables into principal components. *Journal of Educational Psychology*, 24.

Alexander Hoyle, Pranav Goel, Andrew Hian-Cheong, Denis Peskov, Jordan Boyd-Graber, and Philip Resnik. 2021. Is automated topic model evaluation broken? The incoherence of coherence. In *Advances in Neural Information Processing Systems*, volume 34, pages 2018–2033. Curran Associates, Inc.

Jey Han Lau, David Newman, and Timothy Baldwin. 2014. Machine reading tea leaves: Automatically evaluating topic coherence and topic model quality. In *Proceedings of the 14th Conference of the European Chapter of the Association for Computational Linguistics*, pages 530–539, Gothenburg, Sweden. Association for Computational Linguistics.

Stuart P. Lloyd. 1982. Least squares quantization in PCM. *IEEE Transactions on Information Theory*, 28(2):129–137.

Leland McInnes and John Healy. 2017. Accelerated hierarchical density based clustering. In *2017 IEEE International Conference on Data Mining Workshops (ICDMW)*. IEEE.

Leland McInnes, John Healy, Nathaniel Saul, and Lukas Großberger. 2018. Umap: Uniform manifold approximation and projection. *Journal of Open Source Software*, 3(29):861.

Yu Meng, Yunyi Zhang, Jiaxin Huang, Yu Zhang, and Jiawei Han. 2022. Topic discovery via latent space clustering of pretrained language model representations. In *Proceedings of the ACM Web Conference 2022*, WWW '22, page 3143–3152, New York, NY, USA. Association for Computing Machinery.

Tomas Mikolov, Kai Chen, Greg Corrado, and Jeffrey Dean. 2013. Efficient estimation of word representations in vector space. *arXiv preprint arXiv:1301.3781*.

David J Newman and Sharon Block. 2006. Probabilistic topic decomposition of an eighteenth-century american newspaper. *Journal of the American Society for Information Science and Technology*, 57(jun):753–767.

Karl Pearson. 1901. LIII. On lines and planes of closest fit to systems of points in space. *The London, Edinburgh, and Dublin Philosophical Magazine and Journal of Science*, 2.

Alec Radford, Jeffrey Wu, Rewon Child, David Luan, Dario Amodei, Ilya Sutskever, et al. 2019. Language models are unsupervised multitask learners. *OpenAI blog*, 1(8):9.

Nils Reimers and Iryna Gurevych. 2019. Sentence-BERT: Sentence embeddings using Siamese BERT-networks. In *Proceedings of the 2019 Conference on Empirical Methods in Natural Language Processing and the 9th International Joint Conference on Natural Language Processing (EMNLP-IJCNLP)*, pages 3982–3992, Hong Kong, China. Association for Computational Linguistics.

Suzanna Sia, Ayush Dalmia, and Sabrina J. Mielke. 2020. Tired of topic models? Clusters of pretrained word embeddings make for fast and good topics too! In *Proceedings of the 2020 Conference on Empirical Methods in Natural Language Processing (EMNLP)*, pages 1728–1736, Online. Association for Computational Linguistics.

Silvia Terragni, Elisabetta Fersini, Bruno Giovanni Galuzzi, Pietro Tropeano, and Antonio Candelieri. 2021. OCTIS: Comparing and optimizing topic models is simple! In *Proceedings of the 16th Conference of the European Chapter of the Association for Computational Linguistics: System Demonstrations*, pages 263–270. Association for Computational Linguistics.

Laure Thompson and David Mimno. 2020. Topic modeling with contextualized word representation clusters. *arXiv preprint arXiv:2010.12626*.

Chong Wang, David Blei, and David Heckerman. 2008. Continuous time dynamic topic models. In *Proceedings of the Twenty-Fourth Conference on Uncertainty in Artificial Intelligence*, UAI'08, page 579–586, Arlington, Virginia, USA. AUAI Press.

Xuerui Wang and Andrew McCallum. 2006. Topics over time: A non-markov continuous-time model of topical trends. In *Proceedings of the 12th ACM SIGKDD International Conference on Knowledge Discovery and Data Mining*, KDD '06, page 424–433, New York, NY, USA. Association for Computing Machinery.

Zihan Zhang, Meng Fang, Ling Chen, and Mohammad Reza Namazi Rad. 2022. Is neural topic modelling better than clustering? An empirical study on clustering with contextual embeddings for topics. In *Proceedings of the 2022 Conference of the North American Chapter of the Association for Computational Linguistics: Human Language Technologies*, pages 3886–3893, Seattle, United States. Association for Computational Linguistics.

He Zhao, Dinh Phung, Viet Huynh, Yuan Jin, Lan Du, and Wray Buntine. 2021. Topic modelling meets deep neural networks: A survey. *arXiv preprint arXiv:2103.00498*.

Concreteness vs. Abstractness: A Selectional Preference Perspective

Tarun Tater[1] **, Diego Frassinelli**[2]**, Sabine Schulte im Walde**[1]
[1]Institute for Natural Language Processing, University of Stuttgart,
[2]Department of Linguistics, University of Konstanz
{tarun.tater, schulte}@ims.uni-stuttgart.de
diego.frassinelli@uni-konstanz.de

Abstract

Concrete words refer to concepts that are strongly experienced through human senses (*banana*, *chair*, *salt*, etc.), whereas abstract concepts are less perceptually salient (*idea*, *glory*, *justice*, etc.). A clear definition of abstractness is crucial for the understanding of human cognitive processes and for the development of natural language applications such as figurative language detection. In this study, we investigate selectional preferences as a criterion to distinguish between concrete and abstract concepts and words: we hypothesise that abstract and concrete verbs and nouns differ regarding the semantic classes of their arguments. Our study uses a collection of $5,438$ nouns and $1,275$ verbs to exploit selectional preferences as a salient characteristic in classifying English abstract vs. concrete words, and in predicting their concreteness scores. We achieve an f1-score of 0.84 for nouns and 0.71 for verbs in classification, and Spearman's ρ correlation of 0.86 for nouns and 0.59 for verbs.

1 Introduction

Concepts can be viewed in accordance with how humans perceive them. Those that are easily perceptible with any of the five senses are referred to as concrete concepts, whereas those that cannot be seen, heard, touched, smelled, or tasted as abstract concepts (Brysbaert et al., 2014). Examples of concrete concepts are *axe*, *cup*, *salt*, and *elephant*, whereas examples of abstract concepts are *belief*, *spirituality*, and *intuition*. Based on an analysis of noun concepts from the University of South Florida dataset (Nelson et al., 2004) and their occurrence in the British National Corpus (Leech et al., 1994), abstract words tend to be much more common in everyday usage (Hill et al., 2014).

The distinction between concrete and abstract concepts is quite important in linguistics, psycholinguistics, as well as computational linguistics. Furthermore, studies have shown that concreteness measures are useful in a number of applications, such as lexicography (Kwong, 2011), document comprehensibility (Tanaka et al., 2013), and figurative language detection (Turney et al., 2011; Köper and Schulte im Walde, 2016; Aedmaa et al., 2018; Piccirilli and Schulte im Walde, 2022).

Theories of cognition contend that concrete and abstract words should co-occur most frequently with concrete words because concrete information connects the actual use of both concrete and abstract words to their mental representation (Barsalou, 1999; Pecher et al., 2011). However, previous corpus-based empirical studies do not show the same pattern. Bhaskar et al. (2017), Frassinelli et al. (2017), and Naumann et al. (2018) found that concrete words tend to co-occur with other concrete words, whereas abstract words tend to co-occur with other abstract words. Zooming into more specific co-occurrence conditions, Frassinelli and Schulte im Walde (2019) however demonstrated a more diverse empirical picture: they investigated interaction patterns of abstract and concrete English nouns and verbs in subcategorisation relations, and found that specific combinations indicated specific types of literal vs. figurative language usage, e.g., strongly associated abstract verbs subcategorising concrete direct objects often exhibited metonymy (e.g., *recommend a book*), while concrete verbs in the same relationship more often indicated literal language use (e.g., *write a book*).

In this study, we focus on selectional preferences as a way to investigate the inconsistencies between cognitive theories and empirical results reported above. Selectional preferences indicate the tendency that predicates impose semantic restrictions on the realisations of their complements, i.e., co-occurrence in a syntactic predicate-argument relationship (Resnik, 1993; Brockmann and Lapata, 2003; Erk et al., 2010; Schulte im Walde, 2010). For example, see sentences (1)–(3) with the verb *eat*, which requires an edible entity as direct object.

Proceedings of the AACL-IJCNLP 2022 Student Research Workshop, pages 92–98
November 20, 2022.

(1) Amy is eating *chocolate*.

(2) *Chris is eating *justice*.

(3) Joe had to eat *dirt* for his earlier statement.

While the example in (1) is perfectly plausible, the example in (2) is not, because *justice* violates the selectional preferences of the governing predicate *eat*. Similarly, in (3) we see a violation that can only be resolved as a metaphorical reading.

Our study investigates whether selectional preferences represent a semantic criterion to establish empirical differences between the two semantic classes of abstract vs. concrete words. We thus suggest a more in-depth look into co-occurrence conditions in comparison to previous work that explored either window-based or purely syntactic co-occurrence. In this vein, we present two data-driven experiments focusing on (i) selectional preferences of English verbs regarding their subcategorisation of subjects and direct objects, and (ii) inverse selectional preferences of English nouns being subcategorised as subjects and direct objects. We use selectional preferences as features (a) in a binary classification task, to distinguish between more abstract vs. more concrete nouns/verbs, and (b) in a regression analysis, to predict the concreteness ratings of nouns and verbs.

2 Related Work

Frassinelli et al. (2017) quantitatively investigates differences between abstract and concrete words by analysing the abstractness of their respective context words. They showcase that concrete words tend to co-occur with other concrete words whereas abstract words co-occur with abstract words. Naumann et al. (2018) and Frassinelli and Schulte im Walde (2019) analyse the interactions of nouns and verbs in verb-noun subcategorisation by looking at types of syntactic relations between nouns and verbs (see above).

Another strand of research has exploited multimodal approaches to infer concreteness. Hill et al. (2014) investigates which aspects of concreteness can be learned using multi-modal models and which are the most salient linguistic features contributing to it. Bhaskar et al. (2017) combine visual properties extracted from images and distributional representations built from textual data to distinguish between abstract and concrete words.

3 Dataset

For our research, we utilise the concreteness ratings for approximately $40,000$ English words from Brysbaert et al. (2014) (henceforth, *Brysbaert norms*). The ratings were collected via crowdsourcing on Amazon Mechanical Turk. Each word was presented to at least 25 participants who were asked to rate the word on a scale from $1-5$ where 1 indicates clearly abstract and 5 indicates clearly concrete concepts. The scores were then averaged across participants to obtain a mean concreteness rating for each word. The ratings were collected out-of-context and without providing any information about part-of-speech (POS). In a post-processing step, part-of-speech tags and frequencies were added to the target words, based on the SUBTLEX-US corpus (Brysbaert et al., 2012).

Following Schulte im Walde and Frassinelli (2022), we extracted and added frequency information based on the English web corpus ENCOW16AX[1] (Schäfer and Bildhauer, 2012; Schäfer, 2015), as well as the most frequent POS tag associated with each target word. In our final dataset, we only included targets where the POS provided in the original collection corresponded to the POS extracted from the ENCOW16AX corpus, the corpus that we use in our experiments. We also removed words for which their predominant POS tag does not represent at least 95% of all POS tags of the target, to reduce ambiguity, and all words with a frequency below $10,000$, to remove infrequent words. After filtering, the resulting collection includes $5,438$ noun targets and $1,275$ verb targets.

4 Methods and Experiments

In the following, we present our two experiments exploiting selectional preferences to distinguish between degrees of abstractness. The selectional preference features for our verb and noun targets are induced from the ENCOW16AX corpus mentioned above, which contains 20 billion sentences and is syntactically parsed. We focus on two word-class interactions regarding our verb and noun targets.

- *Verb-Noun Interaction*: The verbs interplay with nouns in two ways: verb-object interaction and subject-verb interaction. We investigate these two scenarios in the following way:

[1] `https://www.webcorpora.org/encow/`

- A root verb having a direct object (dobj) as a syntactic child. For example: *Filip* baked a *cake*. Here, the noun *cake* is a direct object argument of the verb *bake*.
- A root verb with a syntactic child as a nominal subject (nsubj). For example: The *student* is *sleeping*. Here, the verb *sleep* takes the noun *student* as subject.

- *Noun-Verb Interaction*: We consider the inverse selectional preferences from the point of view of nouns (Erk et al., 2010), again as two sub-cases.
  - A nominal subject (nsubj) which is a singular noun (NN) whose syntactic parent is a root verb.
  - A direct object (dobj) which is a NN whose syntactic parent is a root verb.

We now discuss how selectional preference features for these two cases were computed and used.

4.1 Selectional Preference Features

For each of the above four sub-cases, we calculate the (inverse) selectional preference scores for each verb and each noun in three ways:

(i) *Frequency-based*: number of times a noun represents an argument (subject/direct object, depending on the sub-case) of a particular verb.

(ii) *Feature normalisation*: min-max normalisation of selectional preference frequencies in (i) by normalising the co-occurrences for a *particular noun across all verbs.*

(iii) *Row normalisation*: min-max normalization of selectional preference frequencies in (i) by normalising the co-occurrences for a *particular verb across all nouns.*

In this way, we construct three variants of (inverse) selectional preference vectors for all our verb targets across all subject/object nouns, and for all our noun targets as subjects/objects across all subcategorising verbs (i.e., the reverse syntactic dependency direction). These variants are assessed and compared against each other as well as against co-occurrence irrespective of any syntactic relationship (i.e., "just" co-occurrence within the same sentence context, because previous studies looked at any co-occurring words), for each of the abovementioned sub-cases, and in two experimental setups.

4.2 Binary Classification

In this first set of experiments, we classify both the $5,438$ nouns and the $1,275$ verbs into abstract vs. concrete words. Since the concreteness ratings range from $1-5$, we treat words with ratings ≤ 3 as abstract and those with ratings > 3 as concrete. The resulting two classes are henceforth referred to as ***Complete*** set.

Given that mid-range concreteness scores are generally more difficult in their generation by humans and consequently noisier in their distributional representations (Pollock, 2018; Schulte im Walde and Frassinelli, 2022), we additionally construct the following variants of our target sets.

- We exclude target words that have concreteness scores between 2.5 and 3.5. These words can be difficult to classify because they are neither clearly abstract nor clearly concrete. After excluding these 'neutral'/'mid-scale' words we have $4,061$ nouns ($2,757$ concrete and $1,304$ abstract), and 769 verbs (118 concrete and 653 abstract). We call this set the ***Extremes*** set.
- We exclude target words with a standard deviation > 1.3 because in these cases annotators strongly disagreed. We refer to the set of words excluding these 'disagreed' words as ***Agreed*** set, containing $3,456$ nouns and 766 verbs.

The distribution of the *Brysbaert* norms for nouns is skewed heavily towards high scores (concrete) and, on the contrary, for verbs towards low scores (abstract). For example: the most concrete $1,000$ nouns can be found in the interval $4.86-5.00$ whereas the most abstract $1,000$ nouns range from 1.00 to 1.92. So, instead of considering the extreme $1,000$ abstract and $1,000$ concrete nouns or 500 concrete and 500 abstract verbs, as done in some of our previous studies (Bhaskar et al., 2017; Naumann et al., 2018; Schulte im Walde and Frassinelli, 2022), we investigate how words in different ***binned*** ranges of concreteness ratings differ. To do this, we binary classify target words that have scores in the range of $1-2$ against words with scores $2-3$, $3-4$, and $4-5$. In this way, we manage to overcome the skewness in the distributions albeit with a trade-off for class imbalance. The binary classification between words having ratings $1-2$ vs. $4-5$ is similar to classifying only the most abstract and concrete words.

Datasets		Train			Test		
		Total	Abstract	Concrete	Total	Abstract	Concrete
Nouns	All	$4,350$	$1,628$	$2,722$	$1,088$	407	681
	Extremes	$3,248$	$1,043$	$2,205$	813	261	552
	Agreed	$2,764$	851	$1,913$	692	213	479
Verbs	All	$1,020$	774	246	255	194	61
	Extremes	616	522	94	155	131	24
	Agreed	572	463	109	144	116	28

Table 1: Data split $80 : 20$ across experiments.

Targets & Selectional Preferences		Accuracy	Precision	Recall	F1-score
Verbs	Subject	0.80	0.75	0.63	0.65
	Direct Object	0.77	0.70	0.72	0.71
	Co-occurrence	0.77	0.78	0.77	**0.77**
Nouns	Subject (inverse)	0.84	0.83	0.84	0.83
	Direct Object (inverse)	0.85	0.84	0.84	0.84
	Co-occurrence	0.87	0.86	0.87	**0.87**

Table 2: Evaluation of binary classifications using SVMs with row-normalised features.

In the binary experiments we use three different classifiers: Support Vector Machines (SVMs) with *rbf* kernel, Random Forests and Logistic Regression. The binary classification is evaluated using accuracy, precision, recall, and f1-score to address the data skewness between classes. We use an 80:20 data split between train and test set using stratified sampling for our experiments, see Table 1. We also perform a hyper-parameter search optimising the parameters.

4.3 Regression: Predicting Concreteness Ratings

This task pertains to predicting the concreteness ratings from $1-5$. We use Gradient Boosting to predict the concreteness scores of $5,438$ nouns and $1,275$ verbs. The predicted concreteness ratings are evaluated using Spearman's rank-order correlation coefficient ρ against the average human ratings from the *Brysbaert* norms.

5 Results and Discussion

Table 2 reports the accuracy, precision, recall and f1-score results for our binary classifications across subject and direct object selectional preference conditions in comparison to simple co-occurrences. Using SVM with row-normalised features and the regularization parameter $C = 5$ for both the verb-noun and the noun-verb settings,[2] the best f1-score results are achieved when relying on co-occurrences (0.87 for noun targets and 0.77 for verb targets), while selectional preference features reached 0.84 for nouns and 0.71 for verbs when relying on selectional preferences for direct objects, and 0.83 for nouns and 0.65 for verbs when relying on selectional preferences for subjects.

Figure 1 shows accuracy scores of the binary classification for nominal subjects (left) and direct objects (right) across our *binned* ranges of concreteness ratings, i.e. classifications between words in the concreteness ranges $1-2$ vs. $2-3$, $3-4$, and $4-5$. Unsurprisingly, accuracy increases with stronger differences between the ratings of the two classes. We also indicate the results for binary classification of the *Complete* sets (red dotted lines, also see accuracies in Table 2), and results for distinguishing the *Extremes* sets (green lines), which are similar as for distinguishing between bins $1-2$ and $4-5$, as expected.

Table 3 shows the results for our regression experiments, which are more difficult because they target the whole range of scores. We report best Spearman's ρ correlations of 0.865 for predicting noun scores, and 0.596 for predicting verb scores. In these experiments, the best results are reached

[2]Results obtained with Logistic Regression and Random Forest classification models are comparable.

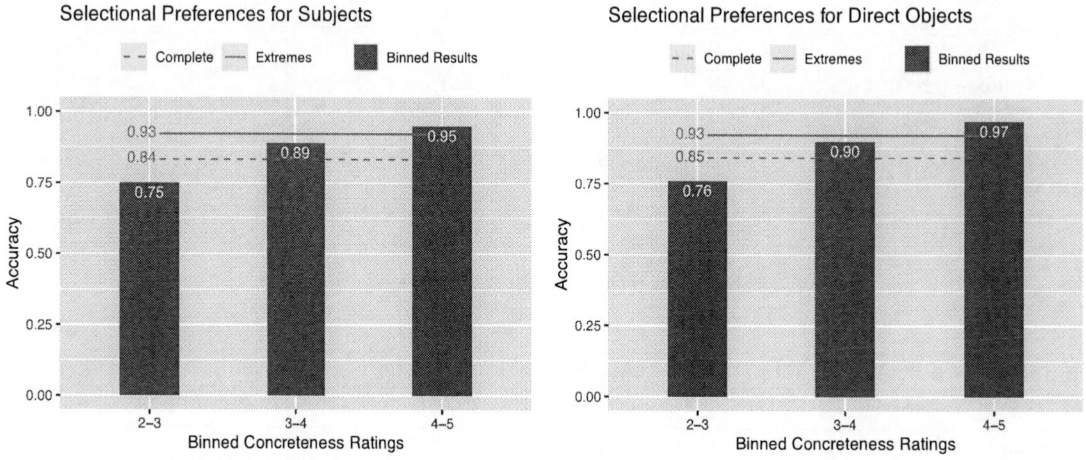

Figure 1: Classifying abstract vs. concrete nouns based on selectional preference features.

Targets & Selectional Preferences		Freq-Based	Feature Norm.	Row Norm.
Verbs	Subject	0.479	0.479	0.520
	Direct Object	0.548	0.552	**0.596**
	Co-occurrence	0.424	0.462	0.473
Nouns	Subject (inverse)	0.795	0.795	0.809
	Direct Object (inverse)	0.851	0.858	**0.865**
	Co-occurrence	0.822	0.822	0.861

Table 3: Spearman's ρ correlations across regression experiments.

when using direct object selectional preferences, outperforming both subject selectional preference features and co-occurrences in all conditions, with various difference strengths for feature-based and normalisation variants. Between feature-based and normalisation variants we do not observe strong differences. The reported best results relying on direct object selectional preferences are obtained with the following hyper-parameters for verb targets: 200 trees, with a depth of 3 and learning rate of 0.05, and for noun targets: 200 trees, with a depth of 7 and learning rate of 0.05.

Across binary and regression experiments and experiment settings, the obtained results are better for noun targets than for verb targets, which is in line with our previous work (Schulte im Walde and Frassinelli, 2022). On the one hand, we hypothesise that this is due to the smaller number of data points and higher data skewness for verbs in comparison to nouns, as depicted in the data split in Table 1; on the other hand, we assume that verbs are semantically more difficult to distinguish regarding any meaning aspects, because they are more ambiguous (which is presumably also reflected in their concreteness ratings).

Comparing selectional preference features relying on subjects vs. direct objects, we consistently observe that selectional preferences across direct objects provide more salient features for distinguishing between abstract and concrete nouns and verbs than subjects do.

In comparison to previous work, our Spearman's ρ correlations for predicted noun ratings (0.865) and direct objects selectional preference features are comparable to Bhaskar et al. (2017), which shows a Spearman's ρ correlation of 0.86 for 9, 241 nouns and 0.78 for the extreme 2, 000 nouns. However, their best-performing models utilise both textual embeddings as well as image embedding. Our results are able to achieve similar performance on our 4, 538 nouns with only textual selectional preference features.

6 Conclusion

In this study, we explored the use of selectional preferences as a linguistically more specific semantic criterion than purely sentential co-occurrences, when establishing empirical differences between the two semantic classes of abstract vs. concrete English verbs and nouns. Within a set of binary classification experiments varying selectional preference features, normalisations, classifiers, and more or less extreme differences in concreteness scores of the words in the classes, simple co-occurrence generally outperformed the semantically more fine-grained selectional preferences; in contrast, selectional preferences for direct objects improved over subject preferences and co-occurrences when used in the more fine-grained concreteness predictions of regression models. So overall, the more fine-grained semantic features are helpful in the more fine-grained perception-based semantic distinctions, and the core information in these combinations are verb-object semantic subcategorisations.

Acknowledgements

This research was supported by the DFG Research Grant SCHU 2580/4-1 *Multimodal Dimensions and Computational Applications of Abstractness.*

References

Eleri Aedmaa, Maximilian Köper, and Sabine Schulte im Walde. 2018. Combining Abstractness and Language-specific Theoretical Indicators for Detecting Non-Literal Usage of Estonian Particle Verbs. In *Proceedings of the NAACL 2018 Student Research Workshop*, pages 9–16, New Orleans, LA, USA.

Lawrence W. Barsalou. 1999. Perceptual Symbol Systems. *Behavioral and Brain Sciences*, 22:577–660.

Sai Abishek Bhaskar, Maximilian Köper, Sabine Schulte im Walde, and Diego Frassinelli. 2017. Exploring Multi-Modal Text+Image Models to Distinguish between Abstract and Concrete Nouns. In *Proceedings of the IWCS Workshop on Foundations of Situated and Multimodal Communication*, Montpellier, France.

Carsten Brockmann and Mirella Lapata. 2003. Evaluating and Combining Approaches to Selectional Preference Acquisition. In *Proceedings of the 10th Conference of the European Chapter of the Association for Computational Linguistics*, pages 27–34, Budapest, Hungary.

Marc Brysbaert, Boris New, and Emmanuel Keuleers. 2012. Adding Part-of-Speech Information to the SUBTLEX-US Word Frequencies. *Behavior Research Methods*, 44:991–997.

Marc Brysbaert, Amy Beth Warriner, and Victor Kuperman. 2014. Concreteness Ratings for 40 Thousand generally known English Word Lemmas. *Behavior Research Methods*, 64:904–911.

Katrin Erk, Sebastian Padó, and Ulrike Padó. 2010. A Flexible, Corpus-Driven Model of Regular and Inverse Selectional Preferences. *Computational Linguistics*, 36(4):723–763.

Diego Frassinelli, Daniela Naumann, Jason Utt, and Sabine Schulte im Walde. 2017. Contextual Characteristics of Concrete and Abstract Words. In *Proceedings of the 12th International Conference on Computational Semantics*, Montpellier, France.

Diego Frassinelli and Sabine Schulte im Walde. 2019. Distributional Interaction of Concreteness and Abstractness in Verb–Noun Subcategorisation. In *Proceedings of the 13th International Conference on Computational Semantics*, pages 38–43, Gothenburg, Sweden.

Felix Hill, Roi Reichart, and Anna Korhonen. 2014. Multi-Modal Models for Concrete and Abstract Concept Meaning. *Transactions of the Association for Computational Linguistics*, 2(1):285–296.

Maximilian Köper and Sabine Schulte im Walde. 2016. Distinguishing Literal and Non-Literal Usage of German Particle Verbs. In *Proceedings of the Conference of the North American Chapter of the Association for Computational Linguistics: Human Language Technologies*, pages 353–362, San Diego, CA, USA.

Oi Yee Kwong. 2011. Measuring Concept Concreteness from the Lexicographic Perspective. In *Proceedings of the 25th Pacific Asia Conference on Language, Information and Computation*, pages 60–69.

Geoffrey Leech, Roger Garside, and Michael Bryant. 1994. Claws4: the tagging of the British National Corpus. In *COLING 1994 Volume 1: The 15th International Conference on Computational Linguistics.*

Daniela Naumann, Diego Frassinelli, and Sabine Schulte im Walde. 2018. Quantitative Semantic Variation in the Contexts of Concrete and Abstract Words. In *Proceedings of the 7th Joint Conference on Lexical and Computational Semantics*, pages 76–85, New Orleans, LA, USA.

Douglas L. Nelson, Cathy L. McEvoy, and Thomas A. Schreiber. 2004. The University of South Florida Free Association, Rhyme, and Word Fragment Norms. *Behavior Research Methods, Instruments, & Computers*, 36(3):402–407.

Diane Pecher, Inge Boot, and Saskia Van Dantzig. 2011. Abstract Concepts. Sensory-Motor Grounding, Metaphors, and Beyond. *Psychology of Learning and Motivation – Advances in Research and Theory*, 54:217–248.

Prisca Piccirilli and Sabine Schulte im Walde. 2022. Features of Perceived Metaphoricity on the Discourse Level: Abstractness and Emotionality. In *Proceedings of the 13th International Conference on Language Resources and Evaluation*, Marseille, France.

Lewis Pollock. 2018. Statistical and Methodological Problems with Concreteness and other Semantic Variables: A List Memory Experiment Case Study. *Behavior Research Methods*, 50:1198–1216.

Philip Resnik. 1993. *Selection and Information: A Class-Based Approach to Lexical Relationships*. Ph.D. thesis, University of Pennsylvania.

Roland Schäfer. 2015. Processing and Querying Large Web Corpora with the COW14 Architecture. In *Proceedings of the 3rd Workshop on Challenges in the Management of Large Corpora*, pages 28–34, Mannheim, Germany.

Roland Schäfer and Felix Bildhauer. 2012. Building Large Corpora from the Web Using a New Efficient Tool Chain. In *Proceedings of the 8th International Conference on Language Resources and Evaluation*, pages 486–493, Istanbul, Turkey.

Sabine Schulte im Walde. 2010. Comparing Computational Approaches to Selectional Preferences: Second-Order Co-Occurrence vs. Latent Semantic Clusters. In *Proceedings of the 7th International Conference on Language Resources and Evaluation*, pages 1381–1388, Valletta, Malta.

Sabine Schulte im Walde and Diego Frassinelli. 2022. Distributional Measures of Abstraction. *Frontiers in Artificial Intelligence: Language and Computation. Alessandro Lenci and Sebastian Pado (topic editors): "Perspectives for Natural Language Processing between AI, Linguistics and Cognitive Science".*

Shinya Tanaka, Adam Jatowt, Makoto P. Kato, and Katsumi Tanaka. 2013. Estimating Content Concreteness for Finding Comprehensible Documents. In *Proceedings of the 6th ACM International Conference on Web Search and Data Mining*, Rome, Italy.

Peter D. Turney, Yair Neuman, Dan Assaf, and Yohai Cohen. 2011. Literal and Metaphorical Sense Identification through Concrete and Abstract Context. In *Proceedings of the Conference on Empirical Methods in Natural Language Processing*, pages 680–690, Edinburgh, UK.

Author Index

Association for Computational Linguistics
209 N. Eighth Street
Stroudsburg, Pennsylvania 18360

ISBN 978-1-7138-6312-0

CURRAN ASSOCIATES INC.
proceedings
.com